Business Loans

Rick Stephan Hayes

Business Loans

A Guide to Money Sources
and How to Approach Them Successfully

CBI Publishing Company, Inc.
51 Sleeper Street
Boston, Massachusetts 02210

Library of Congress Cataloging in Publication Data

Hayes, Rick Stephan, 1946–
    Business loans.

    Includes bibliographical references and index.
    1. Loans.   I. Title.
HG2055.H39   658.1'5224   76-56090
ISBN 0-8436-0752-1

International Standard Book Number: 0-8436-0752-1

Library of Congress Card Catalogue Number: 76–56090

Printed in the United States of America

Designed by Lauri Rosser

Third Printing

Contents

Foreword by Cecil Byrd   ix

Preface   xi

1 Sources of Loans

1 Introduction to Sources   3

Advantages of Borrowing   4
How Do You Rate as a Borrower?   4
The Sources   5

2 Banks   7

The Advantages and Disadvantages of Banks   7
Best and Worst Conditions for Borrowing   8
People and Environment of Banks   10
What Kind of Bank Should You Look For?   12

Types and Uses of Loans   13
Summary   21

3 Commercial Financial Lenders   22

Advantages and Disadvantages of Commercial Financing   23
People and Environment of Private Financial Companies   23
Types of Loans Available   28
Other Sources of Private Loans   33

4 Government Financing   34

People and Environment in Government Financial Sources   34
The Loan Process   36
Government Agencies and Types of Loans   38
What are Government Requirements?   44
SBA   44
Economic Development Agency   57
Export-Import Bank of the United States   61
Agricultural Department Loans   68
Federal Reserve Board   71
Other Government Loans   72
Summary   74

II Preparation of Loans

5 Introduction to Preparation   77

6 Preliminaries and Basic Factors   79

Financial Statements and Technical Terms   79
What Data is Necessary?   85
Market Data   87
Information Bibliography   104
Use of Funds Statement   106
Break-Even Analysis   106

7 Financial Data and Analysis   111

Historical Data   111
Expected Expenses, Cost of Sales, and Owner's Draw   114
New Businesses   115
Calculating Loan Repayment   116
Variable and Fixed Expenses   118
Projected Financial Statement   118
Monthly Profit and Loss   119
Cash Flow   123
Supporting Schedules   125
Footnotes   125
Pro Forma Balance Sheets   127
Ratios   129

8 The Presentation Format   131

Sample Loan Proposal   132
Major Sections of Proposal   151

Appendix: Analog of a Loan Proposal   165

Index   178

Foreword

Rick Stephan Hayes and I met in 1969. It was then that we both began cutting our teeth on business loans. The difference between us was that he was just starting the process and I wasn't. He was fresh out of college and I had been in banking for twenty-one years at the time. The environment we were working in (one I found myself in by chance and one he had chosen, for reasons that still elude me) was an environment like no other for testing a person's resources, capabilities, morale, and morality. We worked in an economically-depressed section of South Los Angeles—a black community with some Spanish-speaking and a few Korean families, mostly newly arrived and unsettled. The area's economic life was in total disarray by urban blight, white flight, poverty, and unemployment.

It was in this arena that Rick Stephan Hayes learned his trade working for the Interracial Council for Business Opportunity. It was here that I learned the hard fact, with a great deal of help from Rick, that making loans to small businesses is the most difficult of any banking function I had as yet encountered. Life in this community was hard. There was a hardness in the businesspeople who eked out a living among a hard clientele; made hard by the constant stare of poverty at every turn.

The lessons of the proud new programs that had sprung up in the wake of the Watts riots were beginning to return to us. Many families had been destroyed and lives ruined by the lust and greed these programs had fostered. Black pride was just reaching its stride, however, and there was no end of new entrepreneurs, young and old (mostly young), that came from nowhere to try their luck in the poverty program game, most to fade back to the same obscurity from whence they had emerged.

Many outrageous schemes were hatched to lay hands on some of the easy money that was to be had. Most often these schemes weren't successful but enough of them were to discredit the programs and to serve as excuses for many lenders to get out of the game. Those that stayed in became increasingly gun-shy. Bank of America stayed in and, to my knowledge, never considered getting out but it became pretty tough to get an SBA loan for a while there. It isn't easy now!

The kind of experience Rick Stephan Hayes received in South Los Angeles might be compared to the experience a doctor receives doing his internship and residency at Bellevue Hospital in New York. He was presented with every variety of case imaginable, one on top of another. Mostly poor; mostly desperate. Negotiating cases like this with a bank took the greatest of skill, patience, and perseverance. The insights he gained during those years, along with the sophisticated refinements he has since acquired, are reflected in the pages that follow.

In *Business Loans: A Guide to Money Sources and How to Approach Them Successfully* Rick has done a remarkable job in capsuling his experiences in South Los Angeles and elsewhere but still covers his subject in sufficient detail to provide a thorough step-by-step guide for those seeking business loans. More importantly he provides the kind of insight that is lacking in most other contemporary treatments of the subject.

Pushing thirty years as a banker, I'm naturally most interested in those sections dealing with banks and banking, debt capital opposed to equity capital, and the other areas in which he shows unusual perception of my calling. He will be taken to task by many, but not by those of us who have shared some of Rick Stephan Hayes' experiences. He doesn't agree with all of the textbooks on our shelves but he is coming from the real world which afterall is sometimes at variance with the conjectured world of the business school or bank training department classrooms.

CECIL E. BYRD
Vice President
Senior Urban Affairs
Credit Officer—South
Bank of America NT&SA

Preface

The basic problem, to my eyes, is the ever-widening gap between lender and borrower, banker and businessman. The businessman generally doesn't understand the bewildering financial world of the banker and the banker is amazed at how little the businessman knows about finance.

The businessman must know a little bit about all the functions of his business: sales, production, personnel, and finance. Generally, the thing he knows the *least* about is finance. Most businessmen can't look at a balance sheet and profit and loss statement and say: "Well, my materials and labor are up a little in cost, I need more long term financing because of my above-industry-averages dependence on short term capital. There is a recent trend toward lower cost of utilities. Some of my employees must be stealing because my cost of sales is out of line." They look at the sales and bottom line—profit. Most businesses only get balance sheets because they have to. Well, all the stuff a businessman can't tell about his business finances a banker can.

Therein lies the rub.

Technically, there is a wide gap between lender and borrower. The borrower just doesn't understand the financial language, much less the financial tools.

Add to this the fact that lenders are intent on preserving money and businessmen are intent on spending it, and you start to see that there might be a psychological gap as well.

This book is about closing the gaps—technical as well as psychological.

It's really not enough to know the technical aspects of finance, you have to understand the underlying psychological mechanism at work as well. So this book is dedicated to understanding—understanding the whole lending game, from: "Where do I go to get money?" to "How do I prepare my request so that I can get the maximum response?"

To deal with these questions I have divided this book into two basic sections: sources and preparation.

The "Sources" section deals primarily with what money sources are available and which one is the best for your particular needs. It discusses banks, other private sector lenders, and government lending. It also gives an idea of what kinds of loans are available, their definition, and who grants them. Probably most important, the individual chapters on banking, other private sector lenders, and government, give you an idea of what kind of people you are liable to be dealing with in these institutions, their training, their attitudes toward lending, and how they look at businesses, in a special "people and environment" section of each chapter.

The second section—"Preparation"—explains step-by-step the technological process of making a loan presentation to the lender.

"What are the basic elements of finance in a lending situation?" "How do I present the financial management, and marketing aspects of my business?" "How do I get the necessary information to start a new business with a loan?" "How do I find out what my market is?" "How do I find out and show what sales and expenses my business will have one year from now?" "How do I 'project' my sales?" These are all questions that the second section will answer.

The concepts covered in the second section may appear difficult but they are not. The concepts are explained in a manner assuming the reader has no finance background.

I'm very dedicated to the proposition that every businessman can know everything it takes to get a loan and use that knowledge accordingly. I'm sort of a do-it-yourselfer, and enjoy the excitement of everything that further extends my knowledge of my job, myself, or my environment. Hopefully, this volume will let you get a loan yourself, using your own personality and intelligent resources, and probably more importantly, teach you more about your own business or proposed business financially.

I

Sources of Loans

Introduction to Sources

Yes, there is money out there and a large variety of places to go to get it.

Basically, this book will be concerned with debt capital—loans. Money you borrow and pay back.

The type of financing that we *will not* deal with in detail is equity financing—money given to you in return for part of your business.

Briefly, the difference between debt and equity financing is this: When you are given equity money, also called seed capital and injection capital, you also must give something back—specifically, a piece of your business. When you borrow debt money, you are loaned the money and are expected to pay it back plus interest, but you keep all of your business for yourself.

The advantage of equity capital is that you don't have to pay the money back, and moreover, if you are a majority stockholder, you don't even have to declare dividends to the people who gave you the money in return for stock. The major disadvantage of equity capital is that by giving away part of the business, the business is no longer yours and you must constantly deal with the wants, needs, and business opinions of others. If you own less than 50 percent of the business, then there always exists the possibility that the other stockholders might get together and give you the old heave-ho when it's least expected.

Debt capital is money borrowed with the intention of paying it back and there are no other owners except yourself, unless, of course, you default on the loan and the bank claims your assets for liquidation. The advantage of debt capital is you retain ownership and you get "leverage" (a concept we shall discuss later). The disadvantage of debt is that you have to pay the money back plus interest and, if you don't, you lose your business.

In short, debt is better if you are going to be successful, because you will make the company worth more than the debt money borrowed, you will have a smaller personal investment, and you will retain all the control. Equity capital is better if you *aren't* going to be successful for a few years, because there will be little danger of losing your business to liquidation.

There are several sources of financing available for the businessman; this chapter will discuss most of them. The largest loan source, of course, is the commercial bank, which loans practically all short-term (30−90 days) money to business and more than 80 percent of the immediate and long-term funds borrowed by small businesses for expansion. The next chapter goes into some depth about bank lending.

Advantages of Borrowing

You should avoid excessive borrowing, of course, but you should also be aware of the advantages and benefits of borrowing:

1. Borrowed funds can earn more than they cost. The rate of interest that lenders charge is generally lower than the rate of return you expect your investment to earn. As a result, borrowed funds, if they are used successfully, increase the return on your investment over what it would have been without the borrowing.

2. Interest payments on borrowed funds are tax deductible. Dividend payments or other returns to investors are not. These facts should be taken into account, along with other considerations, in deciding on borrowing policies.

3. Some credit is a matter of convenience. Buying merchandise on open account and services on an accrual basis are examples of the credit for convenience. Wages are a specific example. Even a very small businessman would find it difficult to make daily wage settlements.

How Do You Rate as a Borrower?

The lender—who more often than not is a banker—needs certain information on which to base a loan decision. Part of it will be furnished by the borrower, and the rest will come from the banker's own credit files and from outside sources. This information is related to what credit men call the "Cs" of credit—Character, Capacity, Capital, Collateral, Circumstances, and Coverage (insurance).

Character. To the banker, character means two things in particular: 1) The borrower will do everything in his power to conserve his business assets and so ensure repayment of his loan. He will manage his business to the best of his ability. He will not squander his own or other funds. 2) The borrower is a man of his word. When he says that he will repay his borrowing promptly, he means it. If he does not keep his promise, he at least will have made every possible effort to do so.

Capacity. The management skill shown by the small businessman in using his investment and enlarging it is another important business asset. For those just embarking on a business career or entering a new field, however, past performance—however successful—does not qualify a person to direct all the activities involved in operating a machine shop.

Capital. The small businessman's investment in his own business is evidence of his faith in its future. He himself must furnish the management and most of the capital until others have enough confidence in his business to be willing to invest in it.

Collateral. Businessmen who have a high credit standing do much of their borrowing on an unsecured basis. Others are often obliged to back up their credit standing with collateral. This is especially likely to be true of a new small businessman. If he owns a home or other improved real estate, life-insurance policies with a cash surrender value, or marketable securities, he may be able to use such assets as collateral for business loans.

Before borrowing on these terms, however, he should consider the consequences to himself and his family if he should be forced to withdraw from the business before it becomes firmly established. A small businessman who retires from business prematurely usually does so at a loss.

Circumstances. Some factors over which the small businessman has no control may have a bearing on the granting of a bank loan and its repayment. These include:

—Seasonal character of the business
—Long-run business changes
—The level of community business activity
—The competitive position of the firm
—The nature of the product

Coverage. Proper insurance coverage is extremely important. Small businessmen are subject to possible business losses from many causes, such as these:

—The death of an owner, partner, or principal stockholder.
—Physical damage or interruption of operations as the result of fire, explosion, flood, tornado, or other violent cause.
—Theft, embezzlement, or other acts of dishonesty by owners, officers, employees, and others.
—Public liability not covered by workmen's compensation insurance.

A new small businessman may not be able to insure his company as fully as the owner of an established business, but he should recognize the need. A going concern has little excuse for neglecting to establish and maintain adequate insurance protection against basic risks. (See your insurance broker, agent or company representative!)

The Sources

The major categories of sources of debt capital for businessmen are banks; private financial institutions; and the government. Each of these categories will be discussed in the following chapters in detail, but a brief summary for each appears below.

Banks

Banks are generally the best source to approach for all types of loans because:
1. The bank usually charges lower interest rates than finance companies.
2. Because the banker is in the business of dealing with other businesses' finances the banker can give the applicant expert business and financial guidance.
3. The bank relationship will help establish a good basis for credit references.
4. Because a banker can give you access to all forms of loans.

Private Financial Institutions

Private financial institutions are more likely to be in a position to help the smaller businessman because they will make loans more readily to "risky" businesses (translate that, "small business"). When your business is new or your credit isn't sterling, a private financial institution will take a chance on you when a bank won't.

Government Financing

What is the advantage of government financing? The primary advantages are good terms, low interest, and low equity requirements (net worth of present or personal cash injection into a new business) and that's a lot of advantages. The disadvantages are that there are special criteria a businessman must need to be considered and the loan proposal is usually more detailed and more difficult to put together than other financing.

Banks

The bank's business is loaning money. They have to loan money to make a profit. If the bank is a branch of a larger bank, they have a certain "quota" of loans that they should make, a certain amount of deposits they should take in, new businesses they should contact, and so on. In other words, they are expected to loan money and go out and seek new businesses.

The Advantages and Disadvantages of Banks

The *advantages* of getting a loan from a bank are:

1. Generally, with the exception of a few government and private programs, borrowing from a bank is the cheapest way to go. They usually have the lowest interest rates and they can handle financial reporting for you at low cost.

2. A bank's business is dealing with money, money for all kinds of businesses and many personal needs as well. Because they deal with businesses on a full-time basis, they can give you expert business advice about businesses related to yours and general business trends.

3. Borrowing from a bank, as opposed to a government source, for instance, is better for your credit standing.

4. Banks have the largest loan breadth, i.e., more types of loans, than other sources.

5. Banks offer many business services, including: credit references on customers or potential customers; financial, investment, and estate advisory services; loans needed in your business; discounting customers' accounts and notes payable; check certification; safe deposit boxes; night depositories;

collections of remittances (lock boxes); payment of freight invoices; check reconciliation services; and payroll accounting services.

6. After a bank issues you money, they will do all they possibly can to keep you afloat.

The *disadvantages* of dealing with banks include:

1. The conservative nature of banks when considering loans. That is to say, banks are about the most difficult of the loan sources to get loans approved by.

2. The technical requirements (financial spreads, projected budgets) of presenting a loan. Usually, a bank wants more information and more precise information than other sources.

3. In banks that have a large number of branches, there is a tendency to have a branch manager work at one branch for only a couple of years, therefore it is difficult to set up a long-term relationship with that branch manager.

4. Because banks are regulated by the federal government, and are still a profit-making organization, they have to be careful their loans don't fail. The bank will not only be hard to get money from, but they will watch your business like a hawk, whether you like it or not, to make sure you don't go under. For long term loans most banks demand annual, semi-annual, quarterly, or even monthly profit and loss statements and balance sheets so they can observe your business carefully. And remember, they have records of *every* check you ever write. As discussed previously, their monitoring you is an advantage but be aware because it can be a two-edged sword.

Best and Worst Conditions for Borrowing

Let us talk about the best time and the worst time to approach a bank for money. Of course, depending on your personal or company situation, anytime might be a good time or bad time, irrespective of external influences and bank policies. That is, you might fall into one or the other categories of what I call, the unwritten golden rule of borrowing, which says: *If you don't need money, that's the best time to get a loan.* If you need money desperately, your chances of getting it are almost nil. Of course, there is a lot of area between not needing money at one end of a continuum and being dog-desperate at the other, and that's what this book is all about.

Externally, i.e., having to do with the bank and the economy only, here are the best times and situations to borrow and the worst times and situations to borrow:

The best environment for borrowing is:

1. When interest rates are generally low. This means two things, that the bank has more money to loan than it usually does and that the borrower will get a better deal.

2. When a bank has just opened. New banks, especially independent banks, are looking for businesses, especially deposit business. New banks will usually take more chances with a marginal business because they have to build up their loan portfolio. Sometimes you will find, however, that new banks are conservative; but if you start building a relationship immediately, and don't ask

for a loan at the start, the bank will loan to you when they get to know you. Incidentally, if you have a sizable business, banking with a small independent will be very good because you might be their biggest depositor. If you are their biggest depositer, they will bend over backwards (but not break their own backs) to give you service.

3. When the economy is in an up-turn. That is, sales all over the economy are increasing, the stock market is up, and disposable consumer income is up. This might be reflected in lower interest rates, but not necessarily.

4. When banks in a particular area are in heavy competition. This might mean that there are too many banks in a new, developing area. Some ways that you can tell there is a lot of competition is if more than one bank visits your business to start up a relationship (the more the better for you). Another sign is if there are a lot of incentives for deposits. That is, the banks are trying to outdo themselves in premiums (toasters, calculators, etc.) they offer for deposits.

5. When banks are in a generally expansionary process. During the sixties, banks threw down the traditional conservatism and started expanding their branch systems, including international branches, tremendously. Since there was more competition and a downgrading of traditional restraints, money was easier to get. There is a new facet of banking that might spark expansion: electronic banking devices called consumer-bank communication terminals, or CBCT's. These are the electronic devices that banks put outside their branch, or, which is where the expansion would occur, in supermarkets, shopping centers, and so on; electronic devices that dole out money or allow you to deposit without ever going to the bank. If the use of these devices becomes widespread, then the banks that get the most deposits will also have more money to loan, at least for a while.

6. When there is a special program within the bank, usually a large bank, to take high-risk loans as "the bank's moral obligation." An example of this is loans to minorities and special groups like Vietnam veterans, the handicapped, and, in some cases, displaced businesses or disaster victims. The large banks sometimes set aside sums for these "special high-risk" loans: but beware, regardless of the bank's good intentions, if the economy is bad or there is a high demand on loan funds, these special loans have a way of being aced out.

The worst environment for borrowing is:

1. When interest rates are high. When rates are high it means that there is a large demand on bank funds, and in many cases, from large, secure "Fortune 500"-type firms. Also, at these times, the bank might be up to its loan limit as far as loan-to-deposit ratio (discussed shortly). High interest rates don't just mean money is more expensive, it means there is less of it to borrow. This occurred in 1974.

2. When the economy is in a recession. In recessionary times, regardless of other influences, banks tend to be more conservative in their lending. There are more chances for a business to go under in a recession. Furthermore, there is usually high demand for money to tide an established business over.

3. When a bank is up to its lending limit, or when the bank has made a decision to decrease their dollars outstanding to make the bank more liquid. When there is an extremely high demand for funds, the bank is tempted to loan to secure businesses at high rates and therefore make a better profit. There is a limit to how much money they can loan out, however, and that limit is their maximum loan-to-deposit ratio. The loan-to-deposit ratio is simply the total loans they have outstanding divided by the total number of deposits they have. During the dark days of 1974, the banks were sometimes up to 75 percent of their deposits loans out. This was scary for the banks because if only 26 percent of their depositers took out their money, the bank would be in serious trouble, maybe bankruptcy. And even this 75 percent loan-to-deposit ratio might be misleading. Banks have to report their loan-to-deposit ratio to the federal government once a week, so they could borrow money from other banks for 24 hours to bring up their deposits to help the ratio. In the old days, (first part of the twentieth century), the banks would very seldom go above 33 per cent loan-to-deposit ratio. So you can see how 75 per cent is a thin edge to walk on.

In 1975, when money became looser, loans didn't. The reason was that although more money was available to loan out, the banks wanted to keep the money to build up their loan-to-deposit ratio and make the ratio a little healthier.

4. When there is very little bank competition for loans and deposits. A one bank town is a perfect example. When you need money, you go there and the competition is nil. The best thing to do is to go to another town for financing.

5. When the parent bank is in trouble or suffers severe losses. In 1973 when United California Bank had trouble with the Swiss subsidiary, for example, it was very difficult to get financing from the branches. If you read the business section of your newspaper, the *Wall Street Journal, Business Week,* or other business publications, you will learn about your bank's various troubles.

Of course, it is not always possible to wait for the right time to get your loan and chances are good if you are an existing business you will need your money the most when everyone else needs it, but the above ''best and worst'' list will clue you in to how difficult it is going to be to get a loan.

People and Environment of Banks

People get into banking like people get into anything else. Some plan a career as a banker and want most of all to get a job in a bank; others sort of wander into it because they need a job and a banking job is available, so they take it; and still others get into it for a temporary experience on their way to something else.

Who Becomes a Banker and How Are They Trained to Deal with Business

Bankers are human beings. Moreover, they have a family, friends, get stoned occasionally, drive automobiles, and have trouble paying their bills just like all of us do. They watch television, wash dishes, see x-rated movies occasionally, and have a hard time finding a parking place downtown. So why do people get so uptight talking to them? Well, bankers usually dress formally.

Most people are always a little hesitant to ask anyone for money, much less a complete stranger dressed in a three-piece suit. But to most people, the thing that makes a Banker, the Person, into a Banker, the Institution, is tradition. That is, the formal history of banking, the traditional training of the banker, and, if you will, the "bank paranoia" that they are going to lose the bank's money. The one comparison factor in all people who become and are bankers, however, is a basic business background, either a degree in business or a practical business background or both.

As such, bankers are basically interested in business and money. They may become more interested in getting their money back than they are interested in the business they finance being super successful, although generally a successful business also pays back debt. Given a choice, the banks want their money. The basic training of a banker includes an in-depth training in finance and conservation of bank assets and how to deal with people, and, to a lesser degree, how to carry out the bank's "moral and business community responsibility."

Let us talk about financial training because that is what bankers get the most of: most lending officers just starting, or present employees just promoted get an intensive course in financial analysis of a business. This always involves the profit and loss statement and balance sheet of a business as source material. That is where the banks get their ratios, industry average comparisons, repayment ability, and historical comparatives. Balance sheets and profit and loss statements, or more particularly, the accounting involved, is the "language of finance," just like math is the "language of science." The whole point of this financial training is the conviction that financial statements of businesses can predict, to a large degree, whether the business can manage money and whether it will be successful in the future and pay the loan back.

What Does the Bank Look For from Your Business?

"On lending to business, we bankers take into account the borrower's ability, experience, reputation, character, even his personality, and sometimes his influence," wrote Daniel Kiyawa in *Journal of Commercial Bank Lending.* He said the following were considered: deposit balance, collateral, interest rates, past experiences, and economic conditions.

In this portion of "People and Environment of Banks," I would like to give you an idea of what banks want from you as a business when considering a loan request and what they think is important by using direct quotes and summaries of articles and books written by bankers themselves addressing themselves directly to this loan situation. Read carefully and understand.

The bank would like to know everything they can about your business and you. This may seem like a drag, but in fact, it isn't so bad. If you understand what a banker wants, and give that to him at the same time that you request the loan, even before he asks for it, it will help you. I have devised what I call, after myself, of course, the "Hayes Friend Theory." The theory is this: "The more the banker knows about you and your business, the more like a friend you become. And people have a hard time turning down a friend." As a matter of fact, I suggest that you furnish all the information to the bank when you open your account, before you need a loan. That is when the "Hayes Friend Theory" works best. I had a client who had a business that was in terrible shape, but because he was open with the banker, and furnished him with all the information, the bank gave him loans they shouldn't have. My client eventually went bankrupt, after being in bankrupt shape for over two years, but hung-on through his good bank relations. Even after bankruptcy, his banker told me, "He's the most astonishing, hard working man I've ever known." Of all the things the bank wants, financial information is probably the most important, so I want to quote a few of the articles from bankers, further explaining the importance of financial statements to a bank.

I would like to summarize on one brief insight into the thinking process of a banker when he is considering loaning you money. This is an article, from *The Journal of Commercial Bank Lending,* by a man with over 25 years banking experience, Victor D. Smith. The article is entitled "A Reflective Approach to Business Loans" (April 1974, p. 49). Smith concedes that lending is not as easy as one, two, three.

"Despite the efforts of many intelligent lending officers who have done their best to formalize the lending function, it remains an *art* in which no formula nor guidelines nor rule is absolute. . . . The best lender is an individual who brings the entire force of his intellect against a given situation to come to a conclusion which neither he nor his associates can really rationalize."

What can a banker base his decision on, then? Smith answers, "As with any edifice, either tangible or intangible, strength arises from the foundation. *Facts* are the foundation of credit."

He uses as his facts the current ratio, current assets divided by current liabilities, which will be discussed in depth in Part II. If the current ratio is 1 to 1, Mr. Smith suggests that there will be difficulty paying debt. Another ratio he likes is debt-to-worth, the total debt divided by net worth, also discussed in Part II. He suggests that two and one-half times more debt than net worth is the maximum one should consider.

Mr. Smith goes down the list of ratios and financial statements and why they are important, and I will give more of his feelings in Chapter 7, "Financial Data and Analysis." The point is that although Smith says that loan granting is an art, he nevertheless depends heavily on financial data.

I hope this portion of the chapter has given you a good insight as to what the bank wants from you and how the banker thinks about loans. This is very important! If you are aware of what is expected of you, you have a much better chance of getting the loan and having a good banking relationship.

What Kind of Bank Should You Look For?

What should you look for in choosing a bank? There are five main points to consider.

1. Is the banker progressive? Has he kept pace with changing conditions,

and is he alert to the developing requirements of the community? Most of the younger bankers would be more progressive, generally speaking, than the older bankers. Especially consider a banker who manages a large volume bank. He didn't get into that position unless he has something on the ball. But also beware of a young banker who just became a manager, he may tend to be conservative although aware of requirements of the community. It is good to ask other bank-business customers about the manager. That will help.

2. Does the management of the bank combine integrity, experience, ability, and initiative? That is quite a sentence full, and it is a difficult question to answer by looking at the surface. Most large branch banks will have branch managers who will have at least most of these traits, except perhaps initiative. Again, the best way to answer this question is to ask people who have had direct experience with this banker.

3. How does the banker approach your problems? Does he appear interested and helpful? These are questions you can answer only by having a conference with the banker directly. Be straight forward in the interview. Don't hold back. Don't just tell him what you think he wants to know.

4. Can you get the kind of credit you need? Be sure the banker understands your particular needs and is prepared to service them. First, know what kind of credit *you do* need. (The following portion of this chapter on types of loans should give you this information. The rest must come from your interview.)

5. How big is the bank? Generally speaking, size should probably not be the deciding factor in choosing a bank. It may make a difference, however, in the types and amount of credit available, the services offered, prestige, and so on. Sometimes small banks are the best bet because they might be more liberal and offer more personal service. But, of course, if you need special services or large amounts of credit, or international services, a bigger bank is preferable.

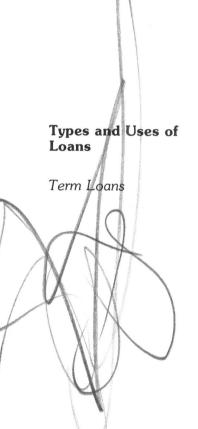

Types and Uses of Loans

Term Loans

Term loans are loans for more than thirty days and generally speaking, are the kinds of loans this book is all about.

In the past, seasonal loans were the best for banks because they gave good liquidity. That is, the money only left the bank for short periods of times and if there was a run on the bank by the depositors, the money would be pretty close at hand. Well, there is a very small chance nowadays of a run on the banks, and even so, all the deposits are insured by the federal government, so banks now accept a certain portion of term loans on the theory that there will always be a basic level of deposits below which liquidation will not be necessary. There are three types of term loans.

Short-term credit is generally considered to be credit extended for one year or less usually thirty to ninety days.

Intermediate-term credit is for more than one year but less than five; and *long-term* credit, for more than five years. (Some authorities distinguish between intermediate- and long-term loans at ten years instead of five). Some bankers will speak of anything over one year as simply a term loan.

Short-Term Loans

Short-term loans for the daily operational needs of the businessman, such as salaries, rent, insurance, advertising, and most importantly to pay suppliers and take advantage of discounts, are a principal type of bank lending. Generally speaking, such loans are written for a short duration (30, 60, or 90 days) and are based upon the operating or business cycle of the individual firm. Operating loans vary in length of maturity since they are adapted to the particular cycle of the business.

Many such loans are "revolving loans," that is, the loan proceeds are used to purchase inventory, pay for manufacturing or processing expenses, or for market and delivery costs. The loan is repaid when the business completes this process and collects from the purchaser. When new sales generate new accounts receivable, new revolving loans are initiated.

Short-term loans are easier to get than intermediate- and long-term loans, especially for small businessmen. They are often unsecured and may be less expensive than longer loans.

Intermediate-Term Loans

An intermediate-term loan (also called simply a term loan) provides the businessman with capital for other than temporary needs without requiring him to yield business control. In this way, it gives him a chance to build up his equity over a period of years.

Suppose, for example, that you need new equipment to increase your output, but don't have the cash to pay for it. With an intermediate-term loan, you will be able to acquire title to the machine right away. During the life of the loan, the equipment will be helping to produce income from which you can pay the installments and interest.

Intermediate-term loans are also used to purchase existing businesses, to help establish new ones, to provide additional working capital, and to replace long-term indebtedness that carries a higher rate of interest. They may be either secured or unsecured. Payment may be made monthly, quarterly, semi-annually, or annually, often with small early payments and a large final payment called a balloon payment.

While a term loan is in force, you will be subject to certain restrictions as to how you manage your business. The loan agreement is usually designed to protect the lender against drastic reductions in the value of collateral or in business income available for repayment of the loan. Also, term borrowers are required to submit periodic financial statements. On the other hand, term lenders often give their borrowers expert advice on business matters affecting the loan. See the next section on long-term loans for some more of the details of term financing. Most of the same rules and restrictions that apply to long-term financing applies to intermediate loans.

Long-Term Loans

When long-term rather than short- or intermediate-term funds are needed, one or more of the following sources may be used:
1. Internal sources such as retained earnings, asset reductions, or the sale of assets not essential to the business (for example, security holdings)

2. Long-term borrowings

3. The investment of new permanent capital

Which kind of financing you use may depend upon what you can get, since sources of long-term loans or new capital for small businesses are not plentiful. But before you begin your search, you should know which type is best for your needs. A small businessman is sometimes reluctant to accept new equity from outside the business because he wants to keep ownership of the business entirely in his own hands. Sometimes, however, more equity capital is what the business needs, rather than a loan.

Furthermore, equity capital may have some real advantages over long-term borrowed funds. It is true that an investor of equity capital often expects to have a voice in the management of the company in which he risks his money, but that prospect is not necessarily a grim one. He may bring new skills or a fresh viewpoint that will add strength and vitality to the business. On the other hand, loans, too, have some advantages. The important point is that all types of funds should be considered carefully in relation to the needs and existing resources of your business.

There is now an ever-increasing need for long-term loans. Because of this, the banks have become more flexible. These loans are not necessarily restricted to collateral loans for purchase of fixed assets. When a business doesn't have access to equity markets, it may get term loans for expanded growth. Long-term and intermediate-term loans in most cases, and for working capital, with the payment of the loan on a monthly or quarterly installment basis.

1. Banks usually take a security interest (require a pledge of the asset financed by the loan) to support term loans.

2. Most term loan repayment programs are either on a monthly or quarterly basis.

3. Term loans offer advantages to the borrower. The installment repayment schedule and amount of payment are usually tailored to fit the borrowers' potential profits and operational capacity. In addition, there will be no acceleration of prepayment unless the borrower fails to meet the agreed terms.

4. A term loan, due to its long maturity, requires constant review and follow-up by the lending officer. This follow-up by the lending officer is not much different than for any other loan except that it is on a continuous basis for the term of the loan. This attention includes analyzing monthly balance sheets and profit and loss statements, visiting the businessman's premises on a periodic basis, requesting a monthly list of accounts receivable and accounts payable showing their current status, and making periodic credit checks on the business through reports from Dun and Bradstreet, Inc., the business suppliers, and the Interchange reports of the National Association of Credit Management.

5. A term loan agreement sets forth in writing the conditions on which the loan is made. The major function of the term loan agreement is to specify certain conditions and restrictions under which the business will operate. These conditions are also aimed at keeping the business viable throughout the period of the loan and at the same time protecting the bank's interest. Included in the

loan agreement conditions can be how much salary or other withdrawals the owner can receive, the loan amount, repayment schedule, the amount of dividends paid, the maintenance of working capital at a given ratio, restrictions on selling fixed assets, and the frequency of financial reports required. For additional support, and particularly in the case of the sole proprietor, the bank may request the borrower to take out a term life insurance policy for the amount and maturity of the loan with the bank as "loss payee."

Unsecured Loans

The unsecured loan is the type of loan in which you don't have to put up collateral because the bank makes the loan based on your credit. This type of loan is used most frequently by banks for short-term loans.

1. An unsecured loan to a business usually indicates that the bank considers that business a priority customer, based on its financial strength.

2. Although the loan does not require the businessman to pledge collateral, most banks will require the personal guarantee of the businessman to support an unsecured loan. A personal guarantee supporting a loan means, in effect, that if the borrowed funds are not repaid, the bank can look to the guarantor and his personal net worth to repay the loan.

3. A business receiving an unsecured line of credit or loan will also receive a plus in its credit rating with its suppliers, since it is recognized that a business must have a sound operation if it is receiving unsecured credit from its bank.

4. A business receiving an unsecured loan may also receive favorable interest rates on the loan because the strong company financial strength indicates there will be reduced risks and because the loan usually will cost the bank less to administer. The loan depends on:

—The business's ability to generate profits.

—Management capabilities, which can best be measured by how well the company is doing in its industry and against local competitors.

—The personal assets of the owner of a small or closely-held business.

On the negative side, a business borrowing on an unsecured basis may find the amount of its borrowings limited and, therefore, may have to switch to secured borrowings.

There are four kinds of loans that are generally unsecured. They are: simple commercial loans; character loans; installment loans, and lines of credit. The following are definitions and ramifications of these loans.

Simple Commercial Loans

Most of these loans are made for periods ranging from 30 to 90 days. They are usually based on financial statements. Often, they are unsecured, and signed by the maker without other endorsement. In most cases, it is expected that they will be paid from the funds produced by normal business activity. This type of loan is used particularly for seasonal financing and for building up inventories.

Character Loans

Character loans are usually made as individual rather than business credit. They are sometimes used for business purposes, however.

Installment Loans	Loans of this type are made for many business purposes, usually by larger banks. They may be extended for almost any period the bank sees fit to offer, with payments generally on a monthly basis.

As the loan is reduced, it is often possible to obtain refinancing at better rates. Also, these loans may be tailored to the seasonal requirements of the business, with heavier payments in peak months and smaller payments during off-season periods.

Lines of Credit

A line of credit is an informal understanding between a businessman and his bank. The bank agrees to grant loans as the businessman requests them so long as they do not exceed at any one time a maximum established in the agreement. The loans are usually unsecured, and are often granted almost automatically during the period of the agreement (usually a year) and up to the total specified. Credit lines are used most commonly by businessmen with seasonal short-term funds.

Secured Loans

A *secured* loan is a loan that requires a pledge of some or all of your business assets. The bank requires security to protect the funds lent, funds that belong to the depositors of the bank, against the risks of business.

1. If a business cannot qualify for an unsecured loan, then the business may be able to borrow on a secured basis.

2. Secured borrowing, whether it is short-term or long-term, requires some acceptable collateral to the pledged support the loan.

3. A secured loan will reduce the bank's risk, and therefore a business can often obtain a larger loan than its statements justify on a secured basis.

4. Depending on the type of collateral pledged, a secured loan usually places a bank in first position over other creditors.

5. A secured borrower, because of the added administrative costs and also due to the possible higher potential risk factor, may pay a higher interest rate for the loan if it is secured by accounts receivable, inventory, or fixed assets. However, if the collateral is what bankers call "liquid" collateral, then this type of collateral, such as a savings passbook, marketable securities, bonds, or time certificates or deposits that can be converted into cash by the bank within a very short period, may reduce the interest rate.

6. A secured loan may enable a new or growing company that does not qualify for unsecured credit to go to the bank and borrow the funds needed for its operation by supporting the loan request with collateral.

7. Of course, the degree of risk in either secured or unsecured loans will also determine the interest rate. Interest rates on secured borrowings are usually higher than on unsecured borrowings, as stated earlier, due to higher clerical service costs, time spent on administering the loan, reviewing reports and checking on collateral.

In this portion of the chapter we will discuss all the different types of secured loans a bank offers, but first, let us briefly discuss three types of secured loans that aren't secured by tangibles; that is, loans endorsed with comakers and/or guarantor, or loans secured by someone else.

First, let me say that I have never met a banker who likes notes secured by another party; too many times the borrower defaults and the bank plays hell to get the money from someone else. Of course, all loans granted to minors have to be cosigned or endorsed.

The *endorsers,* others besides yourself, are contingently liable for the loan they sign. If the borrower fails to pay, the bank expects the endorser to make the payments.

A *comaker* shares the responsibility of a loan jointly with the borrower. The banker may collect directly from either the maker or the comaker.

A *guarantor* guarantees the payment of a loan by signing a guarantee commitment. When you are an officer of a corporation the lender may require a personal guarantee for a loan granted to the corporation. A manufacturer will guarantee a loan to a customer. Bankers like guarantees, unlike comakers and endorsers, because the loan doesn't necessarily depend on the guarantee to be repaid. The Small Business Administration (SBA) and other government organizations offer guarantees through banks for private businessmen, see chapter 4, "Government Financing."

Additionally, *assignment of leases* as security is similar to a guarantee, and is especially used in franchise situations. The bankers take a mortgage on property, then take the lease on the property assigned to the bank for further security. The bank receives the rent payments automatically, therefore, being assured of payment.

There are four basic categories of secured loans: loans secured by liquid assets (stocks and bonds, or cash); accounts receivable loans (accounts receivable loan and factoring); inventory loans; and fixed asset loans.

Liquid asset loans include loans secured by savings accounts, life insurance, or stocks and bonds.

1. Savings accounts can serve as collateral for a loan. The bank gets an assignment from you and also keeps your savings passbook. Your passbook can't be used, then, until you pay off part of the principal (money you pay back besides interest). Passbook loans are usually the lowest interest of secured loans. You put up a $1,000 account and the bank loans you $1000 at one or two percentage points above the interest you get from the passbook.

2. Life insurance cash values can be lent against. You would assign the policy to the bank. Rather than borrow the money directly from the insurance company on the policy, it is sometimes a cheaper interest rate to assign the cash value as collateral.

3. Marketable stocks and bonds can be used as collateral, too; but because of market fluctuations, banks usually loan only up to 75 percent of the market value of a high-grade stock. On bonds, banks will loan up to 90 percent of their market value.

Accounts receivable financing can be used as a basis for short- or intermediate-term loans from your bank, a finance company, or a factor. (A factor specializes in lending money on accounts receivable and/or purchasing them outright.) If your working capital is limited or your sales volume fluctuates, you will find this type of financing particularly useful.

When you obtain an accounts-receivable loan, you pledge or assign all or part of your accounts receivable as security for the loan. The agreement for the loan specifies what a percentage of the volume of receivables you assign will be loaned to you. In the case of the bank loan, this will usually be from 75 to 80 percent of sound receivables; for factor loans, it may be somewhat higher. The agreement also sets forth your rights and liabilities, those of the lender, the conditions under which each assignment is to operate, and the charges, which may include both interest and service charges.

You assign accounts receivable to the lender as you need funds. Each time, you prepare a schedule of assigned accounts and, if a loan is made, you sign a note for the amount. Usually, the lender stamps the assigned accounts in your accounts-receivable ledger.

Factoring Accounts Receivable

In more and more lines of business, factoring companies are being used to convert accounts receivable into cash. This procedure, called "factoring," is not the same as assigning accounts receivable as security for a loan, though most factoring companies handle both types of financing. In factoring, you enter into an agreement under which the factor buys all your accounts receivable as they arise. The accounts sold are no longer among your assets, nor does the amount received increase your liabilities, since it will not have to be repaid. If you borrow on your accounts receivable, on the other hand, they remain as an asset, and the amount of the loan becomes a liability.

With a loan on receivables, you are still responsible for collection, but when you sell the accounts, the factor takes over that function. He assumes all the risk and has no recourse if an account proves uncollectable. Because of this, the factor will pass on the credit standing of your customers. If he does not approve an account, you may still make the sale, but at your own risk. The factor will not buy that account.

The factor typically makes a service charge of 1 or 2 percent on the face amount of the accounts purchased. In addition, he charges interest at the rate of about 6 percent per year for the period between the time you receive funds from him and the average maturity date of the receivables he purchases from you. Factoring is an expensive method of raising funds, but it does away with the need for a credit and collection department. Also, it is often the quickest way for a small business to obtain cash.

There are two bases that banks take receivables on: notification and non-notification. Under the notification basis, the purchaser of your company's goods or services is informed by the bank that the account has been assigned to the bank and payments on the account are made directly to the bank. Under the non-notification basis, the borrower's customers continue to pay the borrower and the borrower pays the bank. (Factoring is discussed in more detail in chapter 3.)

Inventory financing is necessary when a large amount of inventory is tied up for a period of time. Some firms, especially those in manufacturing, have long cycles for purchasing, production, and warehousing, which would make inventory financing important.

In inventory loans the bank does not take physical position of the inventory, they appoint a third party to control the collateral to be released on authorization of the banker. The bank may have a lien on or title to the goods stored separately on the premises or in a storage warehouse. Inventory that would not be held this way are: small quantities of goods, fast moving items, work in process. In floor planning, the dealer has possession of the merchandise (in exchange for a note), but title to it remains with a bank or other lender who has paid the manufacturer. When the dealer sells a unit, he must pay the lender the amount due on that unit. The agreement contains various provisions for the protection of the lender.

The trust receipt is a legal document used for floor planning. It is used in conjunction with several pieces of numbered merchandise. When signed, the person signing it (the businessman-borrower) acknowledges receipt of the merchandise, agrees to keep the merchandise in trust for the bank, promises to pay the bank as the goods are sold.

Loans secured by inventory as collateral present special problems and conditions not ordinarily encountered with other loans. The bank cannot take physical possession of inventory, therefore, he must be certain of the reliability and honesty of the warehouser and the borrower. Any inventory financing will, of course, stifle the flow of inventory in operations and is expensive to administer. The most practical inventory for this type of financing is large quantities of slow moving goods.

Fixed Asset Financing is financing of large capital items (improvements, land and buildings, equipment and fixtures) and is for the longest term of the types of financing already discussed. In most cases loans secured by fixed assets are for in excess of one year.

When you are purchasing equipment as collateral, that is, you make a down payment on the equipment and borrow the rest from the bank, the bank takes a chattel mortgage. The chattel transfers ownership (title) to the bank and the borrower uses the equipment.

A real estate loan, which we are all familiar with, would be handled by the real estate section of the bank and is much like a personal real estate loan except it may require more documentation and a higher down payment.

Another type of long-term loan is the Small Business Administration 90 percent guaranteed loan through the bank. Its term is from five to fifteen years and it can be used for equipment, real estate, improvements, and working capital.

Summary

As I explained in this chapter, banks are the primary source of funding for a small- to medium-sized business. Most people are a little uptight when dealing with bankers, but I hope the "Environment" section has shown that they too are human and their conservative nature is more a product of training and concern for their depositors. I have shown that in certain circumstances, the bank can be a "liberal" institution. There are three time periods for loan repayment: Short-term (30 to 90 days usually, but less than one year), intermediate-term (up to five years) and long-term (five plus years). As far as collateral, loans are extended unsecured (requiring no collateral and usually for a short-term period) and secured, (most loans, those where collateral is used). The most widely used secured are loans secured by liquid assets (cash, etc.), accounts receivable, inventory, and fixed assets.

3 Commercial Financial Lenders

Go to a bank first," financial advisors generally suggest, "and if the bank cannot or will not help you, go to other private financial lenders." Commercial (or private) financial lenders, and I include in that definition personal financial lenders (consumer finance companies), commercial finance companies (including factors, industrial time sales companies, and leasing companies), life insurance companies, credit unions, foundations, and commercial paper houses, usually are more expensive as far as interest rates and will take, consequently, higher risk businesses.

Personal finance companies (or consumer finance companies, as they are sometimes called) take the highest risks of the private financial lenders and also charge the most interest. Commercial finance companies take average risk businesses up to the much higher risks. Pension funds, life insurance companies, and credit unions take the lowest risk of high risk loans, and their interest is the cheapest.

Private financial institutions include: personal (or consumer) finance companies; commercial finance companies (including factoring companies, time sales companies, and leasing companies); life insurance companies; trade credit; and other sources (including credit unions, pension and foundation funds, commercial paper houses, and personal credit).

Advantages and Disadvantages of Commercial Financing

Personal finance company loans offer the advantages of usually loaning more money to you for specific small purchases than the bank; although the credit criteria is about the same as a bank, personal finance companies will accept more debt per income, i.e., a weaker financial structure, and usually they offer much longer terms than a bank.

The major disadvantage of a personal finance company is that the interest is high. In California, for instance, interest is 30 percent per year simple interest on the first $225, 24 percent per annum on the portion of the loan from $225 to $625, 18 percent on amounts from $625 to $1,650, and 12 percent per annum on the portion of a loan over $1,650. Some states don't have any maximum interest on unsecured loans.

Commercial finance companies are willing to loan to businesses that aren't as strong financially as businesses that banks would consider. Furthermore, commercial financial companies are willing to take as security or collateral items banks are more selective about, such as inventories and receivables. In short, commercial finance companies are a lot more flexible than banks.

The disadvantages of commercial finance lending is that interest rates are generally higher, sometimes much higher than banks.

Life insurance companies, pension funds, commercial paper houses, and foundations offer money to businesses for real estate, equipment, leasing, and sometimes working capital in amounts that are usually larger than the typical bank loans. Their interest rates are usually only slightly higher than bank rates.

The disadvantages of these companies is that they usually only make large loans (in excess of $500,000) and require that the companies applying are financially strong.

Trade credit is a loan source without disadvantages. Your suppliers give you terms of up to ninety days and if you pay within the specified period you get the use of the money. The supplies would cost no interest, and if you pay early you sometimes even get a discount.

Personal credit and credit unions offer the advantage of getting small amounts of money quickly. The disadvantage is higher rates than standard bank loans.

People and Environment of Private Financial Lenders

Because each type of private financial company has slightly different environments and training, I will discuss each separately. One of the things that ties them all together is that the people of the institutions are usually experienced in banking or the securities industry.

Personal Financial Companies

Personal Financial Companies are unique in that, as one personal financial officer told me, "When people come in for the first time there is an atmosphere of distrust. They don't trust me and I distrust them." Most of the time customers who come to finance companies have been turned down by the bank. The borrower in this case doesn't have a history of a loan with this particular personal finance company. He wouldn't, of course, have a checking account, savings account, or any other credit background as he would have with a bank. You can get a picture of why the personal financial officer would probably be more apprehensive than a banker.

Most personal financial officers get their training through practical experience rather than through a well-coordinated, continuous training system as in a bank. Many personal financial officers have experience as bankers, and those that were not bankers were probably trained in a short intercompany or apprenticeship program for the chain personal financial companies or by apprenticeship with small finance companies. The pay for personal financial officers is about the same or more than the equivalent position in a bank. Most professional people, however, if given the choice of a job for the same pay at a bank or a personal finance company, will choose the bank job.

Unlike a bank, however, personal financial companies will spend more time soliciting customers. Most of the readers of this book have probably gotten a written solicitation in the mail from a finance company: "Here's a check for $25; all you have to do is come into our office and cash it. You repay it at. . . ." Also, some finance companies use sales contracts with tire companies, appliance companies, and so on. A customer will buy a set of tires on credit and the personal finance will own the payment contract. These sales contracts are usually a money loser for finance companies, because the maximum interest charged is usually restricted by law, but then they have a customer who they can call and say, "Well, how would you like to pay off all your bills and make a payment to one place." That is, they can now solicit a personal loan and make a better interest rate. As a matter of fact, some "bank qualified" people have probably never gone to a bank because it is so convenient to deal with a particular personal finance company, and, after all, the finance company already "trusts" them.

Commercial Finance Companies

Most of the people in commercial financing are brought up in the business, and generally, they don't have a banking background, I was told by the head of a large commercial financing company. Commercial financing is a high-risk kind of financing, or as the same gentleman put it, "we provide quasi-equity lending."

Commercial finance people sometimes get referrals from banks because the account is too difficult for the banks to handle. At the point when the commercial people get some of the business referrals, the bank's files on the business are pretty messy—as a loan gets worse, no one wants to deal with it, no memos are written, the chronology of events starts getting more and more dated.

Commercial finance people deal with more complex lending, of course, than personal finance companies, but they take higher risk loans.

Other Commercial Financiers

Trust directors, insurance companies, and foundation people tend to be long time professional investors who want a *safe* return on investment and are primarily concerned with loaning large amounts. The lenders tend to be removed from the person who makes the loan request by several layers of brokers, managers, and investors, in a complex almost government-like bureaucracy.

To site the example of an insurance company, the applicant must first approach a designated broker for the insurance company, a broker who may handle many insurance companies. Basically it is the broker who makes the decision to proceed, and, depending on the amount of the loan, generally has the final say so, that way the insurance company just gets a report and writes out the check.

These brokers, like the commercial finance company people, tend to be people brought up in the business and probably don't have any banking background.

Personal Finance Companies

There are many licensed consumer finance offices in this country that are widely distributed. They are engaged in making consumer loans to individuals and families for constructive purposes. The most important considerations in granting the loan are the borrower's character and his ability to meet financial obligations. In most cases, however, security such as a lien on household goods or a comaker (see chapter 2 for definition) is taken as further assurance of repayment of the loan.

The personal finance company is not a business loan operation, but sometimes a business in need of small amounts of money will use this source. It would not be considered a business loan *per se,* but a personal loan used for business purposes.

The average size loan is about $750. Most money loaned by personal finance companies is used for consumer loans. The average length of time is from two and one-half to three years and the average interest is usually the highest allowable by law.

As we mentioned that the finance company usually takes a lien against household goods, but generally this is more psychological security, than it is real security. As one finance officer told me, "If a borrower has $2,000 worth of furniture and we loan him $1,000, if he doesn't pay and we repossess, all we can expect to get is about $200 after marshal's fees, court costs, brokers commissions, etc." So the finance company is probably more interested in your character than your furniture.

Generally, personal financial companies do more work on checking your credit than banks. They use direct credit checks, i.e., calling your bank, charge cards, and other previous lenders; they use a credit service like Triple C's Credit or TRW Credit; and they also have access to a "Lenders Exchange" service which lists all people now having loans with these institutions, so if a borrower already has a loan with his dining room set as collateral, the exchange will have that information and he can't borrow from another finance company.

Commercial Finance Companies

For our purposes we will include in our discussion of commercial finance companies not only those companies called "commercial finance companies" but also factors, commercial time sales companies, and commercial leasing companies. Most large commercial finance companies would handle all of these functions anyway.

Commercial finance companies make loans secured by:
—Inventory
—Equipment and fixtures
—Accounts receivable (by both accounts receivable financing and factoring)
Commercial finance companies also provide equipment leasing services.

Most finance companies extend seasonal and term business credit. The majority of loans must be repaid within ninety days to one year. The loan's purpose affects its maturity. For example, if a company loans a retailer funds to build up pre-Christmas inventory, the loan would normally be repaid in January. However, if the company loans a manufacturer funds to purchase production equipment, the loan term could run as long as five years.

Commercial finance companies *do not* make unsecured business loans. Usually the collateral pledged is inventory or accounts receivable. But some loans are secured by the borrower's fixtures, furniture, machinery, equipment, or physical facility. Manufacturers and wholesalers as a rule can obtain accounts receivable financing on more favorable terms than retailers can. Manufacturers' and wholesalers' good shipments can be traced and identified more easily than retail sales items. Manufacturing and wholesaling invoice amounts per customer tend to be higher than retailer customers' bills. When accounts receivable are used to secure a loan, the borrower usually remains obligated to collect unpaid accounts. If a non-notification agreement exists, the borrower's customers are not informed that their accounts are pledged.

Commercial finance companies charge relatively high-effective interest rates. Rates may range from double the prime rate up to whatever a state's usury laws permit. The primary reason businesses apply to commercial finance companies for funding is the high risk nature of their propositions.

In the early 1900s the commercial finance company was created to fill a need of businessmen neglected by the traditional practices of the commercial bank, i.e., the financing of receivables. The idea originated as the story goes, by a Chicago seller of encyclopedias in 1904. He was selling his books on the installment plan, and he found his receivables increasing rapidly as his sales increased. He looked all around for a lender to advance him against his receivables. He found a private person interested and they formed a company. They intended to operate like a factors operation (discussed shortly) by having the borrower's customer pay them directly, but they got a lot of resistance to this idea. So the new company decided to have the borrower assign the receivables to the lender but collect the receivables themselves, as they normally would. By agreement, however, the borrower was legally the agent for the finance company and had to turn over all collections to the finance company in the form they were received (that is, they endorsed the payment check over to the finance company). This form of financing became known as "non-notification accounts receivable financing."

As commercial finance companies increased in number and strength, they employed other methods of financial assistance to their clients. They added financing of inventory and equipment.

Factors are one of our oldest financial institutions. The factor started as a sales agent who would bill buyers for goods that came from the factory through his hands. Even though he was selling the factory's goods he would bill in his name. Then, as now, invoices to buyers bear the sellers name bearing a legend indicating the assignment to the factor and requesting payments directly to the factor. Merchandise is not in the factor's possession. Therefore the factor's advances to the factory are secured by liens.

The basic difference between accounts receivable financing, the traditional field of the commercial finance company, and factoring, the province of the factor, is that in accounts receivable financing, the lender does not indicate on the invoice that the account is assigned and in factoring a legend on the invoice indicates that the account is assigned to a factor. Factoring and accounts receivable financing will be discussed in more detail later.

Industrial time sales financing deals with the acquisition of equipment and certain fixtures for business using the method of installment credit. The equipment financed must be income producing, which is the chief factor in determining whether they can be financed. Real estate and nonincome producing leasehold improvements are excluded.

Industrial time sales is an arrangement between these parties: the seller of the merchandise (or dealer) the purchaser (buyer) of the merchandise, and the financer. Unless all three people are involved it is no longer considered time sale financing. The transaction begins with a credit sale of the merchandise to the buyer, as opposed to a cash sale. The seller wants to make the credit sale but is unable to wait for the money. The seller contacts a financer who purchases the buyer's obligation from the seller for an agreed upon price. In short, the purchaser buys equipment from the seller and the financer buys paper from the seller. This type of financing is done most in the service industries, with the retail trade next and manufacturing third, and is generally used by small- and medium-sized businesses.

One of the most popular, best known uses of industrial time sales contracts was a well-known hoax. Billy Sol Estes, an enterprising Texas businessman, generated time paper involving the sale of fertilizer tanks to farmers. He produced receipts of the sales on credit and sold them to a financer. Many of the farmers who were supposed to have bought the tanks co-operated with Estes by verifying that the tanks had been bought. As it turned out, the tanks didn't exist and the farmers had been bribed.

We will discuss time sales in more detail shortly as we get into the types of loans available.

Types of Loans Available

Types of loans available from commercial finance companies, as we previously discussed include: inventory loans; equipment and fixture loans (including a discussion of commercial time financing); accounts receivable loans (including accounts receivable financing); and equipment leasing (involving a discussion of leasing companies). The types of loans will be covered in that order:

Inventory loans are available to accounts receivable and factoring clients. Such loans are frequently utilized to assist the customer during periods of slow product shipments and inventory build-up or to facilitate bulk raw material purchases at advantageous prices.

Equipment loans include basically two types: money loaned against presently owned equipment, and money loaned to finance new equipment and financed on a time sales financing basic.

On presently owned equipment, commercial finance companies will sometimes make loans. These advances are normally amortized monthly over a period of one to five years or even more. The proceeds from this type of loan may be required by the borrower to increase working capital, discount accounts payable, or simply to purchase new equipment. Very often an equipment loan is accepted in conjunction with accounts receivable or factoring arrangements.

Industrial time sales, as we discussed previously, are the process of a company buying equipment from an equipment supplier and the equipment supplier selling the purchase contract to a financer.

The price you pay for buying installment equipment is usually high; higher, in fact, than the highest interest allowable in your state. How can the additional cost of financing be higher than the maximum allowable interest rate? Because you don't pay "interest" on industrial installment loans—you pay a "time price differential."

The cost of buying on installment, called the "time price differential," has the following rational. A seller is presumed to have two prices. One is the cash price. The other price is the "time price," which assumes that the purchaser, who wants credit over a period of time, must pay an added charge to compensate the seller for his additional burden. The differential between the cash price and the time price is the time price differential. This reasoning assumes that the seller is not a money lender. The price doctrine provides the legal mechanism to remove the time sell from the application of usury laws (the state laws that restrict the maximum interest that can be charged on secured loans) in holding that the transaction is a credit sale and is neither a loan nor a forebearance for money.

Accounts receivable loans are the "bread and butter" of commercial finance companies, and were originally what the commercial finance companies were set up to deal with. Accounts receivable loans fall into two categories: accounts receivable financing and factoring.

Accounts receivable financing is discussed in detail in chapter 2, and accounts receivable financing at banks is practically identical to accounts receivable financing by commercial finance companies.

In short, accounts receivable can be pledged as collateral for loans. Typically, an 80 percent advantage is made against eligible accounts. The assignment is handled on a non-notification revolving basis and is self-liquidating. Interest charges are billed on the basis of actual daily cash loan balances. This monthly charge is frequently less than missed cash discounts. (More detail is given in chapter 2.)

Factoring is slightly different than accounts receivable financing. Factoring is the outright sale of trade accounts on a nonrecourse basis. Factoring enables a business to eliminate a credit and collection department as well as losses due to bad debts. A factor will buy outright all accounts receivable approved by it at a nominal discount. This enables the client to concentrate on production, purchasing, and selling—the profit tools of any business.

As we explained earlier in this chapter, a factor puts his legend ("This account's payment belongs to XYZ Factors") on the bills, and the factor is paid directly by the customer. That is, accounts receivable are assigned on a notification basis.

There are three basic types of factoring: maturity factoring, advance factoring, and drop shipment factoring.

What accounts will a factor or accounts receivables lender take? What are the considerations involved? Those questions are, of course, of great importance when deciding whether to use accounts receivable financing.

A lender's appraisal of what accounts he will take include two key elements: (1) careful appraisal of the nature and value of the accounts that are the collateral for the loan and (2) estimates of the creditor preserve the borrower is currently under.

An accounts receivable borrower must do the following if he gets financing:
—turn over to the lender the checks from his customers in the form they are received
—supply the lender with copies of invoices and the documentary evidence of shipments (usually parcel post receipts).
The lender keeps a control ledger on the borrower for each account, the ledger shows the amount assigned and advanced, the amount remitted, and the balance.

An account of the costs and benefits of financing is well summarized in *Commercial Financing* (R. Monroe Lazere, Roland Press Co., New York, 1968):

"The advantage to the borrower of pledging accounts is that it accelerates his cash flow. It frees his capital from the waiting period required by normal trade terms. In effect, the financer does the waiting (for the payment by the account debtors) and the borrower's capital can be more profitably re-employed for other purposes. The increased rate of turnover of the borrower's capital enhances the leverage of that capital and should produce increased profits. More specifically, the accelerated cash flow can result in any combination of tangible results such as increased volume, earning of trade discounts on purchases from suppliers, or development of ability to make more advantageous purchases by having available cash." (See Table 3.1)

Leasing is also a type of financing; moreover, it is a type of financing for the full amount of the equipment, etc., you need. Leasing is sort of the baby of the traditional, popular, funding methods, and there is still a lot of debate as to

Table 3.1	Summary of Transaction with Secured Financer*					
Date	Accounts Assigned	Cash Advanced	Cash Collected	Equity Remitted	Collateral Balance	Loan Balance
11/1	$10,000	$8,000	—	—	$ 10,000	$ 8,000
11/2	10,000	8,000	—	—	20,000	16,000
11/3	10,000	8,000	—	—	30,000	24,000
11/4	10,000	8,000	—	—	40,000	32,000
11/5	10,000	8,000	—	—	50,000	40,000
11/6	10,000	8,000	—	—	60,000	48,000
11/7	10,000	8,000	—	—	70,000	56,000
11/8	10,000	8,000	—	—	80,000	64,000
11/9	10,000	8,000	—	—	90,000	72,000
11/10	10,000	8,000	—	—	100,000	80,000
11/11	—	—	—	—	100,000	80,000
11/12	—	—	$10,000	$2,000	90,000	72,000
11/13	—	—	10,000	2,000	80,000	64,000
11/14	—	—	10,000	2,000	70,000	56,000
11/15	—	—	10,000	2,000	60,000	48,000
11/16	—	—	10,000	2,000	50,000	40,000
11/17	—	—	10,000	2,000	40,000	32,000
11/18	—	—	10,000	2,000	30,000	24,000
11/19	—	—	10,000	2,000	20,000	16,000
11/20	—	—	10,000	2,000	10,000	8,000
11/21	—	—	—	—	10,000	8,000
11/22	—	—	—	—	10,000	8,000
11/23	—	—	—	—	10,000	8,000
11/24	10,000	8,000	—	—	20,000	16,000
11/25	10,000	8,000	—	—	30,000	24,000
11/26	10,000	8,000	—	—	40,000	32,000
11/27	—	—	—	—	40,000	32,000
11/28	—	—	—	—	40,000	32,000
11/29	—	—	—	—	40,000	32,000
11/30	—	—	—	—	40,000	32,000

*Commercial Financing, R. Monroe Lazere, Roland Press Co., New York, 1968.

whether it's a good method for businessmen. To add to the controversy, there is no standard way things can be leased. You can rent a piece of equipment with or without maintenance, or with partial maintenance, and you can lease by the month, year, or several years. You can also obtain leases with the option to purchase.

As you might have guessed, leasing is a way to finance equipment, fixtures, or buildings. So far no one's figured out a way to lease working capital.

There are advantages and disadvantages to leasing. Some of the advantages are:

1. Leasing offers a tax advantage. When you own something, you have to depreciate it for tax purposes over a lengthy period, so that the cost is recovered only slowly. A lot of bookkeeping has to be done to obtain a tax saving. If inflation proceeds at the same pace as in recent years, the tax saving becomes one of the decreasingly valuable dollars as the depreciation table stretches into the future. Despite current efforts to slow inflation, there is little reason to expect that it can be kept under control.

Leasing expenses are operating expenses and do not have to be depreciated, stretched out, held to future years, or back-charged to years gone by.

2. If you chose to have a maintenance contract with the lease (a good example is maintenance-included leases on copy machines), your maintenance is done by the maintenance company, therefore you can forget about it.

3. You can "walk away" from the lease, return the equipment to the lessor when the equipment becomes outmoded or too slow, without having to finish the payments. In short, leasing is more flexible than ownership.

4. You need not worry about the equipment becoming obsolete, because you just stop the lease.

5. Money that might be tied up in expensive fixed assets can be used for other purposes.

6. The cost of the equipment is fixed by the lease agreement, and this makes the cost predictable for projections.

The disadvantages of leasing include:

1. The counterargument against the oft mentioned tax advantages of leasing holds that a purchaser of equipment may take depreciation and interest as tax deductible expenses. Studies of comparative tables of parallel transactions (utilizing the same depreciation formula, cost of equipment, and interest charge) have been made. The conclusions thus reached clearly indicate that leasing does not increase or decrease the total tax savings. Leasing, however, does enable the lessee to distribute his tax savings more evenly over the term of the lease. Further, as the lease term or purchase period increases, the annual differential on tax savings seems to become less.

2. Down payments from leasing were at one time cheaper than purchase down payments. Now however, the prepayments on leases is only 2 to 5 percent less than the down payment required for a purchase contract.

3. The costs for purchasing or buying are about the same and when the equipment is purchased from the leasing company at the end of the period, the costs of leasing are higher.

4. If your company loses control over maintenance, you are at the mercy of the leasing company as to when the equipment will be fixed and how long the downtime is.

In short, leasing requires a little less down payment at the start but is generally more expensive than standard equipment purchase. Leasing is best if you need the flexibility of temporary use of the equipment.

*Life Insurance
Companies*

Because of the striking growth of the industry, the accumulation of assets in life insurance companies has been rapid and substantial. It has been estimated that these companies are accumulating assets at the rate of $6 billion per year. The outflow of their funds can be statistically predicted. Hence a part of their portfolio is available for long-term financing in the form of mortgages on industrial, commercial, and housing real estate. They also make loans to businesses but require substantial enterprises with long earnings records and dealing in markets not subject to rapid change. The average small- or medium-sized business would not qualify however, because life insurance companies must follow certain loan policies: (1) borrower has to be a corporation, (2) there is a minimum time for the borrower to be in business, (3) the borrower should have sufficient historical and current earnings to meet a formula of established obligations including debt repayments. A life insurance company grants two types of loans: commercial and industrial mortgage loans and unsecured loans. Mortgages by insurance companies cost the same as or higher than orthodox bank loans.

A prevalent type of life insurance company loans is on an unsecured basis to a business in *very good* financial condition. Life insurance lenders are most interested in long-range financial data demonstrated by projected sales, cash flows, and so on.

Trade Credit

Trade credit is the credit extended by a supplier to a buyer for goods purchased. It is the most used form of short-term credit, especially among small businesses. If the goods purchased are paid for in time to take advantage of the cash discounts, trade credit costs the buyer nothing.

Suppose you have an invoice for $1,000 with terms of 2/10, net/30. If you pay the invoice within the 10 days, you will pay $980. But suppose you do not have enough cash to pay the invoice within 10 days, then you will pay the full $1,000. In other words, the extra 20 days' credit will cost 2 percent of $1,000 or $20.

On the other hand, if you borrowed $1,000 from the bank on a 30-day note and paid the invoice within the 30 days, you would pay the bank only $5 interest, a savings of $15.

It pays to use the full cash-discount period, or if no cash discount is offered, the full credit period. Delaying payment beyond the credit period, however, injures your credit rating and may be costly in the long run.

Other Sources of Private Loans

Besides the sources mentioned, there are other, less known sources of capital. These include: credit unions; pension funds and foundations; commercial paper houses; and personal credit.

1. *Credit unions* make loans. If you are a member of a credit union you can get reasonable interest loans for small amounts. Credit union services are offered only to members of credit unions; the credit union law restricts membership within any single credit union to a more or less homogeneous group of members having a common bond of interest. Credit union laws restrict the rate of interest change and the amount of loan that may be made to a single borrower.

2. *Pension funds and foundations,* because of their investment money coming in, have experienced a rapid and large accumulation of assets and have a predictable outflow. Their standards of investment are also similar to those of the life insurance companies, and they charge about the same interest rates.

A good percentage of pension funds is used for sale-leasehold arrangements. Large foundations make loans in excess of $1,000,000 for periods averaging ten years. When they evaluate applicants, special emphasis is placed on: company management, business background, and realistic projections.

3. *Commercial paper houses* are firms that broker sales of short-term promissory notes of the borrower to individuals or institutions or other business entities. Only large firms with long histories of sound operation are eligible for this type of financing.

4. And last but not least, a source of small, quick loans is your own *personal credit.* One form of personal credit is your BankAmericard, Mastercharge, American Express, or other charge card. In the state of California interest rates are 18 percent per year, which is relatively high, but credit is pretty easy. You can borrow up to your credit limit on each card.

One trick is to borrow, say $500 each on BankAmericard and Mastercharge then, using that money as your personal cash equity, you can borrow another $1,000 from the bank to start a business.

Another source of credit is automatic overdraft checks. You can write a check for up to your maximum overdraft limit and it automatically becomes a loan.

Personal credit is best for short-term quick cash, and not really a good idea for long-term purposes.

In summary, there are resources for loans other than the banks and these sources are more flexible than banks, but usually more expensive.

Government Financing

The largest single lender to business in the United States is the federal government, followed by state and local governments. The federal government's lending program is larger than the loan programs of the Bank of America, Chase Manhattan, City National Bank, J. P. Morgan, and a lot more of the biggest banks in the United States. The US government loans over $1.852 trillion dollars per year to businesses. In light of this, it would seem foolish for a business of any size (breakeven-small to multi-national corporations) to ignore the federal, state, and local government lending programs.

People and Environment in Government Financial Sources

Bureaucracy has been described as everything from "where the civil servant is the uncivil master" to "a lot of government officials whose job someone else wants." The people of the government bureaucracy—the employees of the government lending agencies—are pretty reasonable and quite different from what one would expect from the bad press they have received.

The individual bureaucrats are simply the processors of information. They are given information (a loan request), asked to evaluate whether this specific request meets all the criteria for acceptance (usually the most difficult of all the hurdles), then they, or another bureaucrat makes a decision on the approval of the loan.

The people in government financing are not so much interested in conserving government money (like a banker and bank money) but in adhering to the specific requirements stated in the law and rules passed down from the agency directors. If all the forms presented to the bureaucrat are properly completed, he will have much more time to consider your request. Filling out the forms correctly does not seem like too much to ask of a businessman. The problem is not that the forms are complicated but that an effective loan presentation entails a great deal more information than just filled-out forms.

Background of the Government Loan Officer

Like many of the lenders in banks and commercial finance companies, government lending persons come from banking and technical financial backgrounds. Some also come from liberal arts and sales backgrounds, but this is a smaller percentage. Generally, the backgrounds of the government people are more homogeneous than banks or commercial finance companies. The regional, local, and national heads of government lenders tend to be appointed politically and most do not have bank backgrounds. They are more likely to be people from the business community. Very seldom is someone appointed as a director of an agency who has worked for a considerable time within that agency. In short, the top positions are not very often filled by people who started out as a clerk, became a loan officer, a supervisor, local head, then regional and national director.

What does this mean? To the bureaucrats at the top, it means that decisions will be made providing for a smooth-running organization, loaning out the total monies available by people in a politically precarious position.

The bureaucrats are probably going to be interested in an efficient organization that is cost effective (doesn't cost more than it is worth to run). The objective of the official is to assure that all subordinates' time is effectively occupied, the subordinates follow all the rules of the organization, and they make regular reports to him. These reports are extremely important to him as they are essentially the only tool in which to evaluate the organization. Moreover, the reports he sends to his superiors are based on the reports he receives. As one US Department of Commerce official once told me: "When they want us [the heads of the government agencies] on the Hill for a review, we need good reports, we don't want to have to make up fiction."

I could give a lot of examples of how reports are important and why the bureaucrats are so fanatical about them, but I will let it suffice to say the head people are more interested in their reports than your loans.

This means that the people you talk with, the loan officers, are the people who, for a borrower, are the most important link in the chain.

So how about the loan officers? What are they like? Loan officers are usually more liberal than their bosses. Generally speaking, the loan officers (especially in large agencies like the SBA) are younger and less experienced than the loan review committee. This is purely a matter of economics. The loan officers who do the initial review are the bottom of the professional ladder and

GS pay-scale ratings. There is usually a fairly large turnover at the entry level, as well, since the young officers, once trained, can easily slip into banking, industry, or other government posts.

The typical loan officer is between twenty-five and thirty-five years old, has a college degree, probably in business, and has had a sparse background of experience since college graduation. His experience could have been in banking at a junior level. He is usually married and could have children. He is rather conservative philosophically and from a middle-class background or wishes he was.

The application that the loan officer is reviewing *has* to be in perfect order and, if he recommends a loan, it should conform to all the criteria of lending. In other words, the loan should not violate the agencies' "nos" list and should be on the conservative side of the agencies' "maybes."

Training in-house for the loan officers is similar to bank training except the government puts more emphasis on training in reporting.

The Loan Process

Figure 4.1 illustrates the flow of your loan from the time it is presented until it is approved. After the analysis and proposal is prepared (explained in Part II), the loan is submitted either directly to the government agency or to a bank or other lender who will submit it to the loan officer for approval.

If the loan is submitted to the agency it must go through a review person or committee. (1) If the information is incomplete or the applicant does not meet the legal requirements for the loan, the application is returned to the applicant. If all requirements are met and the information is complete, the loan application goes to a loan officer or committee. Time required in this process is from one day to two weeks.

If the loan is the type submitted to a lender first (1A) to be approved by the government agency as a guarantee, the applicant submits the loan request to the lender. If the loan is approved by the lender, it is sent directly to the agency loan officer, bypassing the review committee. If rejected by the lender, the loan goes back to the applicant. Time required is one week to six weeks before the loan is submitted to the agency.

The loan officer or committee (2) reviews the loan to see whether there are any observable problems that would cast aspersions on either the company, the management, or the ability to repay. Time required is one week to three weeks. If the loan is approved, it goes to the final approval authority with recommendations for approval. If the loan is rejected, it is returned to the applicant or the lender. In most cases, it is unlikely that the loan officer will disapprove a loan submitted by a lender for a guarantee.

The approval committee or person (3) generally acts on the recommendations of the loan officer and unless there is a shortage of funds and a large number of approved applications, the approval person or committee will more or less rubber stamp the recommendations of the loan officer. Time required is from one week to three weeks (or longer in the case of a shortage of

Figure 4.1
Chart Illustrating Flow of the
Loan

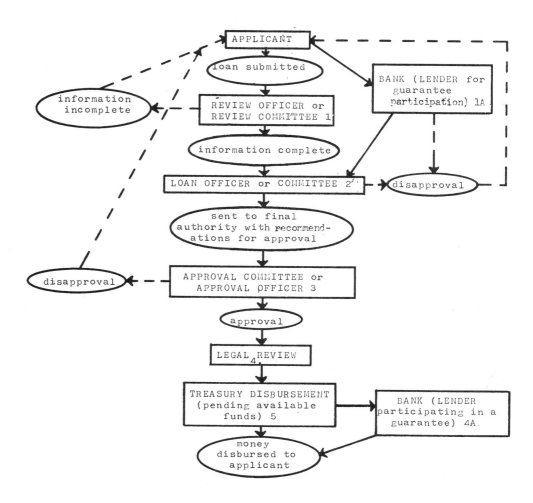

Rectangles represent persons, companies or committees
Ovals represent action
Straight, solid lines represent action <u>toward</u> approval
A broken line represents return of the loan proposal to the applicant

money). If the loan is approved, it goes to the legal department to see that all the final papers are in order. If rejected, it either goes back to the loan officer for reworking or it goes back to the applicant.

The legal department (4) prepares the final papers and checks for any legal problem. When it is approved by the legal department, it goes to the bank or lender for disbursement in the case of a guarantee, or to the treasury for disbursement in the case of direct loans. Time required may be from one to six weeks.

When the bank gets the agency's approval (4A) they prepare the necessary documents, then disburse the loan to the applicant. No negative response ever happens here. Time required for disbursement is from one day to ten days.

The treasury holds the disbursement of the funds until money is available (5). If money is already available, they disburse the funds immediately. Some agencies have money available only in advance. Time required is from one day to five months depending on the money available.

The total time required from submittal of the application until the application is approved and the money disbursed is from three and one-half weeks to eight and one-half months. This time, of course, is from the time the loan is prepared and submitted. The average time required to process government loans is two and one-half months. It has been my experience over the last six years of dealing with government loans that the time period is becoming progressively longer and I suspect, barring any unusual reorganization, the average time will be about three months by 1980.

A consideration of the time required to process these loans is necessary. If you need the money tomorrow, next week, or next month, forget about getting a government loan! You should allow at least three months for the money to get to you *after submittal.* You should also realize that the time required to gather the necessary information about your company and yourself and prepare the loan can take up to two months. The total average time required from when you begin the loan until the time it is disbursed is three and one-half months.

Time is a very important consideration with most business loan requests. The fastest source generally is the bank, with commercial companies following, and with government loans being the slowest of the sources. If your business cannot be slowed down and your belt tightened until the government loan comes through, you are in trouble.

Government Agencies and Types of Loans

The following is a list of all the government agencies that make business loans, and the types of loans they make.

	Type of Loan	Purpose	Who May Apply	Where to Apply
Small Business Administration				
	Business Loans	To assist small firms to finance construction, conversion, or expansion; to purchase equipment, facilities, machinery, supplies or materials; and to acquire working capital. Loans are direct or in participation with banks.	Small businesses	Nearest SBA Field Office
	Economic Opportunity Loans	To assist small firms operated by those who have marginal or submarginal incomes or those who have been denied equal opportunity (Title IV of the Economic Opportunity Act).	Low-income disadvantaged persons desiring to strengthen or establish a small business	Nearest SBA Field Office

	Type of Loan	Purpose	Who May Apply	Where to Apply
	Disaster Loans	To assist disaster victims to rebuild homes or business establishments damaged in SBA-declared disaster areas.	Individuals, business concerns, and nonprofit organizations	Nearest SBA Field Office
	Economic Injury Loans	To assist small concerns suffering economic injury resulting from: (1) a major or natural disaster declared by the President or Secretary of Agriculture; (2) Federally-aided urban renewal or highway construction programs; (3) inability to market or process a product because of disease or toxicity resulting from natural or undetermined causes; (4) US trade agreements.	Small business firms suffering such economic injury	Nearest SBA Field Office
	Development Company Loans	To assist small firms by helping to establish and finance the operation of state and local small business development companies which make loans to small firms for equity capital, plant construction, conversion, or expansion.	State and local development companies	Nearest SBA Field Office

Economic Development Administration (EDA)

	Type of Loan	Purpose	Who May Apply	Where to Apply
	Business or Public Loans	To aid unemployment and underemployment areas in their economic development	States or components, nonprofit organizations, and private borrowers	Administrator, Economic Development Administration, Washington, DC 20230

Export-Import Bank of the United States (Eximbank) and Overseas Private Investment Corporation

Export-Import Bank of the United States (Ex-Im Bank):
To assist in financing US foreign trade through the following programs (in all cases, advance commitments are available without charge).

	Type of Loan	Purpose	Who May Apply	Where to Apply
		Authorizing the Foreign Credit Insurance Association (FCIA) to issue policies covering commercial and/or political risks on short and medium-term credit extended by US exporters to their overseas customers.	Exporters or banks	Exporters' insurance agent or broker, or directly to FCIA, 250 Broadway, New York, NY 10007
		Guaranteeing payment of medium-term export paper purchased without recourse by commercial banks.	Commercial banks and Edge Act Corporations	Commercial banks apply to Eximbank (exporter applies to his bank)

Type of Loan	Purpose	Who May Apply	Where to Apply
	Guarantees directly to US firms covering commercial and political risks involved in the performance of services abroad and in the leasing, consignment, or exhibition of US goods in foreign markets.	Exporters	Eximbank, Washington, DC 20571
	Direct loans to overseas buyer of US goods and services, enabling them to pay cash to the US exporters.	Overseas buyers or interested exporters	Eximbank, Washington, DC 20571
	"Discount" loans against eligible export debt obligations held by commercial banks, providing liquidity to banks financing US exports and, where necessary, more competitive interest rates.	Commercial banks; Edge Act Corporations	Eximbank, Washington, DC 20571

Overseas Private Investment Corporation (OPIC)

Type of Loan	Purpose	Who May Apply	Where to Apply
Private Enterprise Development	OPIC offers a variety of services to private US companies interested in establishing new businesses or expanding present facilities in less developed countries. These services include investment information and counseling; preinvestment and project development financing; project insurance against the risks of currency inconvertibility, expropriation, and war, revolution or insurrection; and project financing through loan guaranties and direct dollar and local currency loans.	US citizens or corporations, partnerships, or associations substantially and beneficially US-owned	OPIC, Washington, DC 20527

Agricultural Business Loans Commodity Credit Corporation (Department of Agriculture)

Type of Loan	Purpose	Who May Apply	Where to Apply
Agricultural	To provide nonrecourse loans on commodities stored on the farm or in commercial warehouses in order to provide price support and enable farmers to carry out an orderly marketing program.	Farmers	The local county office of the Agricultural Stabilization and Conservation Service

Type of Loan	Purpose	Who May Apply	Where to Apply
	To expand or build farm storage facilities, or to buy drying equipment for use with stored commodities.	Farmers	The local county office of the ASCS

Farmers Home Administration (Department of Agriculture)

Type of Loan	Purpose	Who May Apply	Where to Apply
Operating	To family farmers for land improvement, equipment, labor, and development resources necessary to successful farming including the development of recreational and other nonfarm enterprises to be operated on the farms.	Operators of not larger than family farms	Local farmers Home Administration office
Farm Ownership	To buy, improve, or enlarge farms and to provide essential services including buildings and land for nonfarm enterprises needed to supplement farm incomes.	Farmers and ranchers who are or will become operators of not larger than family farms	Local FHA office
Irrigation	Loans to develop irrigation systems, drain farmland, and carry out soil conservation measures.	Groups of farmers and ranchers	Local FHA office
Grazing and Forest Lands	Loans for shifts in land use to develop grazing areas and forest lands.	Groups of farmers and ranchers	Local FHA office
Rural Housing	To construct and repair needed homes and essential farm buildings, purchase previously occupied homes, or buy sites on which to build homes.	Farmers and other rural residents in open country and rural communities of not more than 5,500	Local FHA office
Rural Rental Housing	Loans to provide rental housing for the rural elderly and for younger rural residents of low and moderate income.	Individuals, profit corporations, private nonprofit corporations	Local FHA office
Housing for Labor	Loans to finance housing facilities for domestic farm labor.	Individual farmers, groups of farmers, and public or private nonprofit organizations	Local FHA office
Conditional Commitments	Assurance to builder or seller that homes to be constructed or rehabilitated will meet FHA lending requirements if built as proposed and that the agency would be willing to make loans to qualified applicants who may want to buy homes.	Individual, partnership, or corporations engaged in construction of homes	Local FHA office

Type of Loan	Purpose	Who May Apply	Where to Apply
Disaster	Emergency loans in designated areas where natural disasters such as floods and droughts have brought about a temporary need for credit not available from other sources.	Farmers	Local FHA office

Farm Credit Administration (An independent agency that supervises nationwide farmer-owned and controlled Farm Credit System.)

Type of Loan	Purpose	Who May Apply	Where to Apply
Banks for cooperatives	To provide complete loan service for farmer cooperatives.	Farmers cooperatives	Bank for cooperatives serving area
Federal Land Banks	To provide long-term mortgage credit to purchase, enlarge, or to improve farms, to refinance debts, and other purposes.	Farmers (full-time or part-time) and farming corporations	Federal land bank association serving area
Production	To provide short- and intermediate-term credit for farm production, farm home, or farm family purposes.	Farmers (both full-time or part-time) and farming corporations	Production credit association serving area

Federal Reserve Board Guarantee

Type of Loan	Purpose	Who May Apply	Where to Apply
Defense Production	To facilitate and expedite the financing of persons having contracts or engaged in operations deemed necessary for national defense.	Contractors, subcontractors, and others, doing business with Army, Navy, Air Force, Defense Supply, Agency, Interior, Agriculture, Commerce, GSA, AEC, or NASA	At a bank or other financing institutions, which in turn applies through a Federal Reserve Bank to the appropriate government department or agency for a loan guarantee

Other Loans

Other loans include, for the federal government: Veterans Administration; Maritime Administration; and Natural Resource Loans under the Department of the Interior. For state and local governments, loans include: State of California Job Creation Law Board; and local development companies.

Veterans Administration

Type of Loan	Purpose	Who May Apply	Where to Apply
Real Estate Loans for Business	For the purchase of land or the purchase, construction, repair, alteration, or improvement of buildings to be used for the purchase of engaging in business or pursuing a gainful occupation.	Eligible World War II, Korean Conflict, and Vietnam veterans	Nearest VA Office for approval of eligibility. Loan application is made to a bank or other private lender
Farm Operation Loans	For the purchase of property other than real estate, such as supplies, equipment, machinery, etc. or for working capital required in operation of a farm.	Eligible World War II, Korean Conflict, and post-Korean veterans. Servicemen with at least two years active duty	Nearest VA Office for approval of eligibility. Loan application is made to a bank or other private lender

Type of Loan	Purpose	Who May Apply	Where to Apply
Business Loans	For the purchase of property other than real estate such as inventory, equipment, or machinery; or for working capital required for engaging in business or pursuing a gainful occupation.	Eligible World War II and Korean Conflict veterans	Nearest VA Office for eligibility. Loan application is made to a bank or other private lender
Housing Credit Shortage Loans	Direct Loans to provide for homes in certain designated housing credit shortage areas.	Eligible World War II, Korean Conflict, and post-Korean veterans. Servicemen with at least two years active duty	The VA office having jurisdiction over the area where the home is located

The Maritime Administration

Type of Loan	Purpose	Who May Apply	Where to Apply
Shipbuilding	To insure construction loans and/or mortgages to aid in financing the construction, reconstruction, or reconditioning of vessels.	Private ship owners	Maritime Administration, Washington, DC 20235

Natural Resource Loans, Department of Interior

Bureau of Indian Affairs

Type of Loan	Purpose	Who May Apply	Where to Apply
	To encourage industry and income producing enterprises and for the education of certain Indians needing funds for that purpose.	Indians, Eskimos, and Aleuts	The Indian Agency Superintendent or a local Indian relending organization

Geological Survey

Type of Loan	Purpose	Who May Apply	Where to Apply
	To encourage domestic minerals exploration by providing financial assistance on a participating basis.	Individuals, partnerships, corporate enterprises	Field Offices and Washington, DC, Office of Minerals Exploration, Geological Survey

Bureau of Commercial Fisheries

Type of Loan	Purpose	Who May Apply	Where to Apply
	To assist in strengthening the domestic fishing industry, loans are made to finance and refinance the cost of purchasing, constructing, equipping, maintaining, repairing, or operating new or used commercial fishing vessels or gear.	US citizens, as defined in Section 2 of the Shipping Act, 1916, as amended, who have the qualifications necessary to operate and maintain the vessel or gear to be used	Division of Loans and Grants of a Regional Office of the Bureau of Commercial Fisheries, US Dept. of Interior

Bureau of Reclamation

Type of Loan	Purpose	Who May Apply	Where to Apply
	Loans and grants for the development of small reclamation projects, primarily for irrigation, in the seventeen western states and Hawaii.	Nonfederal entities having authority to contract with the US under federal reclamation law	Regional Offices of Bureau of Reclamation

What are Government Requirements?

Guidelines differ with each organization, of course, but generally, the government tries to aid business in order to increase employment when it would otherwise be difficult to do so. The government funds or guarantees loans to businesses that banks and other financial institutions are not able to or will not make, either because the loan is too big, too risky, or does not fall into traditional lending categories.

Government loans are not easy to get. Yet, sometimes the agencies give money to extremely high risk businesses and the interest rate is usually low. However, the loan operation and requirements to make the loan are generally quite complicated.

The technical requirements, i.e., the package, the analysis of your business that you present to the lender, requires a lot of technical and detail work, all of which will be explained in detail in the second section of this book.

Getting government loans also takes considerable time and effort, not the least of which is the time required to prepare the necessary documentation. There is also considerable effort required to understand and follow the government process.

The Small Business Administration (SBA)

The Small Business Administration (SBA) is an independent agency of the federal government, established by Congress to advise and help the nation's small businesses. Its four major areas of activity are:
1. Helping small companies find adequate capital and credit.
2. Providing management, financial, and production counsel.
3. Licensing and regulating small business investment companies.
4. Helping small businesses secure a fair share of government procurement contracts and surplus sales.

Who is Eligible?

To qualify for a loan a business must be a small business concern and must meet certain credit requirements. The Small Business Administration publishes regulations that provide detailed information on the size standards for loan applicants. These regulations may be obtained from any SBA office.

A small business concern is defined by the SBA for the purpose of receiving an SBA loan as a concern, including its affiliates, which is independently owned and operated, is not dominant in its field of operation, and can further qualify under the maximum criteria as set forth below:

Construction. Any construction concern is small if its average annual receipts do not exceed between $5 million and $12 million (depending on type of construction company: dredging, plumbing, etc.) for the preceding three fiscal years.

Manufacturing. Any manufacturing concern is classified:
1. As small if its number of employees does not exceed 250 persons.
2. As large if its number of employees exceeds 1500 persons (and therefore is not eligible for SBA loans). Note: certain companies may be considered small if

they have more than 250 employees but less than 1500. In these situations it would be advisable to contact the SBA to determine if the business concern qualifies as a small business.

3. As small if it is primarily engaged in the food canning and preserving industry and its number of employees does not exceed 500 persons exclusive of agricultural labor as defined in subsection (K) of the Federal Employment Tax Act.

Retail. Any retailing concern is classified as small if its annual sales do not exceed $2 million. Certain industries or subindustries, as set forth in Schedule D of Part 121, SBA Rules and Regulations, can have sales in excess of $2 million and still be classified as a small business. These exceptions include the following:

1. Clothing stores (men's and boys', family, or women's ready to wear): $2.5 million
2. Shoe stores: $2.5 million
3. Household appliance and radio-television stores: $2.5 million
4. Variety stores: $3 million
5. Farm equipment dealers: $4.5 million
6. Motor vehicle dealers (new or used): $6.5 million
7. Grocery stores, and meat markets (a part of meat and fish or seafood markets): $7.5 million

Services. Any service concern is classified as small if:

1. Its annual receipts do not exceed $1.5 million to $9 million depending on type of service industry ($1.5 million for cleaning and drying and $9 million for marine engineering). (With respect to trailer courts or parks, 50 percent of the receipts must be from rental of space to tourist trailers for periods not in excess of thirty days).
2. It is primarily engaged in the industries shown below and the annual receipts do not exceed the dollar figure shown:

    Hotel-motel: $4 million

    Power laundry: $4 million

    Motion picture production or services industry: $8 million

    Rendering general engineering services: $7.5 million

3. It is primarily engaged in owning and operating a hospital and its capacity does not exceed 150 beds; (convalescent and nursing homes are classified under the $1.5 million in annual receipts restriction).

Shopping Centers. Any concern primarily engaged in operating shopping centers is small if:

1. It does not have assets exceeding $8 million.
2. It does not have a net worth in excess of $4 million.
3. It does not have an average net income in excess of $400,000 (average net income to be computed without benefit of any carryover loss).
4. It does not lease more than 25 percent of the gross leasable area to concerns that do not meet the SBA's small business definitions.

For the purpose of size determinations, shopping center operations will not be considered affiliated with their tenants merely because of lease agreements.

Transportation and Warehousing. Any concern primarily engaged in passenger and freight transportation or warehousing is classified as small if:

1. Its annual receipts do not exceed $1.5 million.

2. It is primarily engaged in the air transportation industry and its number of employees does not exceed 1,000 persons.

3. It is primarily engaged in the storage of grain and it does not have more than 1 million bushels capacity in owned and leased facilities, and its annual receipts do not exceed $1.5 million.

4. It is primarily engaged in trucking, warehousing, packaging and crating and/or freight forwarding, and its annual receipts do not exceed $6.5 million.

Wholesale. Any wholesaling concern is classified as small if:

1. Its annual receipts do not exceed $9.5 million. There are exceptions to this as firms in some lines of wholesaling can have annual receipts of $14 million to $22 million. If you have a firm with annual receipts in excess of $9.5 million, SBA can be contacted to see if it qualifies as a small business concern.

2. It is a business concern primarily engaged in wholesaling, but also engaged in manufacturing, and it qualifies under both the manufacturing and the wholesaling standards.

Farming and Agriculture Related Industries. According to Section 112 (a) Section 2 of the Small Business Act as amended June 4, 1976, "It is the declared policy of the Congress that the Government, through the Small Business Administration, should aid and assist small business concerns which are engaged in the production of food and fiber, ranching, and raising of livestock, aquaculture, and all other farming and agriculture related industries." Until this amendment was passed, the SBA would assist only limited categories of agriculture businesses, primarily custom livestock feeding.

Special Exceptions to Maximum Sizes for Those Firms Considered Small

If your company conducts at least 50 percent of its business in the following states or territories, you qualify for higher gross allowances on the size of your business: Alaska, Hawaii, Virgin Islands, Puerto Rico, and Guam. According to the chart, companies in these areas may exceed the maximum gross sales allowances set above by specific percentages.

Area	% gross sales allowed over maximums set in Part 121
Alaska	25.0%
Hawaii	12.5%
Virgin Islands	10.0%
Puerto Rico	7.5%
Guam	7.5%

In other words, Part 121 of the SBA Rules and Regulations, as stated above, says that the maximum gross annual sales allowable for retail variety stores is $3 million. In Alaska, a variety store would be allowed to have maximum sales of $3.75 million, and in Guam a variety store could have maximum sales of $3.225 million and still be considered a small business for loan purposes.

Part 121 of the SBA Rules and Regulations, the section that states size standards, is updated periodically. In most cases the size of businesses that are considered small have increased over the years. Using the example of the variety store cited before with maximum sales allowable of $3 million; only two years ago, the maximum size allowed was $2 million. If your business is one that exceeds the size standards I've recorded, before you give up it is best to check with the local SBA office.

Money to Buy and Refurbish Houses for Sale

Up until this year (1976) the SBA was specifically prohibited from loaning money to small contractors to buy and build houses that would later be used for sale. This was considered speculation and did not qualify for SBA financing. Now, however, the SBA has started a limited loan program to small contractors who construct three to five houses per year. Recently, when I talked to several people at the SBA, they had not heard of this program, but I'm sure that the SBA will have standard procedures on this type of loan by the end of 1977.

Practical Credit Requirements

In addition to the small business criteria, a loan applicant must meet certain credit and policy requirements established by the SBA. Some of the requirements for the agency's loans are:

1. An applicant must be of good character.

2. There must be evidence the applicant has the ability to operate the business successfully.

3. The applicant must have enough capital in the business so that, with loan assistance, it will be possible for the applicant to operate on a sound financial basis.

4. As required by the Small Business Act, the proposed loan must be "of such sound value or so secured as reasonably to assure repayment."

5. The past earnings record and future prospects of the applicant must indicate ability to repay a loan out of earnings from the business.

Ineligible Applications

Since it is a public agency, using taxpayers' funds, the SBA has an unusual responsibility as a lender. The agency's loans must meet the loan requirements established by Congress and the SBA. Accordingly, the SBA will not make certain types of loans under certain circumstances.

Loans will not be granted:

1. If the funds are otherwise available on reasonable terms (a) from a private financial institution, (b) from the disposal at a fair price of assets not required by the applicant in the conduct of its business or not reasonably necessary to its potential growth, (c) through the use of personal credit and/or resources of the owner, partners, management, or principal stockholders of the

applicant, (d) from other government agencies that provide credit specifically for the applicant's type of business, or (e) from other known sources of credit.

2. If the loan would be for the purpose of (a) paying off a creditor or creditors of the applicant who are inadequately secured and are in a position to sustain a loss, (b) providing funds for distribution or payment to the owner, partners, or shareholders of the applicant, (c) refunding a debt owed to a small business investment company, or (d) replenishing working capital funds previously used for such purposes.

3. If the loan will provide or free funds for speculation in any kind of property, real or personal, tangible or intangible.

4. If the applicant is an eleemosynary institution or nonprofit enterprise, except for cooperatives that carry on a business activity for the purpose of obtaining pecuniary benefit for their members in the operations of their otherwise eligible small business concerns.

5. If the applicant is a newspaper, book publishing company, magazine, radio or television broadcasting company, or similar enterprise.

6. If any of the gross income of the applicant (or any of its principal owners) is derived from gambling activities, except for those small firms that obtain less than one-third of their gross income from income or commission from the sale of official state lottery tickets under a state license.

7. If the loan is to provide funds to an enterprise primarily engaged in the business of lending or investments or to any otherwise eligible enterprise for the purpose of financing investments not related or essential to the enterprise.

8. If the effect of the granting of the financial assistance will be to encourage monopoly or will be inconsistent with the accepted standards of the American system of free competitive enterprise.

9. If the proceeds of the loan will be used for moving an eligible business when the move is for other than a sound business purpose.

10. If the business is a multilevel sales distribution plan, this type of plan usually involves selling such soft goods as cosmetics, household cleaners, or utensils on a door-to-door or house party basis. The key factor is the recruitment of an endless chain of subdistributorships. Generally all of these types of organizations are ineligible; however, if you have any questions about a particular enterprise, SBA can be contacted.

11. To any enterprise that has a principal (owning 10 percent or more) who is a government civilian employee or military person. This also includes concerns where a close relative of an SBA employee owns 10 percent or more of the company applying or a substantial debt is owned by the applicant to the close relative of the SBA employee. Note: Any applications that would tend to come under this section or loans to a concern involving directors, officers, and employees of public and private community organizations that cooperate with the SBA should be discussed with the SBA before proceeding with the loan request. In this way, eligibility can be determined before effort is extended by the bank or the prospective applicant.

Every district and branch office of the SBA has a designated Veterans Affairs Officer whose job it is to facilitate the delivery of SBA services to veterans. This office was created under Public Law 93-237 which directs that SBA give "special consideration to veterans of the Armed Forces of the United States and their survivors and dependents."

For financial assistance, in addition to Veterans Affairs Officers whose job it is to see that special consideration is given veterans, SBA has instituted:

—Prompt processing of all loan applications.
—Extension of maximum loan maturity to veterans.
—Liberal interpretation of their present deferment policy on direct loans.
—A no-declination policy solely because of lack of collateral.

In their management assistance programs, in addition to the standard program, there is special consideration for veterans. This consists of indepth management assistance counselling, including a complete briefing on SBA's programs and benefits available.

Types of SBA Loans

The following is a list of the types of loans available from the SBA, either guaranteed or direct. Each one will be discussed in turn in the accompanying text.

1. The 7(a) loan which is the standard SBA loan.
2. Economic Opportunity Loan (EOL) for economically disadvantaged businesses.
3. Displaced business loan for businesses displaced by government projects including: road projects, urban renewal, armed forces base closing (base closing economic injury loan EIL), and strategic arms EIL;
4. Economic Injury Loans caused by US government regulations such as: occupational safety acts, consumer protection acts; environmental acts (7(B) (5) loans); and water pollution control acts.
5. Disaster loans to businesses occasioned by: federally declared natural disasters, physical disaster, or energy shortage economic energy.
6. Handicapped Assistance Loans (HAL) for owners who are physically handicapped.
7. Revolving line of credit loan.

The 7(a) Loan has two components, direct loans from the SBA and SBA-guaranteed loans from banks. The most frequently used loan is the SBA-bank guaranteed loan. SBA direct loans under the 7(a) program are small in number and are generally discouraged. Figure 4.2 illustrates the SBA direct and bank participation loans.

I would first like to go into some detail about the participation loans, since they are the most widely used. In participation loans, the bank makes the loan upwards to $555,555 (the SBA's 90 percent equals $500,000), and the SBA guarantees 90 percent of the loan against loss. In other words, if the bank loans

KEY FEATURES
OF SBA'S PRINCIPAL LENDING PROGRAMS

U.S. SMALL BUSINESS ADMINISTRATION • WASHINGTON, D.C. 20416

	BUSINESS LOANS	ECONOMIC OPPORTUNITY LOANS
	Direct, Immediate Participation and Guaranty Loans	Direct, Immediate Participation and Guaranty Loans
WHO IS ELIGIBLE?	Most businesses that are: (1) independently owned and operated and not dominant in their fields; (2) unable to obtain private financing on reasonable terms; (3) not eligible for financing from other government agencies; (4) qualified as "small" under SBA's size standards, based on dollar volume of business or number of employees.	Low income or disadvantaged persons who have lacked the opportunity to start or strengthen a small business and cannot obtain the necessary financing from other sources on reasonable terms.
LOAN PURPOSES	Business construction, conversion or expansion, purchase of equipment, facilities, machinery, supplies or materials and working capital.	Any use which will carry out the purposes shown above; generally, the same as other business loans.
MAXIMUM AMOUNT	$ 500,000 to any one borrower. This is the maximum SBA share of an immediate participation loan, where SBA and private lending institution each put up part of loan funds immediately; or a guaranteed loan, made jointly by SBA and a private lending institution and maximum SBA direct loan, one made entirely by the Agency.	$100,000 to any one borrower, as SBA share of loan.
INTEREST RATE	Maximum 5½% per annum on direct loan and SBA share of an immediate participation loan. However, If participating institution sets a lower rate, SBA will match this rate to a minimum of 5% on its share. On the bank's share of an immediate participation loan, the lending institution may set reasonable and legal rate with a maximum ceiling set by SBA from time to time. On a guaranty loan, bank may set legal and reasonable rate, with a maximum ceiling set by SBA from time to time. If SBA purchases its share, rate on this share is 5½%.	On direct loans and SBA share of immediate participation loans, the rate is set periodically, based on a statutory formula. Bank rate same as on other business loans.
MATURITY	Maximum of 10 years as a rule. However, working capital loans generally are limited to 6 years, while portions of loans for construction may have maximum of 15 years.	Maximum of 15 years. Working capital loans generally limited to a 10-year maximum.
TYPE OF COLLATERAL	Real estate or chattel mortgage; assignment of warehouse receipts for marketable merchandise; assignment of certain types of contracts; guarantees or personal endorsements; in some instances assignment of current receivables.	Any worthwhile collateral which is available or will be acquired with the proceeds of the loan.

*At times, SBA may have lower ceilings in order to conserve limited funds.

Figure 4.2

Figure 4.3

Analysis of
SBA Business Loans

TYPES OF LOANS	Loan Limit *	Maximum Loan Maturity	Maximum Interest Rates	Maximum SBA Participation	SBA Guaranty Fee	Collateral	Service Fee Paid Participating Institution	Prepayment Fee	SBA Closing Fee
Regular business Direct	$500,000		5½%.	100%	Not Applicable	Mortgage on land, buildings, machinery and equipment, automotive equipment, furniture and fixtures, warehouse receipts on inventory, accounts receivable; personal guarantees; assignment of life insurance, etc.	Not Applicable	None	Greater of: $10 or 1/8 of 1% of SBA share of loan (paid by borrower).
Regular business Guaranteed	$500,000 (SBA Share)	10 years. (up to 15 for construction portion)	5½% on SBA portion. Participating institution may set higher rate on its portion & on SBA portion of guaranteed loan, until SBA purchases its share.	Not in excess of 90%	1% of guaranteed portion, payable at first disbursement (or in 2 installments if SBA share exceeds $100,000).		¼% or 3/8% of the unpaid principal balance of SBA portion, depending on the amount of SBA's guaranteed portion, when and if purchased by SBA when serviced by participating institution.	None	Not Applicable
Regular business Immediate Participation	$500,000 (SBA Share)			Not in excess of 90%	None		¼% or 3/8% of the unpaid principal balance of SBA portion, depending on the amount of SBA's participation, when made and serviced by participating institution.	None	If closed and serviced by SBA, greater of: $10 or 1/8 of 1% of SBA share of loan. (paid by borrower)
Economic Opportunity Direct	$100,000	15 years.		100%	Not Applicable	Fixed assets purchased with loan proceeds and whatever other worthwhile collateral is available. Personal guarantees may be required.	Not Applicable.	None	Not Applicable
Economic Opportunity Guaranteed	$100,000 (SBA Share)	15 years.	Set by statutory formula for direct and SBA share of IP loans. For guaranteed, legal and reasonable.	Up to 100%	Same as Regular Business		¼% or 3/8% of the unpaid principal balance of SBA portion, depending on the amount of SBA's guaranteed portion, when and if purchased by SBA when serviced by participating institution.	None	Not Applicable
Economic Opportunity Immediate	$100,000 (SBA Share)	15 years.		Not in excess of 90%	None.		¼% or 3/8% of the unpaid principal balance of SBA portion when made and serviced by participating institution.	None	Not Applicable
Revolving Line of Credit (Guaranty only)	$500,000 (SBA Share), or $50,000 if made under EOL program	18 months	Normal bank rate	90%	¼%	Assignment of proceeds of contract; other similar to regular business loans.	Not Applicable	None	Not Applicable

If lending institution has prior indebtedness of borrower which is to be paid from proceeds of SBA loan, the institution ordinarily will be required to participate in SBA loan at least to the extent of borrower's prior indebtedness to the institution.

* The limits shown are the maximum permitted by law. At times SBA has lower administrative limits, in an effort to assure that limited funds are made available to the maximum number of small firms.

you $100,000 on a guarantee and you take the money and run off to Brazil, the bank will be reimbursed $90,000 by the SBA and their actual loss is only $10,000 or 10 percent.

There are two types of participation loans: immediate and guaranteed.

In an immediate participation loan, either the participating institution or the SBA makes the loan and the other participant purchases immediately upon disbursement its agreed percentage of the loan.

In a guaranteed loan, the participating institution makes and disburses the entire loan. The SBA executes an agreement that upon default it will purchase an agreed percentage of the unpaid balance of the loan within a stated period, subject to the terms and conditions of such agreement.

In guaranteed loans, the SBA charges a one time guaranty fee to the lending institution. The one time charge, which shall not be borne by the borrower, is one percent of the portion of the loan that the SBA guarantees.

There are certain advantages a bank enjoys when making an SBA loan over and above their 90 percent guarantee.

Although there are some differences in the regulatory requirements imposed on banks depending upon whether they are chartered by the federal government, or by a state government, the following generally applies:

1. The bank may carry the SBA guaranteed portion of the loan as a nonrisk asset.

2. Examining authorities generally eliminate the guaranteed portions of SBA loans in computing the various ratios (e.g., loan-to-deposit ratio) used to measure bank liquidity and the adequacy of its capital structure.

3. The guaranteed portions of SBA loans may be used as collateral security for: treasury tax and loan accounts; Federal Reserve Bank advances; public funds (in applicable states, cities, school districts, etc.); and uninvested trust funds.

4. With national banks, the SBA guaranteed portion may be carried without being chargeable against legal lending limitations. The same is true for state banks in a number of states. State banks should obtain clarifying ruling from appropriate supervisory agencies.

5. The guaranteed portion of an SBA loan may be sold to and serviced for a secondary participation (pension fund institutional investor, correspondent bank, or other). This can provide the primary participant with liquidity and increase its earnings due to the servicing fee on the guaranteed portion of the loan, the relending of the proceeds of sale of the guaranteed portion, and float on repayments. Banking Circular No. 50, dated June 27, 1972, enables a national bank to secure liquidity by selling the guaranteed portion of an SBA loan subject to a repurchase agreement and exclude such guaranteed portion in computing the bank's total borrowing limitation. Similarly, a national bank purchasing such a guaranteed portion from another institution subject to resale to that institution does not include the guaranteed portion in computing the national bank's lending limit to that institution.

Collateral

The Small Business Act requires that the Small Business Administration's business loans be of such sound value or so secured as to reasonably assure repayment. Therefore, the proposed collateral for a loan must be of such a nature that, when considered with the integrity and ability of the management, and the applicant's past and prospective earnings, repayment of the loan will reasonably be assured. The lending institution should give a realistic opinion of the value of the collateral offered.

Collateral may consist of one or more of the following: a mortgage on land, buildings, and equipment; assignment of warehouse receipts for marketable merchandise; assignment of certain types of contracts; a mortgage on chattels; or, in some instances, assignment of current receivables. As a rule, a pledge or mortgage on inventories is not considered satisfactory collateral unless the inventories are stored in a bonded or otherwise acceptable warehouse, or unless the applicable state law provides for creating and maintaining a satisfactory lien on inventory not so warehoused.

Interest rates

Interest rates for SBA participation loans are now set at 3½ percentage points maximum over prime. If prime interest rates published by the bank is 9½ percent then the SBA guaranteed loan would be 13 percent maximum. Some banks go below the maximum when they set their rates, and the banks have the option of charging any rate above 6¾ percent they like.

The banks also have the option of setting the rates at one interest rate determined at the time of approval and not changing for the term of the loan or, if agreed to by the borrower and the participating bank, a fluctuating rate is permitted as often as semi-annually. However, the rate must rise or fall on the same basis, and will be based on current commercial rates such as the prime rate. The note will reflect the rate at the time of approval, and the basis for utilizing a fluctuating rate.

Maturity

The final maturity of a loan will be geared to the borrower's ability to pay the type of collateral offered, but may not exceed the SBA's statutory limitation of ten years (fifteen years for portions used for construction). Maturity of working capital loans, however, usually is set at not more than seven years.

Repayment

Generally, loans shall be repaid in equal monthly installments including principal and interest except where the borrower's income is received on an annual or seasonal basis. All or any part of a loan may be repaid without penalty before it is due. The lending institution should comment on applicant's ability based upon an analysis of past and projected earnings, the overall debt structure, and the fixed annual obligations the applicant must meet if the loan is approved.

Economic Opportunity Loans (EOL) are loans for economically disadvantaged businesses. This means all minority businessmen (Black, Mexican-American, Asian American, and American Indian) as well as special groups, such as armed forces veterans (especially Vietnam veterans) and the handicapped, qualify almost without exception. There are also special conditions under which others may be qualified.

SBA is authorized by Title IV of the Economic Opportunity Act to make loans or guarantees to small business concerns that are either located in urban or rural areas with high proportions of unemployed persons, or are owned by low-income individuals. Such loans may be made either to established small firms or to new businesses.

Applicants must demonstrate that their total family income from all sources other than welfare is not sufficient for the basic needs of the family, or that due to social or economic disadvantage they have been denied the opportunity to acquire sufficient business financing through normal lending channels on reasonable terms. Specifically included in the eligibles are honorably discharged veterans (especially Vietnam veterans) who are unable to obtain financing on reasonable terms either from usual commercial sources or other SBA financing programs.

The SBA has a large direct loan program under EOL, but there are also participation loans available.

Bank participation is encouraged to the extent that SBA may fully guarantee an economic opportunity loan; however, agency policy is to restrict its guaranty to 90 percent.

Economic opportunity loans may be made for up to $100,000 as the SBA share, may have a maturity of up to fifteen years, and may be made for any reasonable business purpose. SBA may require recipients of these loans to acquire management skills through SBA-approved training courses.

The interest rate on SBA's share of EOLs is set up by a statutory formula. On its share, and on guaranteed loans prior to SBA purchase the bank may set the rate, provided that it is legal and reasonable. Maximum allowable bank rates are set by SBA from time to time.

Displaced Business Loans and Economic Injury Loans are those loans that are made to businesses that have been put into a disadvantaged position because of government policy or a federal resource emergency or shortage. They are made only by the SBA and have no participation with banks.

Applicants eligible for displaced business loans are small business concerns that are economically injured as the result of their displacement by, or proximity to federally-aided urban renewal, highway, or other construction projects. Loans may be used for construction of new facilities, and to nonowners of real property as well. Loan proceeds may also be used for working capital for operation at a new location for a reasonable period, for purchase of machinery and equipment, and for purchases of inventory. Upgrading is permitted up to 50 percent for land, and 33⅓ percent of building.

Strategic Arms Economic Injury Loans (EIL) and Base Closing EILs are for small business concerns that are economically injured as the result of cutbacks in federal projects relating to the development of strategic arms or the installation of such arms or facilities. The applicant must demonstrate that the economic injury suffered is the result of international strategic arms limitation treaties. A SBA loan may be used for working capital and to pay financial obligations that the applicant would have been able to meet had he not lost income because of significant reduction of the scope or amount of federal support for the strategic arms project. Refinancing of debt is permitted under this program.

Occupational Safety and Health Loans are available to most types of small concerns that are seeking either voluntarily or because of a notice of deficiency to meet the requirements of the Occupational Safety and Health Act of 1970, and standards set up by that law. Applicants must demonstrate the economic injury caused by their inability to conform to such standards without SBA assistance, either voluntarily or because of the deficiency notice. In the case of those attempting to meet such standards on a voluntary basis, the report of a licensed professional engineer or architect must be submitted with the loan application. Loan proceeds may be used only for additions to or alterations in equipment, facilities, and methods of operations considered to be necessary by the Occupational Safety and Health Administration of the Department of Labor or the appropriate state authority. Working capital may be provided to replace working capital used for compliance, such as meeting construction time limits, to make payments on equipment notes or mortgage payments, or to finance changes in methods of operation as required by the examining authorities.

For Consumer Protection Loans, eligible applicants are small businesses engaged in meat, poultry, or egg processing, and the loan proceeds must be used to effect additions or alterations in the equipment, facilities, or methods of operation of such firms so that they will be able to comply with requirements established by the Eggs Products Inspection Act, the Wholesome Poultry Products Act, and the Wholesome Meat Act, or state laws enacted to conform with these acts. Such firms must be able to demonstrate that they will suffer economic injury without SBA assistance, and must produce a notice of deficiency from an authorized inspection authority that they are not in conformity with the appropriate requirements. Loan proceeds may be used only for additions to or alteration in equipment, facilities, and methods of operation considered necessary by the US Department of Agriculture or appropriate state authority. Working capital may be provided for the same purposes as Coal Mine Health Safety Loans.

Disaster Loans can be utilized by businesses, but also, and most frequently, by private citizens involved in some natural disaster declared as such by the US government.

In addition to its regular business, economic opportunity, and development company loan programs, SBA has a physical disaster program for the victims of floods, hurricanes, earthquakes, and other such phenomena, and in addition a number of economic injury disaster programs. The authorizing legislation for three of these programs—physical disaster, economic injury caused by physical damage, and economic injury sustained as the result of diseased products from undetermined causes—in recent years has included such factors as very low interest rates and cancellation, or forgiveness benefits. Therefore, SBA has not encouraged bank participation in these three programs, since to do so would be a financial disservice to victims of forces beyond their control. Banks are, however, urged to participate to the extent of providing interim financing to their customers and other disaster victims in appropriate cases. In order that banks may be aware of these programs, and be able to advise those who seek these three types of disaster loans, a brief description of each follows:

Physical Disaster Loans

This is the oldest of SBA's disaster programs, begun in 1953 with a flat 3 percent interest rate and a maturity of up to twenty years. Legislative changes since that time have lowered the interest rate to 1 percent under certain circumstances, and extended the maturity to as much as thirty years. While repayment ability must be shown, the emergency conditions always existing in a disaster situation have naturally resulted in a less stringent credit analysis, particularly in the smaller loans that have a forgiveness feature. Physical disaster loans may be made to individuals for personal property loss, homeowners, business firms of any size, and to charitable and nonprofit institutions. While there is no statutory ceiling on the size of these loans, the SBA from time to time has set various administrative ceilings on size. In the case of larger business firms needing funds in excess of such ceilings, the agency will guarantee bank loans for the excess, without dollar limitation but not exceeding 90 percent of the bank loan. Generally, loan funds cannot exceed the physical damage sustained; in some cases refinancing of previous debt is permitted, both for businesses and home mortgages.

Economic Injury Disaster Loans

Closely linked to the physical disaster program is the economic injury disaster loan program, except that the latter is available only to small businesses. Whenever the President or the SBA Administrator determines that a specified geographical area has suffered from a major or physical disaster, SBA is then authorized to make EIDLs to those suffering economic injury as the result. These loans have the same interest rates, maximum maturity, and forgiveness feature as physical disaster loans. In some cases EIDL assistance is available when a natural disaster has been declared by the Secretary of Agriculture, but such loans do not carry forgiveness provisions. The burden of proof is on the applicant to demonstrate the claimed economic injury; normally, the proceeds of these loans are for working capital to keep the small firm in business until conditions previously existing are restored.

Product Disaster Loans

An infrequently needed program authorizes the SBA to make loans to small firms suffering economic injury as the result of diseased products. Such disease must be from unknown causes, and most frequently has involved diseased seafood. The interest rate, maximum maturity, and forgiveness feature of physical disaster loans also apply to this program.

The SBA also has some bank participation programs for disaster loans. Figure 4.4 is a graphic presentation of the types of loans available under the disaster program, summarizing eligibility, interest, and so on.

Handicapped Assistance Loans (HAL) are devised to help the handicapped start businesses of their own. It follows most of the same criteria as the Economic Opportunity Loan (EOL) but the interest charged is about half as much. The interest on these HAL loans is only 3 percent, the lowest interest rate the SBA charges. The only catch is that direct SBA funds allocated for this program are small, therefore, unless he is lucky, the applicant will probably have to go after a loan under the EOL program at a higher percent. Remember also that if the applicant goes to a bank for a guarantee on this loan, it will be at the prevailing bank-SBA-guarantee rate.

The Revolving Line of Credit Program is mostly restricted to businessmen who are contractors or who have government or other contracts. Under this plan, which was started on a pilot basis in January 1971 and was made available nationwide in May 1971, SBA may guarantee a line of credit to small construction contractors, or manufacturing and service firms, who provide a specific product or service under an assignable contract. The firm must have been in operation for at least a year and must be unable to obtain a bank line of credit without the SBA guaranty.

The amount guaranteed may be up to $500,000 as the SBA share, if made under the regular business loan program; or up to $100,000 if made under the Economic Opportunity Loan program. The bank may charge its normal rate of interest without regard to the SBA's published maximum guaranty rate. The maturity may be up to one year, or eighteen months for larger contracts. The guaranty fee paid to the SBA by the bank is ¼ percent of the amount guaranteed for up to twelve months, payable at the time of SBA approval of the guaranteed line of credit. For periods in excess of twelve months, ¼ of 1 percent per annum will be charged on a pro rata basis.

Economic Development Agency (EDA)

Most people have never heard of the EDA, but they are a pretty potent, and difficult, funding source in government financing. Unlike SBA, EDA funds both business, local, and state government projects, and in addition, the EDA has no upwards limit on the amount of funding available. As a matter of fact, according to a regional director of EDA, "EDA likes to dovetail on top of SBA loans," i.e., loan amounts above $555,000. However, EDA is a tough source of financing to secure. Out of 1,820 requests for loans in a regional area in 1974, there were only 19 granted.

Figure 4.4
Disaster Loans

	PHYSICAL DISASTER		ECONOMIC INJURY		
	Storms, Floods, Etc.	Natural Causes & Diseased Products	Displaced Businesses	Health & Safety	Consumer Protection
WHO IS ELIGIBLE	Individuals, businesses, nonprofit organizations such as churches provided: (a) they have suffered tangible property loss from a disaster and; (b) SBA has declared their area a disaster loan area. "Forgiveness" up to $5,000 is available to victims of disasters occurring in 1972 and until June 30, 1973.	Any small business located in area of physical or natural disaster as determined by the President, SBA, or Secretary of Agriculture, provided business has suffered substantial economic injury, or, as determined by SBA, from inability to process or market a product for human consumption because of disease or toxicity from natural or undetermined causes.	Any small business suffering substantial economic injury as a result of displacement by, or proximity to, urban renewal, highway, or other federally-aided construction projects.	Any small business judged to have suffered economic injury caused by requirements of the Coal Mine Health and Safety Act of 1969 or the Occupational Safety and Health Act of 1970.	Any small business judged to have suffered economic injury caused by requirement to meet the standards set up under the Egg Products Inspection Act of 1970, the Wholesome Poultry and Poultry Products Act of 1968, or the Wholesome Meat Act of 1967.
LOAN PURPOSES	To restore a home, business, or nonprofit institution to pre-disaster condition. For repair and replacement of real estate, furnishings, equipment, fixtures and inventory. For refinancing, if the uninsured damage exceeds 30% of the pre-disaster value of the property.	Working capital and payment of financial obligations (except long-term bank loans) which small business could have met had it not suffered revenue loss because of disaster conditions. To reestablish or continue a small firm injured economically by diseased products.	To help firm obtain comparable space. For purchase of land and buildings, moving expenses, replacement of machinery and equipment, increased rent, inventory, working capital, etc.	To help firm meet standards by upgrading plant or equipment. Proceeds of loan can be used for working capital only under certain conditions.	To help firm meet standards by upgrading plant or equipment. Proceeds of loan can be used for working capital only under certain conditions.
MAXIMUM AMOUNT	For businesses, direct or immediate participation, $500,000 limit on SBA share; on guaranteed loans, no dollar limit, up to 90% guarantee. For homes, direct or immediate participation, $50,000 structural damage; $10,000 furniture and personal effects; combined limit, $55,000; guaranteed loans, no dollar limit, up to 90% SBA guarantee.	Determined by economic loss suffered by applicant as result of disaster and cost of reestablishment or continuation for diseased products economic injury. Same limits as Physical Disaster, either separately or combined with physical loss.	No dollar limit. Loan is based on reasonable estimate of cost of reestablishing business consistent with economic injury suffered. Loan cannot exceed cost of reestablishment, less net funds received for moving expenses and condemnation.	No dollar limitation. Limit of 90% SBA share of immediate participation and guaranty loans.	No dollar limitation. Limit of 90% SBA share of immediate participation loans and guaranty loans.
INTEREST RATE	1% on direct loans and SBA's share of participation loans due to disasters occurring in 1972 and until June 30, 1973. Participating private lender may set reasonable rate on its share of immediate participation loan or on entire guaranty loan but not to exceed prevailing rate for regular SBA business loans.	Same as physical disaster loans.	Set annually by statutory formula on SBA share of loans. Private lending institution my set reasonable interest rate on its share of loan, with a maximum ceiling set by SBA from time to time.	SBA share set annually by statutory formula. Banks may set a legal and reasonable rate with a maximum ceiling set by SBA from time to time.	SBA share set annually by statutory formula. Banks may set a legal and reasonable rate with a maximum ceiling set by SBA from time to time.
MATURITY	Maximum of 30 years.	Maximum of 30 years.	Maximum of 30 years.	Maximum of 30 years.	Maximum of 30 years.
TYPE OF COLLATERAL	No specific requirements. Applicants must pledge whatever collateral is available.	No specific requirements; applicants must pledge whatever collateral they can provide.	No specific requirements; applicants must pledge whatever collateral they can provide.	Whatever can be pledged must be. If fixed assets are acquired with proceeds of an SBA loan, these assets must be pledged. An assignment of any existing leases is required.	Whatever can be pledged must be. If fixed assets are acquired with proceeds of an SBA loan, these assets must also be pledged. An assignment of any existing leases shall be required.

EDA administers several programs. Title I, public works grant; Title II, public works and business loans; Title III, technical assistance and research grants; Title IV, economic adjustment loans; and Title V, emergency job grants.

Who is Eligible?

EDA business development loans are made for one purpose: to upgrade an area economically, primarily through new, permanent jobs and better incomes for local residents. Businessmen, public agencies, Indian tribes, and local development groups are eligible to apply for EDA business loans to establish new businesses or to expand existing firms. New businesses or expanded firms must be located in EDA Redevelopment Areas or development district centers.

A listing of all EDA-designated areas is maintained by EDA offices. As of 1975, there are 18,005 counties and Indian reservations approved by EDA which include almost every major urban area and Indian reservation in the United States.

EDA will not help a business to relocate from one area to another. When a business loan applicant wishes to expand to a new location, while continuing operations at a previous location, EDA must check carefully to determine that employment will not be reduced at the older place of business.

Some of the businesses funded in Los Angeles county in 1975 included an Indian-owned trailer park, a fish farm, an industrial park, and a meat packing plant.

Loan Terms

Although there is no limitation on the amount the Agency may lend to any one applicant, EDA may not lend more than 65 percent of the cost of land, buildings, and machinery and equipment for industrial and commercial enterprises. Depending on the circumstances of an application, EDA may limit its loan to less than 65 percent of these costs.

Maturity on an EDA business loan may extend to twenty-five years. However, maturity on EDA business loans is ordinarily based on the useful life of the fixed assets being acquired.

Interest rates are determined by the cost of government borrowing.

Collateral requirements vary, but the EDA must have at least a second lien position on the fixed assets being purchased.

Repayments are generally made in regular monthly installments. There is no penalty for repayment of an EDA business loan in its entirety prior to the maturity date.

EDA may guarantee loans for working capital made to EDA borrowers by private institutions upon application from the lender and upon appropriate terms and conditions.

An EDA guarantee may not at any time exceed 90 percent of the unpaid balance of funds made available by the lender to the EDA borrower. The applicant should furnish sufficient initial working capital from his own funds.

EDA Requirements

In addition to the conditions that an applicant must be located in an EDA-designated area and may not borrow to relocate his business, other EDA requirements are:

—the project may not be in an industry experiencing a long-run overcapacity situation.

—there must be reasonable assurance of loan repayment.

—the project must be consistent with the EDA-approved Overall Economic Development Program (OEDP) for the area.

—each applicant has to be approved by an agency of the state or political subdivision directly concerned with economic development.

—the project construction contractors must pay prevailing wages to meet requirements of the Davis-Bacon Act, and employment in the construction of the project and operation of the new or expended business has to comply with the nondiscrimination provisions of the Civil Rights Act of 1964.

—at least 15 percent of the total eligible project cost must be supplied as equity capital or as a subordinated loan, repayable in no shorter period of time and at no faster amortization rate than the EDA loan.

—at least ⅓ of the 15 percent is to be supplied by the state or a community or area organization. There is an exception for projects involving financial participation by Indian tribes.

The requested funds may not be obtainable from other sources on terms that will permit the accomplishments of the project.

EDA also may waive the "5-percent community requirement" in certain hardship cases and allow the applicant or other nonfederal sources to supply the funds directly to the project.

To stimulate investment by private lenders, the EDA encourages the applicant to borrow as much as possible of the project cost, above the first 15 percent, from private lending institutions. Such loans may be repaid before the federal loan and may be secured by a lien having precedence over the federal lien, if the assistant secretary determines it necessary for the project.

A summary of the loan program is as follows:

The Applications

Form EDA-201 is a business loan application for use by industrial enterprises, such as corporations, partnerships, and proprietorships.

Form EDA-202 is for use by local development and other community groups, Indian tribes, and public agencies.

The applicant may obtain these forms from his local EDA field office, where EDA financial specialists are available to assist in planning the project and preparing the application.

The forms are designed to give EDA the basic outlines of the applicant's plans. The information given should be in sufficient detail to show that the proposed project is eligible for an EDA loan.

Time and Expense

Processing an application for an EDA loan will be thorough and will entail considerable time and some expense to the applicant.

EDA makes a preliminary review to determine whether the project is feasible. The agency may obtain advice from other government agencies that have expert knowledge of the kind of business involved. If the loan is approved, the applicant has an opportunity to review its terms and conditions at preclosing and closing conferences. According to EDA brochures, applications are processed as rapidly as possible, but making loans designed to create permanent employment requires careful study and review. The applicant's prompt cooperation will enable EDA to act with all possible speed.

The period from the time of initial submittal to disbursement is usually one and one-half years. After the OEDP Committee has approved it, the EDA's processing time is about sixty days.

Properly completed applications are important. Applicants should state the case as clearly and completely as possible. This is the starting point and the basis of actions taken on the loan. Potential borrowers should review the application from the standpoint of EDA to make sure it presents a full and fair picture of the merits and problems inherent in the proposal. This will speed consideration of the project.

Export-Import Bank of the United States (Eximbank)

There is a great market overseas for US products, and if you are a manufacturer and have considered exporting, you night get some help from the US Eximbank. The Eximbank has a half-billion dollar fund earmarked for credit guarantees to US exporters and their banks under the following types of circumstances:

—sales to foreign buyers
—increases in Eximbank exposure in certain right-risk countries
—export transactions promising more future sales or better balance of payment advantages

The Export-Import Bank of the United States, familiarly known as Eximbank, is an independent agency of the US government whose primary function is to aid in financing and to facilitate exports of US goods and services.

Eximbank has implemented a variety of programs to meet the needs of the US exporting community, regardless of the size of the transaction. These programs take the form of direct lending or the issuance of guarantees and insurance, so that exporters and private banks can extend appropriate financing without taking undue risks.

Eximbank's direct lending program is limited to larger sales of US products and services around the world. The guarantees, insurance, and discount programs have been designed to assist exporters in smaller sales of products and services.

Eximbank has two basic "exporter credit programs:" (1) the Exporter Credit Insurance Program, which is administered by, and operated in cooperation with, the Foreign Credit Insurance Association (FCIA), and (2) the Commercial

Bank Exporter Guarantee Program, which is operated between Eximbank and US commercial banks. These programs are mutually exclusive and the exporter can choose either one.

Under both programs, financing is done in the private sector with Eximbank or FCIA protecting the financing bank of the US exporter against defined commercial or political risks. The commercial risks covered under the programs are insolvency of the buyer, or the failure of the buyer to pay the amount due at due date (protracted default). The political risks covered are transfer delays in converting local currency payments into dollars, cancellation of export or import licenses, expropriation or confiscation, and losses due to war, revolution, or civil disturbance.

Under either program, the exporter may be a US corporation, partnership, or individual, or a foreign corporation, partnership, or individual doing business in the United States. However, only financing for the export of US goods and services is eligible for coverage under the programs. Applications for assistance of Eximbank under these two programs can only be initiated by the US exporter or the exporter's US commercial bank. In order for a buyer outside the United States to receive benefits under these programs, it is necessary that the overseas buyer request credit terms from the US supplier, and that the US supplier or the supplier's US commercial bank make application to FCIA or Eximbank.

Credit and financial information on the foreign buyer should be sufficient to enable the commercial bank, Eximbank, and FCIA to evaluate the credit-worthiness of the transaction. Repayment terms should not exceed those considered commercially customary in international trade for the type of goods shipped.

Foreign Credit Insurance Association/Eximbank Coverage

Foreign Credit Insurance Association (FCIA), whose membership consists of some fifty of the nation's leading insurance companies, operates in cooperation with Eximbank to assist US exporters by facilitating their extensions of credit to overseas buyers. Under this cooperative arrangement, FCIA issues all insurance policies and handles underwriting matters on behalf of its member companies and Eximbank. The member companies of FCIA insure against the commercial risks, and are reinsured for a portion of these risks by Eximbank. Political risk coverage under the policies is underwritten solely by Eximbank. By providing insurance to exporters against loss due to nonpayment by their overseas credit customers, FCIA credit insurance takes most of the risk out of export credit sales, and thereby encourages the exporter to expand his credit sales overseas.

The insurance is useful both to the exporter who holds (self-finances) his own foreign receivables as well as to the exporter who discounts his foreign receivables with financial institutions. FCIA does not finance export sales, but the exporter who insures his accounts receivable against commercial credit and political risk loss is usually able to obtain financing from commercial banks and other lending institutions on more favorable terms than would otherwise be possible. As a result, he can extend larger amounts of credit on more favorable

Figure 4.5

General Term Guidelines

Product	Minimum Cash Payment (Down Payment on or Before Delivery)	Maximum Payment Term
Raw materials, consumer goods, general merchandise, parts, supplies, small unit value products FCIA only	None	180 days
Agricultural commodities	10% of contract price (none if covered under FCIA Short-Term Policy)	One year
Capital and quasi-capital goods and equipment for use in industrial, commercial and agricultural business	Minimum of 10% of contract price	Up to five years, depending on contract price of sale, and whether the buyer is an end-user or dealer/distributor

terms to his overseas customers. The exporter, by financing his receivables, frees his working capital for use in his internal operations. The premium charge to exporters for insuring their export credit sales may be largely offset in many instances by the lower cost of financing their exports, resulting in a very low net cost to the exporter for the significant risk-taking by FCIA and Eximbank.

Several types of insurance policies are available to exporters, the choice of policy being indicated by the product mix, desired terms of repayment, extent of the exporter's overseas business activity, type of buyer (end-user, dealer, and so on) and average amount of credit extended on individual accounts.

To introduce the new or small exporter to foreign trade, FCIA provides a small business policy which, in contrast to a master policy, allows a selection of either markets or buyers to be insured. It is offered to firms whose annual export volume over the preceding three years did not exceed $200,000. The policy covers both commercial credit and political risks. It may remain in force for a period not to exceed two years, or until the exporter has insured the aggregate contract value of exports of $500,000, whatever comes first.

One of the areas that most businessmen reading this book are concerned with is the Bank Guarantee Program. The Export-Import Bank of the United States will guarantee repayment of medium-term (181 days to five years) export debt obligations acquired by US banking institutions from US exporters. Any US commercial bank or Edge Act corporation is eligible for guarantees under the Commercial Bank Exporter Guarantee Program. One purpose of this program is to encourage and assist greater participation by banks in supporting US exporters who must provide deferred credit terms on their sales.

Upon receipt of an overseas order, an invitation to bid, or other inquiry, the exporter is encouraged to discuss the case promptly with this commercial bank to determine, in advance, the availability and costs of financing. The commercial bank determines the acceptability of the transaction, for the amount and on the credit terms proposed, and if guarantee coverage is desired applies to Eximbank for a guarantee against the credit and political risks of nonpayment. When shipment is made, Eximbank's guarantee is issued to the commercial bank upon advice from the bank that it has purchased the buyer's promissory notes without recourse to the exporter.

The commercial bank makes the loan to the exporter without recourse, being protected by Eximbank's guarantee against defined credit or political loss. The exporter eliminates the risk of loss and receives his money to put to use in his continuing business operations. In some instances application may be made for political risks guarantee coverage only, in which case the commercial bank is permitted to take recourse on the exporter for the commercial risks, if desired.

A master guarantee agreement is issued to each participating commercial bank. This agreement specifies the terms and conditions of the protection afforded by the guarantees, and each guarantee authorized is subject to those terms and conditions. Briefly stated, these terms and conditions are as follows:

1. Buyer Payment. The exporter will receive from the buyer a cash payment of a specified percentage (minimum 10 percent) of the contract price on or before delivery. The remainder of the contract price (i.e., the financed portion) shall be evidenced by promissory notes or other acceptable obligations of the buyer providing for payment in US dollars in approximately equal installments of principal, with interest on unpaid balances payable concurrently with payments of principal (level payment notes may be acceptable in some instances). In most cases, installments shall be payable not less frequently than semi-annually.

2. Exporter Retention. The exporter shall retain not less than 10 percent of the financed portion (2 percent for agricultural commodities), in equal amounts of each installment, for its own account and risk. The remainder of the financed portion is financed by the commercial bank, without recourse to the exporter.

3. Commercial Bank Responsibility and Eximbank Comprehensive Guarantee Coverage. The commercial bank will be permitted to choose between the following two types of coverages:

Plan I, which requires the commercial bank to take 100 percent of the commercial credit risks on the ''early installments'' (i.e., the first half of the installments of one, two, or three year credits, but not more than the first eighteen months of longer credits up to five years). Eximbank's guarantee under this Plan covers commercial credit risks on the remaining installments (the ''later installments'') and covers the political risks on all installments.

Plan II, whereby Eximbank will issue a comprehensive guarantee of 85 percent of the commercial bank's participation in all installments and a political risks guarantee for the remaining 15 percent of the bank's participation, with the provision that for those transactions with a final maturity date of three years or more, the applicant bank can receive full comprehensive coverage of the last half of the installments at the midpoint of payment for the exporter, commercial banks are permitted to take recourse on the exporter for the commercial risks under the political risks only guarantee. Guarantee fee rates for this coverage are proportionately lower.

4. Level Payments of Principal and Interest. In order to make medium-term export financing more attractive to potential buyers, commercial banks are permitted to schedule repayment of a guaranteed loan with level payments of principal and interest rather than the usual system of equal principal installments with interest on a declining balance. On large transactions, however, Eximbank reserves the right to require the usual method of equal installments of principal with interest paid on the outstanding balance.

5. Guarantee Charges. Eximbank fees on guarantees vary, being based on the length of the credit period and the classification accorded the country of import because of economic and political conditions. The "Instructions to Banks" issued to each participating bank include a table of fees applicable to the various credit periods, and a list of all eligible countries indicating the fee classification of each country.

Since this is a support program for commercial bank financing, Eximbank relies to a considerable extent on the credit judgment of the commercial bank in approving the transaction. Banks experienced in export financing are granted discretionary and delegated authority, permitting them to commit Eximbank to the issuance of guarantees, within specified limits, without prior Eximbank approval.

If discretionary or delegated authority is not being used, but instead prior approval of Eximbank is desired or required, the applicant bank submits necessary financial and credit data with a formal application. In consideration of the credit investigations and other services rendered, upon issuance of a guarantee, the commercial bank retains a portion of the fee paid by the exporter.

When shipments are on a continuous and repetitive basis to distributors or other buyers, a revolving guarantee is available, thereby eliminating the need for arranging a separate guarantee for each shipment.

Political risk guarantees are available for equipment on consignment abroad and guarantees may be provided to cover the deferred sale from consignment. Also, guarantees are available to provide preshipment cover for the exporter to protect against insolvency of the buyer and political risks occurring during the period of manufacture of specially fabricated products. Guarantees are also available to cover a commercial bank's financing of service contracts being repaid on deferred terms.

There is no specification as to the interest rates to be paid by the buyer but Eximbank guarantees payment of interest at 1 percent above the US Treasury borrowing rate for comparable maturities, (with a minimum coverage of 6 percent per annum) or such lesser rate as the paper may bear.

Discount Program

Besides Edge Act and "Agreement" corporations, Eximbank will consider applications from commercial banks operating under sections 25 and 25(a) of the Federal Reserve Act (hereinafter called bank) for loans to assist the banks in financing current exports of US products and services.

Eximbank will make advance commitments to make discount loans for up to 100 percent of the Eligible Export Debt Obligation arising from current US exports. Eximbank will also give advance commitments to purchase on a case-by-case basis Eligible Export Debt Obligations, satisfactory to Eximbank, with full and unconditional recourse on the commercial bank.

Eligible Export Debt Obligations

Eligible Export Debt Obligation means the indebtedness of a foreign obligor, incurred in financing the acquisition of products or services exported from the United States, generally having an original maturity of twelve months or longer. The evidence of the foreign obligor's debt obligation may be in any form satisfactory to Eximbank, including, but not limited to, a promissory note, draft, or contract. Eximbank reserves the right to decline on a case-by-case basis to make a loan against or to purchase any particular obligation.

Advance Commitment and Discount Loans

In order to obtain a Discount Loan for any Eligible Export Debt Obligation, a bank must have applied for and received from Eximbank an advance commitment to obtain such loan. Application must be made before shipment of the products or services. Requests for advance commitments may be submitted to Eximbank by telex or letter, or by telephone with confirming information sent by mail. Eximbank's telex number is 89-461.

Need for Financing

Each application for an advance commitment for a discount loan or purchase must be accompanied by the following statement from the bank: "The exporter has informed us that financing is necessary to complete the export transaction. This bank is not prepared to extend financing on the terms indicated unless Eximbank will commit to make a discount loan." In addition, the bank must describe what, if any, direct or indirect ownership interest, or family relationship, exists among the supplier, obligor, or guarantor.

Availability Date

Advance commitments to make discount loans or purchases will be made without charge and will be valid for the entire term of the Eligible Export Debt Obligation.

Interest Rate and Purchase Price

The interest rate Eximbank will charge the commercial bank on discount loans will be 1 percent less than the interest yield on the export obligation but not less than the applicant bank's prime rate (in effect on the date the application is received) if a loan based on its advance commitment is requested within ninety days after the bank has disbursed against the Eligible Export Debt Obligation.

If the applicant bank requests a discount loan based on its advance commitment after ninety days, the interest rate Eximbank will charge on the discount loan will be the higher of (a) 1 percent less than the interest yield of that Eligible Export Debt Obligation to the bank, or (b) the Eximbank borrowing rate in the private market, as determined by Eximbank, for comparable maturities rounded to the next higher ¼ percent. Comparable maturities shall mean the remaining term of the underlying Eligible Export Debt Obligation.

Eximbank will, on a monthly basis, announce to interested banks its borrowing rate for maturities similar to those that may be presented to it under this discount program. These rates will then remain in effect as the rate referred to above until a new schedule of rates is announced by Eximbank.

Repayment

Discount loans will be repayable in approximately equal quarterly, semiannual, or annual installments, as appropriate, over such period as the bank may request but no longer than the remaining term of repayment of the Eligible Export Debt Obligations will have terms customary in international trade but normally not exceeding five years. However, to meet demonstrated foreign competition, Eximbank will consider on an ad hoc basis making discount loans on longer terms.

Prepayment of Loans

A bank may prepay discount loans and repurchase obligations previously sold to Eximbank at any time without premium or penalty. The bank thereafter may offer the same Eligible Export Debt Obligations for another loan or loans in accordance with the formula described above.

Promissory Notes of Banks and Custody of Eligible Export Debt Obligations

Loans will be made against a promissory note issued and delivered by the bank to Eximbank. The bank shall not deliver the Eligible Export Debt Obligations to Eximbank except when Eximbank purchases the Export Debt Obligation. Eximbank reserves the right to inspect all records relating to any Eligible Export Debt obligations upon which it has been requested to grant a discount loan upon giving reasonable notice to the respective bank.

Financial Statement

When a bank applies to Eximbank for a loan or purchase under the discount program, it shall submit or have on file with Eximbank its most recent statement of financial condition and will provide whatever other information as may be reasonably required by Eximbank.

Ineligible Obligations

Export debt obligations ineligible for discount loans or purchase include obligations arising out of exports:

1. of defense articles or defense services

2. of any product or services to or for use in a communist country unless the President of the United States has determined that Eximbank support of sales to that country are in the national interest and has reported that determination to the US Senate and House of Representatives

3. of any product, technical data, or other information to or for use by a national or agency of any nation that engages in armed conflict, declared or otherwise, with armed forces of the United States

Cancellation

The respective banks shall submit to Eximbank at least once a year, upon request of Eximbank, a list of all advance commitments issued to that bank that should be cancelled for any reason whatsoever.

The Discount Program	This is frequently used in combination with the various exporter credit programs listed herein. However, it is not necessary for the export debt obligation to be insured or guaranteed in order for the bank to use the discount program.

The Eximbank also has other programs such as a lease guarantee program and a program of loans to foreign countries (their largest loan program). If you want to use their programs, contact the Eximbank office in Washington, DC, or the international department of your bank.

Agriculture Department Loans

Before you back off from this loan category and say, "Well, why do I need this source, I am not a farmer," stop! The Agriculture Department does not just make loans to farmers. They make loans to nonfarm enterprises built in rural communities such as: "swimming facilities, tennis courts, riding stables, vacation rental cottages, lakes and ponds for fishing and boating, docks, camping or picnic grounds, repair shops, roadside markets, service stations, small grocery stores, water and waste disposal systems" and loans to "promote development of business and industry . . . in towns or cities of below 50,000 population." Okay, now that you know you don't have to be a farmer to get money, let me briefly illustrate the programs.

The Commodity Credit Corporation loans money and guarantees loans for the purpose of supporting the price of domestic commodities. The commodities loaned against serve as the collateral. The amount loaned is based on a percentage of parity prices established at the beginning of each year. This agency also helps support farm prices by outright purchase and storage of various farm crops.

The Farm Credit Administration

The Land Bank Service

This division supervises twelve federal land banks that make long-term mortgage loans to be used for agricultural purposes. A loan may not exceed 65 percent of the value of the agricultural facilities. These loans are negotiated through federal land bank associations that are cooperative credit organizations composed of farmers in local areas. Each member purchases stock in the association to the extent of 5 percent of his loan. Interest rates are regulated to be not more than 1 percent above the interest rate on the last series of bonds issued by the bank making the loan.

The Federal Short-Term Credit Service

Intermediate- and short-term financing is available by the establishment and functions of twelve intermediate credit banks. These banks do not make direct loans to the farmer, but make loans to local financing institutions that finance the farmer. Another function of the banks is the discounting of agricultural negotiable paper. Loans for farm operations are usually for a term of one year, but may extend for maturities of up to five years. Interest rates are restricted to not more than 1 percent over the rate paid by the member credit bank in its debenture borrowings.

Farmers can also borrow from Production Credit Associations which obtain funds from the local intermediate credit banks. Borrowers are required to purchase stock in the association to the extent of 5 percent of the loan. These loans are secured by a chattel on equipment, livestock, or crops, and are short-term with interest rates averaging about 7 percent.

The Cooperative Bank Service

There are twelve district banks and a Central Bank that provide extensive financing for farmers' cooperatives. Borrowing cooperatives must purchase $100 stock for $2,000 in borrowings. The banks make loans for (a) short-term loans secured by commodities in storage, (b) operating capital loans, and (c) loans to expand physical facilities. Maturities for such loans may extend to twenty years, but the usual period is considerably less.

The Farmers Home Administration

The Farmers Home Administration of the US Department of Agriculture channels credit to farmers, rural residents, and communities. It helps borrowers gain maximum benefit from loans through counseling and technical assistance.

Farmers and rural people have several credit programs they can call upon through FHA to help purchase or operate farms, provide new employment and business opportunities, enhance environment, acquire homes, and upgrade the standard of living for all who wish to live in small towns or open country.

Some loan programs are strictly for individuals and their families. Some involve associations of people. Other loans are made to partnerships, corporations, or public bodies. FHA employees work in concert with all types of borrowers as well as with state and local officials, planning groups, and government agencies.

The agency's loan authorities provide a supplemental source of credit, augmenting the efforts of the private lenders rather than competing with them. Most FHA programs require that a borrower "graduate" to commercial credit when able to do so. The nature of the agency's operation makes it possible for Farmers Home Administration to increase the supply of rural credit by drawing money from the major finance centers of our nation.

Major business purposes of FHA's rural credit programs include:

—To expand business and industry, to increase income and employment, and control or abate pollution.

—To install water and waste disposal systems and other community facilities that will help rural areas upgrade the quality of living and promote economic development and growth.

Most of the loan programs fall into two categories:

1. Guaranteed Loans, in which the loan is made and serviced by a private lender. FHA guarantees to limit any loss to a specified percentage. Interest rates are determined between borrower and lender unless the rate is established by law.

2. Insured Loans that are originated, made, and serviced by the personnel of the agency. Notes are sold to investors, backed by the full faith of the government, and the investors' money replenishes a revolving loan fund. For

most programs, interest rates to borrowers are determined by the current cost of federal borrowing, although some rates are established by statute.

Eligibility

All applications are considered regardless of sex, race, color, creed, or national origin of the applicant. For individual loans, applications from eligible veterans have preference for processing. These general rules of eligibility also apply.

Community Credit

Rural towns of 10,000 population or less and rural areas may borrow to improve or develop community facilities, including waste and water systems.

Business and Industrial Credit

Loans to promote developing of business and industry, or for small business enterprises, may be made for projects in cities and towns below 50,000 population, but not in larger cities or in areas adjacent to them where population density is more than 100 persons per square mile. Preference is given to applications for projects in open country, rural communities, and towns of 25,000 and smaller. Some specific loans follow:

Soil and Water Conservation Loans

Purpose: To finance land and water development measures, forestation, drainage of farm land, irrigation, pasture improvement, and related land and water use adjustments. For: An eligible owner, tenant, leaseholder, partnership, or corporation.

Recreation Enterprise Loans

Purpose: To develop recreation areas, including swimming, fishing, boating, and camping facilities. For: Individual farmers planning income-producing outdoor on-farm recreation.

Youth Loans

Purpose: To establish and operate income-producing projects that will provide practical business experience. For: Rural youths enrolled in an organized and supervised program.

Community Facility Loans

Purpose: To construct community water and waste disposal systems, community centers, fire stations, and other community facilities. For: Public agencies or nonprofit corporations.

Business and Industrial Loans

Purpose: To develop or finance business or industry, increase income and employment, and control or abate pollution. For: Legal entities, including individuals, public and private organizations, and federally-recognized Indian tribal groups in open country or towns of up to 50,000 people. Grants may be available to public bodies.

Repair and Rehabilitation Housing Loans

Purpose: To make repairs to remove health and safety hazards. For: Very low income owner-occupants who have repayment capability for loans of this size.

Rental and Cooperative Housing Loans

Purpose: To build, buy, improve, or repair rental or cooperatively-owned houses or apartments for occupancy by low to moderate income families and persons age 62 or older. For: Corporations, cooperatives, public agencies, individuals, and partnerships.

Federal Reserve Board

The Federal Reserve Board does not make direct loans to business, but it does guarantee loans given by banks to federal procurement contractors and businesses engaged in national defense work under Regulation V, 32A CFR CR XV. (Also, it does not guarantee the loan by the bank giving the loan directly to the Federal Reserve Board.) The loan request by the bank must come through one of the following government agencies: Atomic Energy Commission; Defense Supply Agency; or the National Aeronautics and Space Administration.

As you might have guessed, the source is pretty complicated to tap, but consider this: in most cases, the maximum interest is 7 percent (but it can be higher), there is no maximum amount you can borrow, no equity requirement, and the loan can be guaranteed *up to 100 percent*. The bank must pay a guarantee fee of up to 3 percent of the loan, but the bank can charge a ½ percent commitment fee and get a generous guarantee from the Federal Reserve Board through a government agency.

The objective of the Federal Reserve Board in this capacity will be, according to the act:

to facilitate and expedite to the greatest extent possible the financing of contractors, subcontractors, and other persons having contracts or engaged in operations deemed by the guaranteeing agencies to be necessary to expedite production and deliveries or services under Government contracts for the procurement of materials or the performance of services for the national defense. The Board of Governors of the Federal Reserve System (referred to in this regulation as the 'Board') and the Federal Reserve Banks will cooperate fully with the guaranteeing agencies in order to achieve this objective and will follow in general and to the extent applicable procedures developed from experience obtained in the administration of the V-loan and T-loan programs during World War II.

Procedures are according to the act:

(a) Applications. Any private financing institution may submit to the Federal Reserve Bank of its district on application for a guarantee of a loan to an eligible borrower. Such application shall be in such form and contain such information as the Board may prescribe after consultation with the guaranteeing agencies.

(b) Eligibility of borrower. No loan shall be guaranteed unless it shall first be determined that the contract or other operation of the prospective borrower to be financed by such loan is one which is deemed by the guaranteeing agency involved to be necessary to expedite production and deliveries or services under a Government contract for the procurement of materials or the performance of services for the national defense. Such determination will be made in each case by a duly authorized certifying officer of the appropriate guaranteeing agency or in such other manner as the guaranteeing agency may prescribe. The determination will be made upon the basis of information contained in the application and accompanying papers filed by the applicant financing institution, unless in the circumstances of a particular case it appears that further information is necessary.

(c) Approval of guarantees. Each application by a financing institution for a loan guarantee will be subject to approval by the appropriate guaranteeing agency in Washington or, to such extent as the guaranteeing agency may prescribe, by the Federal Reserve Bank to which the application is submitted. In any case in which an application is required to be submitted to Washington for approval, the Federal Reserve Bank will transmit the application, together with all necessary supporting information and the recommendation of the Federal Reserve Bank, through the Board of Governors to the guaranteeing agency involved. Subject to determination of the borrower's eligibility, if the application is approved by a duly authorized contracting officer of the guaranteeing agency, such contracting officer will authorize the Federal Reserve Bank to execute and deliver the guarantee on behalf of the guaranteeing agency. Such authorization will be transmitted to the Federal Reserve Bank through the Board of Governors; and, thereupon, the Federal Reserve Bank, acting as fiscal agent of the United States, will execute and deliver the guarantee on behalf of the guaranteeing agency in accordance with the terms of the authorization. In any case in which the Federal Reserve Bank is authorized by a guaranteeing agency to approve applications for guarantees, the Reserve Bank, if it approves the application and subject to determination of the borrower's eligibility, will execute and deliver the guarantee without submission of the application for prior approval by any officer of the guaranteeing agency; but the Reserve Bank will promptly notify the guaranteeing agency of the execution of such guarantee.

(d) Other forms and procedures. The Board will prescribe from time to time, after consultation with the guaranteeing agencies, forms to be followed in the execution of guarantees pursuant to this regulation and other such forms as may be necessary. The Board will also prescribe, after consultation with the guaranteeing agencies, procedures with respect to such matters as the purchase of guaranteed loans by the Federal Reserve Banks as fiscal agents, the handling and disposition by the Federal Reserve Banks of guarantee fees and other fees collected, and such other procedures as may be found necessary.

Other Government Loans

The Veterans Administration has a 40 percent guarantee loan for veterans going into business. Unfortunately, the SBA's 90 percent guarantee loan is much more attractive to the banks, therefore the Veterans Administration's program is very seldom, if ever, used.

Maritime Administration guarantees loans for shipbuilding.

Department of Interior has loans and loan guarantees for Indian businessmen (Bureau of Indian Affairs); businesses engaged in domestic mineral exploration (Geological Survey); to fishermen and fishing industries for purchase, construction of, equipping, maintaining and repairing, or operating fishing vessels (Bureau of Commercial Fisheries); and to businesses involved in small reclamation projects (Bureau of Reclamation).

Local Development Corporations. Local and State Development Companies are organizations funded by the SBA under title V of the Small Business Investment Act of 1958 to provide funds to small business.

A State Development Company (SDC) is a corporation organized under a special act of a state legislature to promote and assist in the generation, growth, and development of business and industry within the state. Typical members of SDC's are banks, savings and loan companies, insurance companies, and other financial institutions that are committed to lend funds to the SDC at a fraction over the prime rate in amounts stipulated by the enabling legislation based on a small percentage (e.g., 2 percent) of a bank's capital and surplus.

A state development company may borrow from the SBA an amount equivalent to the total of outstanding borrowings from all other sources. The SDC is required to maintain a portfolio of small business loans or investments with an outstanding principal value of not less than 133⅓ percent of the outstanding balance of the loan from SBA. These loans are on a direct basis and must be reloaned by the SDC within thirty days of their draw down.

The funds borrowed from SBAA can be used by the SDC to assist small business by either equity investments or long-term loans (at least five years) in implementing the expressed policy of the Congress to stimulate the flow of private capital for the sound financing of small business concerns.

The maximum term for an SBA loan to an SDC under Section 501 is twenty years. Repayment without penalty may be made on any interest date. Normally, repayments are scheduled in annual installments over the life of the loan. The term, security, rate of repayment, and interest rate on the SBA loan are the same as are applicable to other borrowings of the SDC. The SBA interest rate is reviewed annually to conform with the rates on other borrowings, but in no event may the interest rate charged by SBA exceed 8 percent.

SDCs are required to use the proceeds of Section 501 loans to assist small business concerns. Funds obtained from other sources may be used for any purpose permitted by the development company charter.

Banks are encouraged to take an active part in the organization of state business development corporations (in those states where such a corporation is under consideration) and are further encouraged to take an active part in its operation because it can be an important adjunct in providing full banking services to the community. The state development corporation can provide nonbankable financing to complement the bankable loans that the bank can make to expanding and new industry in the community.

A Local Development Company (LDC) is a corporation chartered under any applicable state corporation law to operate in a specified area within a state, and which is formed for the purpose of furthering the economic development of its community and environs, with authority to promote and assist the growth and development of small business concerns in the areas covered by their operations. Such corporations may be organized either as profit or nonprofit enterprises.

A local development company must be principally composed of and controlled by persons residing or doing business in the locality. Such local persons will ordinarily constitute not less than 75 percent of the voting control of the development company. No shareholder or member of the development company may own in excess of 25 percent of the voting control of the development company, if he and his affiliated interest have direct pecuniary interest in the project involving the Section 502 loan or in the small business concern that is to be assisted. The primary objective of the development company must be to benefit the community as measured by increased employment, payroll, business volume, and corresponding factors, rather than monetary profits to its shareholders or members. Any monetary profits or other benefits that flow to the shareholders or members of the local development company must be merely incidental thereto.

The development company must provide a reasonable percentage of the project cost, usually 20 percent.

The maximum amount the SBA can lend a development corporation is $350,000 for each identifiable small business to be assisted, though this amount may be limited from time to time by budgetary limitation. The maturity of the loans may be for as long as twenty-five years.

Loan funds may be used to buy land, acquire or build a plant, convert, modernize, or expand facilities, and may include the purchase of machinery and equipment. Loan proceeds may not be used for debt payment or working capital.

Loans to the development company can be made on the following basis:

1. By the bank in participation with SBA under a guaranty of up to 90 percent of the loan amount.

2. By the bank under the first mortgage plan. (Bank or other lender lends a reasonable percentage of the cost of the project and receives a first lien on the collateral. SBA directly or in participation with the bank lends a percentage of the project cost with a second lien position and the LDC finances the balance with a third lien position).

3. The bank can participate with SBA (in 25 percent or more of a loan for the project costs not covered by the LDC's required injection) through SBA's immediate participation program. Under this program the bank can make and service the loan or SBA can make and service the loan.

4. If other financing is not available, SBA can make a direct loan, provided funds are available.

Summary We have covered most of the government loan programs from A to Z. Generally speaking, the applications to these agencies are a complicated affair as far as presentation and preparation, but remember, the most important thing is to get everything in the presentation accurate and make sure you follow the guidelines of the agencies.

Section II, "Preparation" will give you all the technical nuts and bolts to make a good financial presentation.

If any of the foregoing information about loans is unclear or you need more information, contact the agencies mentioned. Many of them have local offices in major cities, and they are very cooperative about giving information.

II

Preparation of Loans

Introduction to Preparation

Common sense tells you that no one is going to give a loan to a business unless that lender can assure itself that that business will be able to repay the money.

The way that you prove, on paper, that your business can take the money, put it to good use, repay the lender, and, why your business is a better investment than some other business is to prepare a "loan package."

First, why do you have to prove your business can make it on paper, in a presentation? There are several reasons for this, perhaps the most compelling of which is the fact that a loan generally has to be approved by many people before the money is finally disbursed, and each person whose hands the loan goes through cannot possibly talk in person to you.

The presentation is perhaps the most effective tool for getting your point across. You have control over it. You can emphasize the good points and explain the poor aspects before the lender has a chance to say "yes, but. . . ."

The philosophy of the proposal, the loan analysis, is to answer all the questions a lender may have before he asks them. A lender doesn't want surprises. If the proposal is thorough enough, conservative enough, and covers all the points good and bad, he won't be surprised. If a lender has no surprises, your proposal has the best chance of success. It's not difficult to put together a loan presentation even though it involves a lot of technical tricks. If you follow the directions of this section, you should be able to prepare a good analysis. I have written the instructions with the assumption that the reader is an average person with some business background but little expertise in finance.

This section is divided into four chapters. Chapter 6, "Preliminaries and Basic Factors," is a discussion of the preliminaries of putting together a loan analysis, including: a basic explanation of what a balance sheet and profit and loss statements are and what elements are important for your analysis; gathering raw material, doing a market study and finding out how much you need and for what.

Chapter 7, "Financial Data and Analysis," shows you how to compare past data and use the information to project sales and the business financial position into the future and how to take this data and compare it with other people in your industry. Moreover, the chapter will show if your business or business idea can make it in the future under the burden of the loan repayment. The chapter includes: calculating future expenses and sales, loan repayment amounts, variable and fixed expenses, breakeven point for sales; how to do annual projections of expenses and sales for your business, monthly projections, supporting schedules, footnotes and pro forma balance sheet; and how to compare your data to national averages, use this information to generate financial ratios, and what the ratios mean.

Chapter 8, "The Presentation Format," tells you how to take all the data discussed in the previous chapters and present it in the most readable form. The chapter includes: a sample of one of my presentations; my loan analysis in the format form; an explanation of each section of the format-application, purpose, use of funds, financial data, personal data, collateral, and business history; and an explanation of what the supporting data should be, including government and lender forms.

Preliminaries and Basic Factors

Financial Statements and Technical Terms
Profit and Loss

The best known financial statement is called a profit and loss statement or income statement. The Internal Revenue Service (IRS) requires that all businesses submit a profit and loss statement at the end of each year to show what their net income was for that year. Figure 6.1 is a sample profit and loss statement.

(1) *Sales or Gross Receipts* represents the total amount of money that the business makes from the sale of their merchandise, generally exclusive of sales tax or discounts.

Figure 6.1

Sample Profit and Loss Statement

Sales or Gross Receipts (1)	$_____
Beginning Inventory	$_____
Inventory Purchased	_____
Less Ending Inventory	_____
Cost of Goods Sold (2)	$_____
Gross Profit	$_____
Less Business Expenses	
Operating Expense (3)	
Rent	$_____
Depreciation	_____
Repairs & Maintenance	_____

(continued)

Salaries & Wages _____
Payroll Taxes & Fringe
  Benefits @ 10% _____
Taxes, Licenses, & Fees _____
Insurance _____
Accounting, Legal and
  Professional Fees _____
Bad Debts _____
Telephone _____
Utilities _____
Supplies _____
Security _____
Auto and Truck _____
Advertising and Promotion _____
Interest _____
Miscellaneous _____

Total Expenses $_____

Net Profit Before Taxes (4) $_____

Federal Income Taxes
(Corporation Only) $_____

Net Profit $===========

(2) *Cost of Goods Sold* is, literally, the cost of the merchandise that the business sells. What those costs are differ with each kind of business. For retail, the cost of sales is the cost of the merchandise bought from the wholesaler or jobber and it is calculated simply by taking the beginning inventory that the business has at the start of the period, adding the purchases of goods during the period and subtracting out the ending inventory that the business has at the end of the period. This procedure will indicate the *exact* amount of goods purchased that are *sold.* For manufacturing, cost of sales will include the inventory as above and also such factors as the cost of labor to manufacture the goods, freight charges, and the direct costs of running the factory (factory overhead) including factory rent, utilities, and supervisory expenses. For all practical purposes if the business already has income statements from the past, the calculation of what is cost of goods has already been performed and the packager should only be concerned with knowing what the cost of goods total is.

(3) *Business Expense,* generally called *Operating Expense,* includes all the costs of the business not directly related to the cost of the merchandise. In other words, the operating expense is the cost of the fiscal plant (store), salaries, and so on, that have to be paid no matter what the merchandise costs, or (and in

most instances) no matter if you sell merchandise or not. Operating expense includes rent on the business (including equipment rental); repairs on the facility or equipment and maintenance of the building and equipment; salaries (except factory salaries which are a cost of sales); payroll taxes that the business has to pay the state, city, and federal governments. Operating expenses include withholding income tax and social security (FICA) taxes; employee benefits such as shared cost, medical, pension, and profit sharing plans; taxes, licenses, and fees which include business licenses, and property tax; insurance; accounting, legal, and professional fees; bad debts such as bounced checks; telephone; utilities; supplies either for the office (such as postage, stationery, and other office supplies) or the store (such as window washing supplies, furniture cleaner, samples, and aprons); security (alarm systems or guards); auto and truck (which includes delivery and business truck expenses); advertising and promotion; interest on business debts; miscellaneous; and depreciation. Depreciation is an expense of the business even though it is not a cash expense. Depreciation is the money the business charges off to pay for the declining value of their machinery.

(4) *Net Profit* equals the sales less the cost of sales less the operating expense.

Balance Sheet   Figure 6.2 is an illustration of a balance sheet from the *Small Business Reporter*, Vol. 7, No. 11, "Understanding Financial Statements."

1. *Current Assets* are cash, accounts receivables, and inventory in the illustration, but also sometimes include prepaid expenses; stocks in other businesses; bonds used for investment, and notes owed the business, payable in one year and other assets that presumably could be turned into cash within one year. In other words you can sell the inventory, collect the receivables, cash in investments, collect on one-year notes and use current prepaids within one year if you closed up tomorrow.

2. *Fixed assets,* or long-term assets, include equipment, real estate, leasehold improvements, depreciation and sometimes long-term investments such as five-year cash deposits (called five-year certificate of deposit) or long-term notes owed the company. Fixed assets are those possessions of the business that are more or less "fixed," that is, the item can't be sold quickly for its market value.

3. *Other assets,* not illustrated, include such items as money (notes) due from officers, or employees of the company as well as prepaid expenses (last month's rent, security deposits, association deposits), that will not be paid back to the company for some time.

4. *Current Liabilities* are notes payable to the bank or others within a year, accounts payable to trade suppliers, and unpaid taxes in the illustration. They also include accrued expenses (expenses not yet paid) and the current portion of long-term debt (that is, that portion of long-term debt due within one year) that have to be paid in one year.

Figure 6.2

BALANCE SHEET
This is how the business looks on a specific date.

ASSETS	LIABILITIES
What the business itself owns.	This side of the balance sheet shows the claims on the assets—by both creditors and owners of the business. The claims of creditors are debts of the business—the LIABILITIES. The owner's claim is his investment in the business—the NET WORTH.

CURRENT ASSETS: In varying states of being converted into cash—within the next 12 months.

 CASH: Money on hand, in the bank.

 ACCOUNTS RECEIVABLE: What the customers owe the business for merchandise or services they bought.

 INVENTORY: Merchandise on hand:
1) ready to be sold
2) in some stage of production
3) raw material

CURRENT LIABILITIES: Debts owed by the business to be paid within the next 12 months.

 NOTES PAYABLE: IOU Bank or Trade Creditors.

 ACCOUNTS PAYABLE: IOU Trade & Suppliers.

 INCOME TAXES: IOU Government.

FIXED ASSETS: Used in the operation of the business. Not intended for resale.

 REAL ESTATE: Land and buildings used by the business. Listed at original cost.

LEASEHOLD IMPROVEMENTS: Permanent installations—remodeling or refurbishing of the premises.

 MACHINERY, EQUIPMENT, VEHICLES: Used by the business. Listed at original cost.

Less Accumulated Depreciation: These assets (except land) lose value through wear, tear and age. The business claims this loss of value as an expense of doing business. The running total of this expense is the accumulated depreciation.

NET FIXED ASSETS: Cost of fixed assets less depreciation = Present Value.

LONG-TERM LIABILITIES: Debts owed by the business to be paid beyond the next 12 months.

 MORTGAGE: On property.

 NET WORTH: Owner's (or stockholders') claim on the assets of the business; his investment. His equity in the business.

For Proprietorship or Partnership:
MR. OWNER, CAPITAL: Owner's original investment plus any profit reinvested in the business.

For Corporation:
CAPITAL STOCK: Value assigned to the original issue of stock by the directors of the corporation. If the stock sold for more than the assigned value, the excess will show as:

SURPLUS, PAID IN: The difference between assigned value and selling price of the original issue of stock. (The subsequent selling price of the stock does not change the assigned value.)

RETAINED EARNINGS: Profits reinvested in the business AFTER paying dividends.

BALANCE SHEET EQUATION:
ASSETS=LIABILITIES+NET WORTH

5. *Long-Term Liabilities* are those debts that are to be paid after this current year. Besides mortgages, as illustrated, long-term liabilities also include the long-term portion of long-term debt (the total debt minus that part of the debt that will be paid off in the next year). For instance, if you borrowed $50,000 for five years, and in the first year you are going to pay off $10,000 of that, then the current portion of the debt (entered under current liabilities) would be $10,000 and the long-term liability portion of the debt would be $40,000.

6. *Net Worth* is the difference between assets and liabilities.

Reconcilement (or Reconciliation) of Net Worth

Currently the SBA and some other government lenders require a Reconciliation of Net Worth Statement in addition to the standard profit and loss and balance sheet. If it is an existing business, the accountant should have one prepared. (See Figure 6.3.)

Figure 6.3

Reconciliation of Net Worth

Net Worth At Beginning of Period	$_____
Add: Net Profit After Taxes (or subtract Loss)	$_____
Other Additions: Sale of Assets, increase in money invested in business, sale of stock, etc.	$_____
Less: Owners' or officers' withdrawals or dividends	$_____
Net Worth as shown on Balance Sheet	$_____

Other Terms and Definitions

In preparing the loan analysis you will run into some financial terms that you might never have heard of. Below is a list of terms and their definitions.

Cost of Sales as a percentage of sales, or Cost of Sales Percentage. Percentage means, as it suggests, if income is 100 percent of sales, then cost of sales is X percent of sales. To derive this percentage just divide cost of sales by sales. For example, if sales are $200 and cost of sales is $100, then the cost of sales percentage is $100÷$200 or 50 percent.

Cash Margin. The amount of cash a business has left over after it pays all expenses, principal loan payment, income tax, and owner's salary.

Cash Flow. A representation of how cash "flows" through the system. For example: A business has $100 cash sales, pays $50 for cost of sales, $40 for expense, $5 for principal loan repayment, and $3 for owner's salary—leaving a $2 cash margin. This shows how the cash comes in and is paid out. If the same business sells $100 on credit, that is, no cash sales, but has to pay out all the cash expenses as above, instead of having in the end a $2 cash margin, it would have a $98 negative cash margin—the business would have paid out $98 more than it took in.

Fixed Expenses. Those expenses that a business has to pay out whether it sells anything or not. Such expenses as rent, insurance, licenses, leases, and for our purposes, most other operating expenses, except commission and percentage leases, are considered "fixed."

Variable Expenses. Those expenses that "vary" as sales do. If sales increase, these expenses increase. One example of variable expense is a salesman's commission.

Cash Flow Monthly. The amount of cash a business has at the end of each month from its operations, i.e., the cash margin for that month.

Cash Flow Cumulative. The total amount of cash the business has at any given time, the "Checking Account Balance" of the business.

Start-up Costs. The costs of getting a business started or the cost of an expansion. Start-up costs would include: equipment, debt repayment, working capital, deposits and prepayments, inventory, purchase price of a business, goodwill, leasehold, improvements, and real estate.

Working Capital. The money that a business has to "work with" to pay for expenses not sufficiently covered by income. Basically, it is an estimate of operating capital for the loan period. For our purposes, working capital will be generally synonymous with cash.

Deposits and Prepayments. Monies that are put up to get into business including such items as utility and phone deposit; rent deposit; buying association deposits and one year's life insurance.

Owner's Salary or Owner's Draw. The amount of money drawn from the business' net profit, if it is a proprietorship or partnership, or charged as an operating expense (officer's salary), if the business is a corporation.

Principal Loan Repayment. The amount of loan repayment the business pays less the interest portion. Each payment to reduce a loan has two parts: principal and interest. The interest part of a loan payment is the amount the bank charges for the borrower's use of the money loaned. The principal portion of the loan payment is a direct reduction in the total amount the business owes and it's not an expense. The business still has to pay it in cash, therefore whenever cash calculations are made, such as cash flow analysis, the principal loan repayment must be considered.

Seasonal Sales Adjustments. The adjustments made each month in preparing a monthly cash flow projection that reflect seasonal changes in sales. For example, most retail businesses sell more merchandise in December than any other month, therefore the sales should be adjusted accordingly.

Financial Comparative. Simply, past financial data set side-by-side to show changes, if any, in the statements. For instance, to do profit and loss comparatives for three years, the 1974, 1975 and 1976 profit and loss statements would be placed side-by-side with all the same expenses, sales, and so on in sequential order, that is, rent 1974, rent 1975, rent 1976. Chapter 7 will show you some illustrations of this.

Projected Financial Data. The financial statements—profit and loss, balance sheet and cash flow—that indicate how the figures will look in the future. The financial data is "projected" into the future.

Depreciation. The calculation of how much in value your assets will lose each year through wear and tear and age. The loss in value of this equipment, real estate (building only) and leasehold improvements is considered as an expense of the business. There are several methods for calculating depreciation, straight-line (S.L.), double-declining balance, sum-of-the-years-digits, and others. For our purposes, we will use straight-line (S.L.) depreciation which is calculated by taking the purchase price, subtracting how much it will be worth at the end of the depreciation period (say five years) which is called salvage value, then dividing by the number of years of the depreciation period. For example, Tap Manufacturing buys a truck for $10,000 and estimates it will last five years. At the end of that five year period, the truck will be worth $2,000, its "salvage value." The calculations to ascertain yearly depreciation on a straight-line basis would be as in Figure 6.4.

Figure 6.4

Purchase Price	$10,000
Less: Salvage Value	$\underline{-\ 2,000}$
	$\overline{\$\ 8,000}$

$8,000 equals $1,600 in straight-line depreciation per year for five years.

What Data is Necessary?

All businesses need a future projection of operating expenses and sales, and a pro forma (projected) balance sheet at the time the loan is disbursed, personal data, an explanation of the uses of the funds, a personal financial statement on the major principals, and a summary of what kind of collateral you are willing to offer the bank. But different kinds of businesses need other, different material.

If you are going to start a new business from scratch, the largest amount of basic data is needed. A new business needs a very good market study explaining where your sales are going to come from and why, and it has to be as complete and convincing as possible. A new businessman is also going to have to scrounge around for something to base his expenses and cost of sales on. Also he will have to be very comprehensive on personal background.

If the business is an existing business and it can make the loan repayment without increasing its sales more than 20 percent, then you don't need a market study, but you do need your last three years (if you've been existing in business that long) financial statements and/or the business's income tax statements and current financial statements (which means profit and loss statements *and* balance sheets). If you don't have balance sheets for the last three years, don't get uptight, it's okay; but you *must* have a current balance sheet. Since the existing business has historical financial data, most of the projections will be based on your historical data.

If the applicant is purchasing an existing business he needs the same data that an existing business needs, i.e., last three years financial data and current financial statements from the business he plans to buy. Additionally, he'll need a buy-sell agreement stating what the business costs and what the applicant gets for his purchase price.

If the business is an existing business that has to increase sales more than 20 percent, you will need a market study in addition to the other materials required for an existing business.

The basic information required for all businesses is the following:
1. Resumes of owners and managers
2. Personal financial statements of owner or major stockholders
3. Personal income tax of owners or major stockholders for the last three years

4. Existing or proposed lease
5. Corporation or partnership papers, if applicable
6. A basic idea of expected expenses and sales for the next year
7. Title of property owned personally by applicants and list of personal creditors, present balances owed, and original balances
8. Some idea of what your market is like

For Existing or Buy-Out Businesses

1. Last three years business income statements
2. Current balance sheet, profit and loss statements, and reconciliation of net worth (less than two months old)
3. Aging of accounts receivable and payable
4. Buy-sell agreement if the business is to be a buy-out
5. Copies of major contracts and list of customers
6. A business history

The rest of the loan analysis you present to a lender is derived from the above sources. How you take this "raw" data mentioned above and turn it into a finished loan analysis is what this section is all about.

Business history, financial statements, and market data will be discussed at some length shortly.

Resumes should be in the standard resume form with special emphasis on experience.

A copy of the proposed lease or present lease is necessary so the lender can see if the business has rental options for the period of the loan and to get an idea of future lease expense.

The lender generally has the option for some loans of taking a lien against personal real estate; therefore, they require a copy of the title. A list of the owner's personal debt with present balances owed and original balances will help the banker check your credit.

An aging of accounts payable and accounts receivable should be a standard practice of all businesses, but if your particular business doesn't have these, it might be advisable to talk to your accountant. Basically, aging of accounts means finding which ones are one month old, two months, and three months plus. The aging will let the businessmen know what accounts haven't paid and which have and which accounts their business owes for the longest period of time.

If you are buying a business you should have a legal agreement showing how much the business costs and what the terms are. This is called a buy-sell agreement.

Business History All businesses that are in existence have a history and this should be included as part of your preliminary work.

Write up a summary of the activities of the business including:
—date founded and the circumstances.
—date incorporated (if applicable).

—key management personnel and owner's history with the business.

—key products and innovations developed by the company.

—a summary of the growth factor, such as increases in sales, net worth, and improvement in financial ratios (to be discussed later in this section).

Financial Information (business and personal)

To put together the loan proposal for a business, it is necessary to collect the last three years income tax statements of the business and a profit and loss statement and balance sheet and reconciliation of net worth not more than two months old. If the business is to be a new operation (not a buy-out), this data, of course, is unavailable.

All loan applicants need a personal financial statement. This is a statement of your personal assets, liabilities and net worth and is a standard form at all banks. Figure 6.5 is a sample personal financial statement.

Market Data

A market study is required of a business that is starting up or that expects to increase sales more than 20 percent in the next projected year. In the next section of this chapter we'll go into market studies in depth. Before you even start thinking of a loan, you should make sure, first, what your market is, and, second, if your market will support the kind of sales it takes to repay the loan out of earnings.

In order to prepare market studies, the applicant has to collect a lot of information. Some information may be had from libraries, the city hall, or trade associations; but a good deal of the research necessary for market studies is calling and getting commitments from expected customers, surveying the geographic area and answering these questions.

1. What products/services will be offered?
2. Who buys and uses such products/services (consumers, businesses, governments, etc.)?
3. Where are these customers located?

—In immediate geographic area of prospective business?

—In general metropolitan area?

—In rural country?

—In multiple countries?

—In state?

—In region and county?

—Nationwide?

Below is a list of what market data is most important to what kind of company, listed in the order of their importance:

Retailer:

1. Market Share Data
2. Location Data, Geographic Area
3. Traffic Patterns
4. Population Data
5. Competition Study

Figure 6.5
Personal Financial Statement

ASSETS	DOLLARS
Cash on Hand and In Banks	$_____
Savings Account(s)	_____
U.S. Government Bonds	_____
Accounts and Notes Receivable	_____
Life Insurance (Cash Surrender Value)	_____
Other Stocks and Bonds (Retirement)	_____
Real Estate (Current Value)	_____
Automobile (Current Value)	_____
Other Personal Property (Current Value)	_____
_____	_____
Other Assets (Current Value)	_____
_____	_____
_____	_____
TOTAL ASSETS	$_____

LIABILITIES	$_____
Accounts Payable	_____
Notes Payable To Bank	_____
Notes Payable To Others	_____
Installment Accounts	_____
Loans On Life Insurance	_____
Mortgage On Real Estate	_____
Unpaid Taxes	_____
Other Liabilities	_____
_____	_____
TOTAL LIABILITIES	$_____
	_____
NET WORTH	$_____

LIFE INSURANCE HELD

Company and Policy Type	Cash Surrender Value	Beneficiary
_____	$_____	_____
_____	$_____	_____
_____	$_____	_____

PERSONAL OBLIGATIONS

Bank Or Other Credit Institutions	Orig. Bal.	Pres. Bal.	Payments Per Mo.	Maturity Date
	$_____	$_____	$_____	
_____	$_____	$_____	$_____	_____
_____	$_____	$_____	$_____	_____
_____	$_____	$_____	$_____	_____
_____	$_____	$_____	$_____	_____
_____	$_____	$_____	$_____	_____

STOCKS	Cost	Market Value
	$_____	$_____
_____	$_____	$_____
_____	$_____	$_____

REAL ESTATE OWNED

Title In the Name Of: ....
Property (Dwelling Type): ....
Orignial Cost To Me: $.......................Date Purchased..........
Present Market Value: $..
Tax Assessment Value: $.....................Rate Of Mortgage:........
Original Mortgage Amount: $.................Balance:$..............
Maturity Date: ....
Terms Of Payment: $_____ per...............................
Name and Address Of Mortgage Holder:_____

Manufacturing or Distribution Companies:
1. Market Share Data
2. Competition Study
3. Population and Trends Studies
4. Traffic Study
5. Location Geographic Area

Service Business:
1. Market Share Data
2. Competition Study
3. Population and Trends Studies
4. Location, Geographic Area
5. Traffic Studies

Market share data is the most important information in *every* case but that's because it's important to know what your product is and who you are selling it to before you collect any more data at all, otherwise you don't know what data to look for. The market share data is just a general sizing-up of the market before you get specific.

Market Share The purpose in estimating market size is to assess the total sales or total purchases of the products or services being offered within the trading area of the business. After estimating this market size (and after making an analysis of competition) then it is possible to intelligently address the question: "Can this trading area support another (gasoline station)?" The method recommended is relatively straightforward:

First, define the "buying unit," i.e., define just what constitutes a customer for these kinds of products and services. For instance, the buying unit or customer for a service station is anyone in the area who owns or operates a motor vehicle. The customer for a photofinishing firm is anyone who uses a camera. A clothing store's customers may be composed of men, women, or family units. A produce wholesaler's customers or buying units might include retail food stores plus restaurants and hotels. A manufacturer of certain home improvements or do-it-yourself materials or tools might include among his customers hardware wholesalers and retailers, home improvement stores or chains, and perhaps even the larger discount chains, department stores, variety stores, or mail order and catalog companies.

Second, determine how many such buying units exist in the trading area previously defined for the business. How many families, how many consumers of a certain type, how many stores, etc.

When it is known (approximately) how many buying units or customers of a certain type exist, the next step is to determine the number of dollars they spend, on an average, in a single year for the type of products or services to be offered. Obviously, this may or may not be an easy figure to determine, depending on the size of the trading area, the number and variety of customers, the nature of the products and services, and the availability of reliable statistics.

The more common or familiar the product or service, the more likely it is that reliable statistics will be available, since both government and trade associations typically collect figures on average annual purchases. However, even with such figures, it will usually be necessary to tailor them to the peculiar and often different social, economic, and other characteristics of the particular trading area. For example, the National Restaurant Association and the larger firms in the restaurant business have figures on how often people eat out, and how much they spend in various types of restaurants. Nevertheless, the accuracy of these figures for a particular restaurant of a particular type in a particular neighborhood will have to be adjusted up or down.

When there is a limited number of customers, such as might be the case for a manufacturer or wholesaler, published figures may be more scarce or even nonexistent, but the limited number may also permit average annual purchases to be secured with relative ease. For instance, a prospective wholesaler can secure such figures both from retail customers directly and in some cases from manufacturers who would be distributing through his firm. Based on the number of buying units or types of customers in the trading area, and their average annual purchases, the total annual purchases in the trading area can be estimated. This, then, is "the market"—the ballpark or field of opportunity open to the client.

A final indicator of market size is suggested, and this is the trend of purchases. Of course, trends are not always obvious, nor can they be trusted altogether without knowing the reasons for the trends. Naturally, a brand new type of product or service has no trend at all, and may not even have an annual purchase figure as a base for decision making. Nevertheless, if there has been a clear trend—up, down, or steady—that has persisted for several years, this is worthwhile information to know. Obviously, if such a trend is detected, you will want to know the reasons for the trend, since this might indicate other business alternatives, or show that the long-term future of a business is unattractive (i.e., in a static or declining market). The following questions summarize how to determine market share:

1. What is the "buying unit"? (Individual customer, family, retail store, retail group, manufacturing company, etc.)

2. Approximately how many such buying units exist in the trading area?

3. Approximately how many dollars are spent per year per buying unit for the type of products/services being considered?

4. What is the total number of dollars spent by all buying units annually? (Question 2 times question 3.)

5. What is the trend in buying? (Percent increase or decrease in recent years.)

Location If the business is a retail business, location is very important, and to a lesser extent, location is important to manufacturing and service businesses.

The primary elements to consider when choosing a location for a retailer is: foot traffic, auto traffic, visibility, population, competition, parking, the complimentary nature of adjacent stores, and the cost of the site.

The visibility of the business is directly related to whether it can be easily seen and from what distance, and how effective your signs, windows, and exterior looks are. Naturally, the more visible a business is from a long distance, the better its attraction. For instance, a liquor store located on a corner lot in a predominately residential area, painted bright yellow with large signs that can be seen from both cross streets will be extremely visible. In short: can your store be seen?

It is a good idea to have stores around you that attract people, especially those that attract people who would shop in your store. For instance, a good men's shoe store next to a men's clothing store is a naturally attractive situation. If the stores around yours are as good-looking on the outside as yours, more people will be attracted than if the stores around yours are run-down and tacky (or worse yet, closed for some time).

The cost of the site should only be high if all the other elements of a good location, discussed in this portion of the chapter, are reasonable.

In the central business district, land values and rents are frequently based on traffic counts. The site in the central business district that produces the highest traffic count with regard to the type of traffic desired by a particular store is considered its 100-percent location. However, a 100-percent location for one type of store may not be 100-percent for other types. For example, a site that rates 100 percent for a drugstore may be only 80 percent for a men's clothing shop and 60 percent for an appliance store.

Data from a traffic count should not only show how many people pass by, but generally indicate what kinds of people they are. Analysis of the characteristics of the passing traffic frequently reveals patterns and variations not readily apparent from casual observation.

For counting purposes, the passing traffic is divided into different classifications according to the characteristics of the customers who would patronize your type of business. Whereas a drugstore is interested in the total volume of passing traffic, a men's clothing store is obviously more concerned with the amount of male traffic, especially men between the ages of 16 and 65.

It is important to classify passing traffic by its reasons for passing. A woman on her way to a beauty salon is probably a poor prospect for a paint store, but she may be a good prospect for a drugstore. The hours at which individuals go by are important. In the early morning hours people are generally on their way to work. In the late afternoon these same people are usually going home from work. When one chain organization estimates the number of potential women customers, it considers women passing a site between 10 a.m. and 5 p.m. to be the serious shoppers.

Evaluation of the financial bracket of traffic is also significant. Out of one hundred women passing a prospective location for an exclusive dress shop, only ten may appear to have the money. Of course, the more experience you have had in a particular retail trade, the more accurately you can estimate the number of your potential customers.

In summary, the qualitative information gathered about the passing traffic should include counting the individuals who seem to possess the characteristics appropriate to the desired clientele, judging their reasons for using that route, and calculating their ability to buy.

Pedestrian Traffic Count   In making a pedestrian count you must decide: who is to be counted; where the count should take place; and when the count should be made.

Before the study begins, consider who, that is, what types of people, should be included. If the directions are not completely clear as to whom to include, the counters will be inconsistent and the total figure may be either too high or too low.

As previously indicated, it is frequently desirable to divide the pedestrian traffic categories into classes. Quite often separate counts of men and women and certain age categories are wanted. A trial run will indicate if there are any difficulties in identifying those to be counted or in placing them into various groupings.

You next determine the specific place where the count is to be taken. You decide whether all the traffic near the site should be counted or only the traffic passing directly in front of the site.

Remember, if all the pedestrians passing through an area are counted, there is the possibility of double counting. Since a person must both enter and leave an area, it is important that each be counted only once—either when entering or when leaving. Therefore, it is essential that the counter consistently counts at the same location.

In order to determine what proportion of the passing traffic represents your potential shoppers, some of the pedestrians should be interviewed about the origin of their trip, their destination, and the stores in which they plan to shop. This sort of information can provide you with a better estimate of the number of potential customers.

The season, month, week, day, and hour all have an effect upon a traffic survey. For example, during the summer season there is generally an increased flow of traffic on the shady side of the street. During a holiday period like the month before Christmas or the week before Easter, traffic is denser than it is regularly. The patronage of a store varies by day of the week, too. Store traffic usually increases during the latter part of a week. In some communities, on factory paydays and days when social security checks are received, certain locations experience heavier than normal traffic.

The day of the week and the time of day should represent a normal period for traffic flow. Pedestrian flow accelerates around noon as office workers go out for lunch. Generally more customers enter a downtown store between 10 a.m.

and noon and between 1 p.m. and 3 p.m. than at any other time. Local custom or other factors, however, may cause a variation in these expected traffic patterns.

After you choose the day that has normal traffic flow, the day should be divided into half-hour and hourly intervals. Traffic should be counted and recorded for each half-hour period of a store's customary operating hours. If it is not feasible to count the traffic for each half-hour interval, the traffic flow can be sampled. Traffic in representative half-hour periods in the morning, noon, afternoon, and evening can be counted.

Types of Customers   Another factor that affects site selection is the customers' view of the goods sold by a store. Consumers tend to group products into three major categories: convenience, shopping, and specialty.

"Convenience" usually means low unit price, purchased frequently, little selling effort, bought by habit and sold in numerous outlets. Examples: candy bars, cigarettes, and milk.

"Shopping" usually means high unit price, bought infrequently, more intensive, selling effort usually required on the part of the store owner, price and features compared, and sold in selectively franchised outlets. Examples: men's suits, automobiles, and furniture.

"Specialty" usually means high unit price although price is not a purchase consideration, bought infrequently, requires a special effort on the part of the customer to make the purchase, no substitutes considered, and sold in exclusively franchised outlets. Examples: jewelry, perfume, cameras, and so on, of specific brands.

For stores handling *convenience goods,* the *quantity* of pedestrian traffic is most important. For stores handling *shopping goods* the *quality* of the traffic is most important.

Specialty goods are frequently sought by customers who are already "sold" on the product, brand, or both. Stores catering to this type of consumer may use isolated locations because they generate their own consumer traffic.

Stores carrying specialty goods that are complementary to certain other kinds of shopping goods may desire to locate close to the shopping goods stores. In general, the specialty goods retailer should locate in the type of neighborhood where the adjacent stores and other establishments are compatible to his operation.

Automobile Traffic   A growing number of retail firms depend upon drive-in traffic for their sales.
Count   Both the quantity and quality of automotive traffic can be analyzed in the same way as pedestrian traffic. For the major streets in urban areas, either the city engineer, the planning commission, the state highway department, or an outdoor advertising company may be able to provide you with data on traffic flows. However, you may need to modify this information to suit your special needs. For example, you should supplement data relating to total count of

vehicles passing the site with actual observation in order to evaluate such influences on traffic as commercial vehicles, changing of shifts at nearby factories, through highway traffic, and increased flow caused by special events or activities.

Automobile traffic may be classified according to the reason for the trip: work or shopping. Knowledge of the type of trip can assist you in making the correct site decision. Careful observation of the character of the traffic and even a few short interviews with drivers who are stopped for a traffic signal will reveal the nature of their trips.

Different types of retailers seek different locations although they are serving the same type of customer. For example, to serve a work-trip customer, a dry cleaner and a convenience foodstore usually desire to be located on different sides of the street. The dry cleaner wants to locate on the going-to-work side of the street while the convenience foodstore wants to be on the going-home side.

A good location for a retailer seeking the customer on a planned shopping trip is along the right-hand side of the main street leading into a shopping district and adjacent to other streets carrying traffic into, out of, or across town. The beginning or end of a row of stores rather than across the street is preferable. Noting on which side the older, established stores are located provides a clue to the best side of the street. But check it out to be sure that these stores are still on the rise rather than the decline.

In smaller communities, where the major streets lead to and from the downtown area, the traffic pattern can be readily identified. In larger cities, where there are suburban shopping center locations, the traffic moves in many different directions. Since shopping centers tend to generate traffic, an analysis of the traffic flow to centers and between centers may show a particular store location is outstanding.

The person on a pleasure or recreational trip is in the market for services such as those offered by motels, restaurants, and service stations. The probability of attracting this type of customer increases if the facility is located alongside a well-traveled highway and adjacent to a major entrance to the community.

Understanding the business of people passing your site in cars also depends on the same analysis of consumer behavior used in classifying pedestrians. There are the same three categories of goods or products to consider: convenience, shopping, and specialty.

In general, the greater the automobile traffic, the greater the sales of convenience goods for catering to the drive-in traffic. For the drive-in store selling low-priced convenience goods, the volume of traffic passing the site is a most important factor in making a site decision. The consumer purchases these goods frequently. He desires them to be readily available. And he is reminded when passing a convenience goods store that he needs a particular item.

If the consumer must make a special trip to purchase such convenience staple goods as food and drug items, he wants the store to be close to his home.

One study of foodstore purchases in the central city area revealed that nearly 70 percent of the women patronized stores within one to five blocks of their homes. Another study of foodstores indicated that for suburban locations the majority of customers lived within three miles of the stores, while the maximum trading area was five miles. For rural locations, the majority of consumers lived within a ten-minute drive to the store, with the maximum trading area within a twenty-minute drive. A west coast supermarket chain wants a minimum of 3,500 homes within a mile-and-a-half radius of a shopping center before considering it for location. Research indicated that 80 percent of the customers of pizza carryouts lived within a mile of the establishments.

On the other hand, a retailer dealing in shopping goods can have a much wider trading area. Without a heavily trafficked location, but with the help of adequate promotion, this more expensive type of store can generate its own traffic. In this case, a location with low traffic density but easy accessibility from a residential area is a satisfactory site. The consumer buys these goods infrequently. He deliberately plans his purchases. And he is willing to travel some distance to make shopping comparisons.

If you offer shopping goods, however, you should not locate too far away from your potential customers. One study of a discount department store showed that 79.6 percent of the shoppers lived within five miles of the store and another 16.1 percent lived within a ten-mile radius. The magnitude of the trading area for a shopping goods store can be determined by a customer survey, automobile license checks, sales slips, charge account records, store deliveries, and the extent of local newspaper circulation.

The same principles of location that are applicable to the walk-in specialty goods stores are appropriate for the drive-in facility. Because this type of retailer generates his own traffic, he can locate away from the major traffic arteries.

Population and Geographic Area

The United States Census Bureau through their census tracts can tell you a lot of things about your particular business and its location. You can use the Census Tracts to answer the following questions:
—How many persons or families are there in the trading area and how has this changed over time?
—Where do they work?
—How many young or old persons are there? How many children or teenagers?
—How many families with children or with teenagers?
—How many one-person households? How many small or large families?
—What is the income of the families or individuals?
—Is the area an older established one or one where most residents are newcomers?
—How many families own their homes? How many rent?
—What is the value of the homes? What is the monthly rent?

—What is the age and quality of the homes?

—Do the homes have air conditioning; other appliances?

—How many of the families own an automobile? How many own two or more?

As you might tell from reading these questions, the answers will tell you a lot about your market area.

In order to use the census tracts, however, it is necessary to determine where your business market will extend to. Of course, for manufacturing the geographic boundaries tend to be countries, states, or counties, but for the retailer his geographic boundaries only extend so far. The larger the business, generally, the larger the geographic area. For small retailers, however, unless they are specialty stores, their boundaries are usually considered to be about a one-mile radius maximum.

How well the small retailer can describe his market area depends, to a great extent, on this locality and on the type of goods he sells.

The market area of a distributor of tractors and other farm implements in a county seat town, for example, may be fairly easy to describe. If he is the only tractor dealer in the county, his trade comes from the county, and if there is no comparable dealer in the adjoining county, he has the opportunity to draw business from it also.

A large men's store in a large city may have a market area of a hundred-mile radius from the metropolitan area. On the other hand, a downtown hardware store draws trade only from the city and its immediate suburbs. And the business of a neighborhood drugstore may be limited to several blocks of the city.

Certain customers can get to Store A easier than they can to Store B. Store A can expect to draw those who can reach it quicker—in four or five minutes—than they can reach Store B, using the road that connects the two stores. But if it takes much longer than four or five minutes to drive to Store A, customers are likely to go to Store B which is closer for them.

The same principle is true for Store C which is twenty-five minutes' driving time from Store A and Store D which is twenty minutes from Store A.

The broken line connecting the Xs surrounds the area from which, other things being equal, Store A draws a big part of its business. Store A will get some trade from outside the broken-lined circle, but the other stores, B, C, and D, will draw more than A because they are closer to the people who live outside the broken-lined circle than A is.

However, keep in mind that distance is only one factor in describing your market area. For example, Store A might use quality, assortment, appealing promotions, and so on to attract many customers from outside the broken lines in Figure 6.6—people who normally would shop in stores B, C, and D.

Therefore, distance is one factor in describing your market area. How long does it take a customer to walk or drive to your store? Can he buy the same items in another store that is the same distance from his home? Is a third store even closer for him?

Figure 6.6

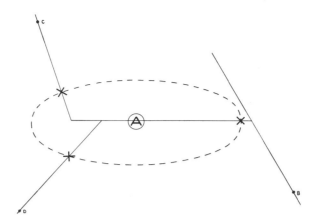

The first step in finding the geographic area and working with it is to get a city (or in some cases, county) map, plot a distance around it that you feel would be the maximum area your store would regularly draw customers, look up the competitors you have within that area and put them on the map. When you finish this, the outline of your map should look like Figure 6.6.

Figure 6.6 represents the trade area that Store A (a small department store) shares with three competitors, Stores B, C, and D. The Xs on the roads connecting the stores represent the halfway mark: for instance, eight minutes in the case of A and B because the driving time between them is sixteen minutes.

Competition

It is perhaps fairly obvious that the ability of any business to enter, survive, and grow in a market is seriously affected by the number and type of competitors in that market. Nevertheless, many market analyses give inadequate attention to competition, resulting in an inflated estimate of probable success. This is especially the case when the market is fairly large, and the client has ability and resources. Under those circumstances, the two positives can easily lead to overoptimism until competition is taken into account.

What is a competitor? To answer that question, it is important to rephrase that question.

How many businesses in the trading area are trying to satisfy or "tap" those same needs? These will not necessarily be businesses of the same type, nor will they necessarily offer identical products and services. For example, a consumer in need of automotive service has the choice of going to service stations, automotive dealerships, independent garages, automotive repair and service departments of discount or department stores, or back yard mechanics. If a person proposes to provide automotive service, then all of these organizations and individuals in his trading area constitute his potential competitors. Similarly, a fast-food restaurant competes not only with other fast-food restaurants, independent or franchised, but with all other kinds of restaurants, hot dog or hamburger stands, and in a sense even with food stores (the "competition of eating at home").

Of course, a true competitor is limited to a company or individual seeking to satisfy the needs of the same customers the client will go after. In the case of automotive service, for example, the fact that there are hundreds of service stations in a city, and dozens of other automotive service establishments need not discourage entry into the market. The main considerations are the market's dollar size, and whether the competitive situation allows another station to profitably share those dollars.

Who are your prominent competitors and what is their share of the market?

While it may be difficult or even impossible to fix their exact market share, that is not nearly as important as knowing that they are predominant. For in any market with one or a few predominant businesses, all other businesses must be able to compete effectively with them. They set the standard, as a rule, for what customers expect, and in most cases the only way to enter, survive, and grow is to emulate or exceed these already predominant businesses.

There are, of course, markets in which no competitors are predominant; in which the business is either split evenly between all existing companies, or where almost no real competition exists. In such cases, it is tempting to conclude that an enviable opportunity exists. But such a condition usually calls into question the nature of the opportunity itself. In a free market economy, it is normally the case that opportunity invites competition. Where real needs exist, and people have the resources to satisfy those needs, someone will step in to reap the profits available. Where you find no one doing that, or no one doing it effectively, it *may* mean that all existing competitors are incapable and inefficient—but it is more likely to mean that the needs you believe exist do not, in fact, exist, or that those with the needs do not have the resources to satisfy them. In short, in any market, where there is real opportunity to succeed, except in the case of brand new products or services, you can almost always assume competitors will be in that market, and that at least a few of them will be the pacesetters.

If and when predominant competitors are identified, much can be learned by examining their marketing operation in microscopic detail. (Fortunately, such a detailed look is not hard to come by, because simple observation of the competitive business normally reveals all you need to know.) There are several possible sources related to marketing, ranging from product/service uniqueness through the reputation or influence of the management of the competitor. Although it is often true that a predominant competitor tends to "score" well on almost all of these points, the idea in making the analysis is to check off those that seem to be particularly critical sources of success (strengths and weaknesses).

For example, location tends to be a critical factor in the success of retail establishments, since location includes closeness to consumers, visibility, ease of entry and exit, parking, and so on. However, important as it is, location *by itself* does not make anyone predominant. Case after case exists in which firms with less desirable locations out-gun firms with the better locations.

The main purpose of making the competitive analysis is not simply to know what they do that leads to success. Instead, it is to know what *your business* must do to lead to its own success. Although there is a good deal of room for speculation in this area, the actions of predominant competitors provide a real-world base. Whatever else is known, there is no denying one thing: the predominant competitor is predominant! What he is doing, while it may not be "perfect," is at least better than what anyone else is doing. Meet or beat what he is doing, and the odds for successful entry and growth increase accordingly.

Bear in mind, in this analysis, you are considering only the predominant competitors, and, in turn, considering only those particularly important success factors accounting for their leadership. Such an analysis need not be used for all competitors. These additional points should be kept in mind:

1. Some competitive success factors (such as location, public image, or perhaps the personal influence of the owner) may turn out to be unbeatable. That is, they cannot be duplicated, nor can they be offset. Fortunately, items in this category are few and far between.

2. Many competitive success factors will turn out, upon further analysis, to be duplicable. The businessman can do the exact same thing just as well, or reproduce the same set of conditions, or, through other tactics, he could offset or neutralize the competitive advantage. For instance, a competitor whose success is partially accounted for by having many salesmen might be neutralized in this area by the person offering more liberal credit, better delivery, and aggressive personal selling. Or a competitor who is on top of the market because of his aggressive local advertising could be neutralized in this area through better pricing or better merchandising.

3. In a few cases, it may even turn out that the very thing the competitor does best can still be exceeded. He may offer liberal credit . . . but there is room to offer still more liberal credit. He runs good promotions, but you could do even better. He delivers within a five mile radius; you could well deliver within a ten mile radius, and so on.

The following is a list of some of the factors that might be responsible for the competitor's success, some of which we discussed.
—Product/service uniqueness
—Product/service superiority
—Range, variety of products/services
—Pricing practices
—Cost/purchasing advantages
—Business location
—External appearance
—Internal appearance and merchandising
—Floor space
—Land
—Equipment and/or machinery
—Credit

—Delivery

—Other convenience services

—Promotional practices

—Quantity and/or quality of advertising

—Personal selling

—Quantity and/or quality of personnel

—Trade/public image or recognition

—Reputation and/or influence of owner or other key personnel

   When you analyze all the factors of your competition you should put it in writing for the loan proposal and weigh it with other factors.

Differences Between Businesses/Marketing Analysis

As you might have surmised from reading the preceding market portion of this chapter, retailers and manufacturers or distributors are interested in different sets of data. Location is very important to a retailer, but less important to a manufacturer except that for him it's a good idea to be located near good highway or rail access.

Estimating Total Sales

After you have collected all the data for the Market Study and have a good idea of what the market looks like, who's buying, who's competing, and how you expect to approach the whole thing, you come to the most crucial part of your market study, namely, "What does all this mean as far as sales? Can the market support my business?"

   There are several ways of taking your data, and using it to predict sales.

   One way of doing it is the *statistical or direct data method.*

   If you have a description of your market area, the next task is gathering figures on the sales of your type of merchandise within its limits. If you sell used cars, for example, how many were sold last year?

   This chore is fairly easy if your market area coincides with a political subdivision such as a city or a county. You can use statistics pretty much as you find them.

   However, in many cases, the boundaries of a retail market will overlap the city or county. When they do, you have to adjust your statistics, using portions of the political areas.

   Figure 6.7 is a simple example of how portions of population figures might be used. It assumes an equal dispersion of population throughout the statistical unit: two countries. In Figure 6.7, the market area is 10 percent of County B and 25 percent of County A. Therefore, you would use those percentages of the total population in each county to determine how many people make up the market area.

   You will want to analyze population figures that show growth or decline to determine whether the change affects your type of business.

   If you find out how much merchandise of the kind you sell was sold last year in the two county area, you can apply the actual sales on your type of goods to your market area directly.

Figure 6.7

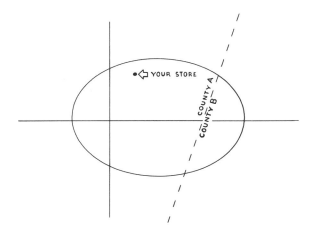

For example, if you sell furniture and you have information on total furniture sales for Counties A and B (see Figure 6.7), you use 25 percent of County A furniture sales and 10 percent of County B's.

Or if you know the per family expenditure for furniture, you can multiply that figure by the estimated number of families in your area. (Number of families can be estimated from your population data; for example: total population divided by three.)

These direct sales figures are sometimes available from the local chamber of commerce, the advertising research department of the local newspaper, or from trade associations, (such as the Local Menswear Retailers Association).

When you have this information, it goes fairly easily, but what do you do when there are no sales figures available for your type of goods or services in your market area? When such is the case, you have to estimate the volume of business by relating sales of your type of merchandise to other merchandise that is sold in conjunction with yours or by relating known national data to known local data.

One approach, the *correllary data method*, assumes a direct relationship between the sales figures for your type of goods and figures for some other type. Tires and automobiles provide an answer.

If you sell tires, you might logically determine that the sales of new cars three years ago have a strong effect on the present retail sales of tires. Your use of this relationship will depend, for one thing, on the kinds of figures available to you. You may, for example, find a consistent relationship by comparing data on the volume of sales of new cars for your area to a similar figure for the sales of replacement tires.

Or suppose that national sales of replacement tires for 1958 were 10 percent of auto sales in 1955. And if this relationship held relatively constant for several years previous to and following 1958, then it would be logical to use 10 percent of the 1962 automobile sales in your area as your market potential for 1965.

For many products or services, it would be much more accurate to use a national or local income figure (such as disposable income or income per capita) to relate to sales in your market. In some cases, you may have to use average per capita or per family purchases of your product. You can get an estimate of total market sales by multiplying the per capita purchase of an item by the population estimates for your market area.

After you have a figure for the total sales of your kind of goods, you are ready to estimate what your share is.

Suppose, again, that you sell furniture. Suppose, further, that you learned through the direct data method that furniture sales in your market area totaled $3 million last year. Your own sales were $750,000.

To find the market share that you got last year, you divide the total sales ($3 million) into your sales ($750,000). Thus your share last year was 25 percent of the total just as it was in the year before last.

However, knowing your percent of the market is not enough. You have to compare it with the trend in furniture sales in the area. For example, suppose that area furniture sales have been increasing an average of 15 percent per year over the past five years. In the face of such an increase, the mere maintenance of last year's market share means that your market share for this year has decreased.

But what if there are no merchandise sales figures? Some small retailers may not be able to get figures for the sales of their type of goods. Or using sales figures may be difficult because the retailer handles several lines, and sales figures may be available on some items but not on others. How does he estimate his market share?

One way is to look at growth trends in the population and retail sales of all kinds of merchandise in his market area. Of course, this method will not give you as good an estimate as one based on sales of a specific type of goods, but it was better than not having any idea of your market share.

For instance, if yours is an existing business and you find that the population has been growing by 20 percent in your market area for the last several years, you could reason that your sales should increase by 20 percent next year just to keep up with the population growth.

Knowing the traffic patterns also could give you a good idea of sales by assuming that since these are X number of qualified customers passing the door everyday, a certain percentage of them should stop in and spend what should be an average purchase for your customers (say $5.00). If you know the total amount of people passing, what percentage will buy, and how much each will spend, by multiplying these factors you should get an idea of sales. For example: 1,000 qualified customers a day walk by the Zap Emporium. (By qualified, I mean people who are of the right income, culture, sex, and interests to buy Zap's products). Ten percent of them will stop in. Of all the people who come in the shop, the average purchase (total sales per day divided by total people walking in) is $5.00. To find out what Zap's average per day is, multiply

1,000 people times 10% (0.10) times the $5.00 average purchase. Answer: $500 expected sales per day. When you add this to a similar traffic count of automobiles and advertising response, the picture of Zap's sales becomes even clearer.

Direct information about what a competitor is doing in sales or what a like business in a similar location is doing is also a good way to show sales. If you have direct information (like a profit and loss statement) from a similar business, you can use the sales that store gets and discount the number or add to it to allow for your particular operation.

Of course, generally when you put together a market study, there is no one thing that will predict sales but a combination of all sales predictions.

For instance, the best way to gauge sales is by predicting sales by the direct data method, the population method, the traffic study method, and so on, and taking the average of all these. The average of all methods would be a far stronger prediction of sales than any one method by itself. To get the average, one simply adds the predictions by each method and divides by the number of predictions. For instance, Zap Emporium's calculation of sales from the direct data method indicates sales of $100,000, population indicates sales of $150,000 and traffic studies show sales of $125,000. Adding the three and then dividing by three, predicts average sales of $125,000.

Furthermore, if one of these methods seems to you the most realistic, then you can give that area more weight in your calculations. This is called taking a *weighted average*. For example, Zap Emporium believes that the direct data information is the most important of the three and reasons that about 70 percent of the calculation should be based on those findings. Zap further believes that the population data should have *weight* of 20 percent of the equation and traffic studies would probably only account for about 10 percent of the accuracy (or weight) of the equations, so Zap makes the following chart (Figure 6.8).

Figure 6.8

Method	Sales	Weight
Direct Data	$100,000	0.70 (70%)
Population	150,000	0.20 (20%)
Traffic	125,000	0.10 (10%)

To get the most logical sales based on these weights, Zap multiplies sales by weight for each method, and adds the results as in Figure 6.9.

Figure 6.9

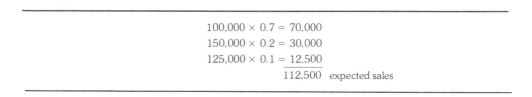

$$100,000 \times 0.7 = 70,000$$
$$150,000 \times 0.2 = 30,000$$
$$125,000 \times 0.1 = \underline{12,500}$$
$$112,500 \quad \text{expected sales}$$

Information Bibliography

Besides such local information sources for data such as the Chamber of Commerce, the advertising research department of local papers, and national statistics available from trade associations, there is also a good deal of information available from the federal government, most of which is available from the Department of Commerce. A list of these publications follows:

Directory of Federal Statistics for Local Areas

This directory describes the information available on standard metropolitan statistical areas, counties, and cities. Other types of areas are indicated for those publication programs that cover them.

Bureau of Census Catalog

The catalog is issued quarterly, with monthly supplements. It furnishes a complete and accurate inventory of available publications, computer tapes, punch cards, and special tabulations available from the Bureau of the Census.

Measuring Markets

A guide to the use of federal and state statistical data. Describes some of the measurable characteristics and dimensions of a market, plus the principal statistical series of interest, and provides series of cases which illustrate how government statistics can aid in measuring markets.

Marketing and Low-Income Consumers

This publication is a single reference source to over 320 articles, reports, and studies on marketing and low-income consumers. Each concise summary tells you how the source is useful to you, giving the author, and the publisher.

A Survey of Federal Government Publications of Interest to Small Business

A listing of Small Business Administration publications.

Retail Data Sources for Market Analysis

Outlines data published by the various agencies within the Department of Commerce for use in analyzing the retail market. The sources listed will assist management in determining the size of the market, market share, allocation of advertising expenditures, alignment of sales territories, effectiveness of sales force, and store location.

Wholesale Data Sources for Market Analysis

Outlines data published by the various agencies within the Department of Commerce for use in analyzing the wholesale market. Sources listed will assist management in determining the size of the market, market share, allocation of advertising expenditures, alignment of sales territories, effectiveness of sales force, and location of distribution centers.

The following publications provide information on trends for major industry segments, but do not provide specific information for local areas:

U.S. Industrial Outlook, 1974

Narrative outlook analyses projecting industrial activity in 1974 and providing a narrative review of 1973, with forecasts for 1980. The analyses cover two hundred industries and forecast trends in major segments of industry.

1972 Census of Manufactures

Final Area Reports

Provides data on value added by manufacturing, employment, payrolls, new capital expenditures, and number of establishments.

Final Industry Reports

Separate reports in this series present data on value of shipments, capital expenditures, value added by manufacturing, cost of materials, and employment for 430 manufacturing industries. These data are shown by geographic region and state, employment size, class of establishment, and degree of primary products specialization.

Subject Reports

Separate reports presenting data on such specific subjects as size of establishments, inventories, type of organization, water use in manufacturing, plant and equipment expenditures, materials consumed, and selected metalworking operators.

Census publications that provide information more localized to the specific trade area of a small business include:

1970 Census of Population, State Reports

Series PC (1) — A. Number of Inhabitants.

Presents final population counts for states, counties, SMSAs (Standard Metropolitan Statistical Areas), urbanized areas, all incorporated and unincorporated places of 1,000 inhabitants, including minor civil divisions.

Series PC (1) — B. General Population Characteristics.

Presents statistics on age, sex, race, marital status, and relationship to head of household for states, counties, SMSAs, urbanized areas, minor civil divisions, census county divisions, and places of 1,000 inhabitants or more.

1970 Census of Housing

Series HC (3) — Block Statistics

A census of housing report was issued by each city with 50,000 or more population. Includes data on average rooms, average contract rent, average value, and other subjects. Includes map.

Series PHC (1) — Census Tracts

These reports present information on both population and housing subjects for small neighborhoods within each of the SMSAs in 1970. Population subjects include those covered in the "C" series. Housing subjects include tenure, number of rooms, plumbing facilities, year structure built, and value of property.

1972 Census of Business

Retail Trade

Presents statistics by kinds of business for states, SMSAs, counties, and cities of 2,500 or more. Includes data on the number of establishments, sales, payroll, and personnel.

Wholesale Trade

Presents data on number of establishments, sales, payroll, and personnel for kinds of business in states, SMSAs, and counties.

Selected Services

Includes data on hotels, motels, barbershops, beauty parlors, and other retail service organizations. Number of establishments, receipts, payrolls for states, SMSAs, counties, and cities.

County and City Data Book, 1972

This comprehensive basic reference book, a supplement to the Statistical Abstract, gives data for counties, larger cities, SMSAs, counties, and cities. Data presented are taken from the 1967 Censuses of Business, Manufactures, and Governments, 1969 Census of Agriculture, 1970 Census of Population, and others.

County Business Patterns, 1972

Based on Social Security tax records, a series of separate reports for each state and United States Summary gives data on employment, size of reporting units, and taxable payrolls for various segments of the economy. Useful for analyzing market potentials.

Use of Funds Statement

The use of funds statement is, as the name suggests, a statement of what you will use the loan funds for.

Zap Manufacturing wants $100,000 in debt to expand their business. Their use of funds statement is shown in Figure 6.10.

Figure 6.10 illustrates most of the items that would be included in the loan proceeds. Note that any equipment or improvements that are to be bought should be based on written estimates from suppliers or contractors. Don't try to estimate these expenses without an estimate in writing because, nine times out of ten, your estimates out of your head will be too low. Another note of caution: when the business calculates how much money it needs, do not forget deposits and prepayments. In the case of Zap Manufacturing, the deposits amount to 4 percent of the loan. Always footnote these items and explain them fully.

Break-Even Analysis

Break-even analysis is important for two reasons: (1) to determine how much sales it will take you to pay all your expenses and other obligations and (2) to determine if it's even possible to go into business; that is, if the sales requirements are too high or too difficult to achieve, either the business won't make it or you have to reconsider some of your expenses.

Traditional break-even analysis uses charts and different formulas, but for our purposes, we want to determine the *cash* break-even, and one particular formula is perhaps the easiest.

First, why do we want to know cash break-even and what are the components? Cash break-even is, literally, the amount of cash you are going to need to pay not only your expenses and cost of sales but also your taxes, your owner's salary, and the principal portion of the loan. We are going to assume

Figure 6.10

Equipment		$ 20,000 (1)
Leasehold Improvements		40,000 (2)
Repay Debt		20,000 (3)
Deposits and Prepayments:		
Rent deposit	$2,000	
Utility deposit	500	
Licenses	100	
Legal	1,000	
Insurance	400	4,000 (4)
Inventory		26,000 (5)
Total Cash Requirement		$110,000
Less: Applicants injection		10,000 (6)
Total Loan Required		$100,000

Footnotes:
(1) Equipment includes the following:
One XEL Stamper	$13,280
One Zip Smasher	817
One Elec. Thrasher	5,903
	$20,000

(2) Leasehold improvements includes remodeling of the proposed new facility, see written estimates, Exhibit II
(3) Bank of Zarb, loan number 316119, original loan-$40,000 for three years at 12% interest, present balance $20,000. Payments are _____ per month
(4) All deposits and prepayments are based on written estimates, Exhibit II
(5) Inventory represents sufficient inventory to cover expanded operations for one month.
(6) Zap Manufacturing's owners intend to inject $10,000 in cash to help pay for the expansion requirements.

that the best way of generating sufficient cash is through sales. So how much sales are you going to need? The components of the break-even analysis are:

—Cost of sales percentage, that is, for every dollar you make by selling some item, how much do you spend on materials, labor (if the business is a manufacturing company), freight and other overhead (for manufacturing)? For example, if an item sells for $1.00 and you have to buy it for $.75, then your cost of sales percentage is 75 (cost ÷ Sale price).

    —Depreciation
    —Variable operating expenses
    —Total fixed operating expenses including interest
    —Total principal loan repayment
    —Total owners salary
    —Estimated income tax requirement

By now, if you are intending to make a projection you should have a good idea what your expenses and cost of sales percentage are. If the business is an existing one, either requesting money for expansion or for a buy-out, the cost of sales percentage and expected operating expenses should be pretty consistent with historical data. If it is a new business you should have an idea of expected expense and cost of sales. Also, after reading chapter 7, you will know what the principal loan repayment for the year should be. The proper income tax percentage can be derived by consulting Figure 6.11. It must be noted that this chart will not always be a totally accurate picture, but for utilitarian purposes it works fine.

Figure 6.11

Income Tax Percentage Chart

If principal loan repayment + owner's salary − depreciation equals	then the income tax percentage equals
$1 to 15,000	10%
15,000 to 30,000	20%
30,000 to 50,000	30%
50,000 to 99,000	40%
100,000 plus	45%

The formula for calculating cash break-even sales is seen in Figure 6.12.

Figure 6.12

Cash Break-Even Sales Formula

$$\frac{\dfrac{\text{Owner's salary + principal loan repayment − depreciation}}{1 - \text{income tax percentage}} + \begin{matrix}\text{Fixed} \\ \text{Operating} \\ \text{Expense}\end{matrix}}{1 - (\text{cost of sales percentage + variable cost percentage})}$$

In other words, to get the cash break-even sales you *add* owner's salary (the money you will draw from the business) to the principal loan repayment for the year and *subtract* the amount of depreciation for the year. The number thus arrived at is *divided* by one (1) *minus* the income tax percentage that is arrived at by using the income tax percentage chart (Figure 6.11). Take the answer of this division and *add* to it the total fixed operating expense.

Take the new number arrived at and *divide* it by one (1) *minus* the cost of sales percentage *plus* the variable cost percentage. The answer is the exact cash break-even sales required for the year. Please note: In many cases your company probably won't have variable operating expenses, so for 'variable cost percentage' in the calculation, you would substitute the number zero (0).

Figure 6.13 is an example based on the formula in Figure 6.12. The solution for Zap Manufacturing is that break-even cash sales equals $222,222 for the first year. When we reintegrate all our numbers we see how this is true. The example may be reintegrated as shown in Figure 6.14.

Figure 6.13

Zap Manufacturing has the following cash expenses and percentages for the year:

Fixed operating expense	$80,000
Variable costs — commissions	10% of sales*
Cost of sales	48% of sales
Owner's salary	$12,000
Principal loan repayment	8,000
Depreciation	8,000

Calculations:

$$\frac{\frac{12,000 + 8,000 - 8,000}{1 - 0.10} + 80,000}{1 - (0.48 + 0.10)} = \frac{\frac{12,000}{0.9} + 80,000}{1 - 0.58}$$

$$= \$222,222.22 \text{ or rounded } \$222,222$$

*The income tax percentage of 10% (or 0.10) is arrived at by adding owner's salary ($12,000) and principal loan repayment ($8,000) and subtracting depreciation ($8,000) to arrive at $12,000 total and then using the income tax percentage chart (Figure 6.11)

Figure 6.14

Sales	$222,222
Cost of Sales (48%)	106,667
Gross Profit	115,555
Less:	
Fixed operating expen.	80,000
Variable Op. Ex. (10%)	22,222
Total Operating Expense	102,222
Net Profit	13,333
Add:	
Depreciation	8,000
Less:	
Owner's salary	(12,000)
Income Tax (10% of N.P.)	(1,333)
Principal loan repay.	(8,000)
Total cash outflow	(13,333)
Cash margin	$ - 0 -

The cash break-even formula that we have been using is to the best of my knowledge the *only* cash break-even formula in all the business literature that takes into consideration all the cash outlays including income tax in determining cash break-even sales. This formula was developed by me, and later perfected by Jeff Malzahn, one of my co-workers. It is always accurate and it will always come out to the exact dollar. I call the formula the Hayes-Malzahn Cash Break-even formula.

I would like to add one more thing to the discussion of break-even analysis before we go on. Most lenders want to have sales projected slightly higher than break-even so that there is a positive cash margin in the end, therefore it is advisable that you add from $10,000 to $20,000 to the break-even sales to guarantee a small cash margin.

Financial Data and Analysis

You have the raw information (financial statements of the business, market study, and what you will use the money for—use of funds). Now, you can combine this information to estimate, or project, what your business will do next year. This is called a projection. If you project what the financial information will look like next year, this is called "financial projection."

There are two bases for financial projections: historical financial data and data arrived at by reasonable approximation.

Historical Data

If you have existing historical data to work with, your projections will probably be the most accurate. Before you try to project from historical data, you should first take the last three years and current profit and loss statements and place them side by side in what is called a "comparative statement," as illustrated in Figure 7.1.

You should take these statements one step further by taking the current statement, if it is for less than one year, and change it into a one-year statement by "annualizing" it. That is, one would take the six-months' operating expenses and multiply them by two so that they become a reasonable approximation. To find out what number to use to annualize the current operating expenses, simply divide the number of months the statement is for into twelve months, then multiply by that figure. For example, the total operating expenses for

Figure 7.1

Zap Men's Clothing

	12/31/74 12 months Income Tax	12/31/75 12 months Income Tax	12/31/76 12 months Income Tax	9/30/77 7 months P & L
Sales	$ 72,814	$ 40,256	$ 63,577	$ 314,213
Cost of Sales	60,197	29,778	39,126	232,896
Gross Profit	12,617	10,478	24,451	81,317
Operating Expense	24,453	40,176	61,120	60,000
Net Profit	(11,836)	(29,698)	(36,669)	21,317

year-to-date (July) is $60,000 in the example, so what is the total operating expenses (annualized) for the year? See Figure 7.2 for the calculations.

Figure 7.2

$$\frac{12 \text{ months}}{\text{No. of months in interim statement}} = \text{Number of times interim statements operating expenses are multiplied by to get "annualized" expense}$$

In the case of the example:

$$\frac{12 \text{ months}}{7 \text{ months}} = 1.71$$

$1.71 \times \$60,000 = \$102,600$ annualized expenses

Sales, however, can't be annualized so easily. Sales, unlike expenses, generally fluctuate on a seasonal basis, i.e., sales for most retail stores are larger in December and September, and lower in the summer. Therefore, it would be unrealistic to "just" take the first six months' statement and multiply the sales by two. In order to annualize sales, you need to use a seasonal index like Figure 7.3, from *Accounting Corporation of America's Small Business Barometer, Yearbook 1973.*

To determine what the sales would be when annualized, first add up the index numbers to get the total index number for the year. In Figure 7.3, the total number would be 1209.

Next add up the index numbers up to the last month of the interim statement. If the last month of the statement is July, that is, the interim statement is year-to-date July 30, 1977, as in the example, then you would add the index numbers up to July (or 653).

Then take the index figures up to July and divide them into the year's index total, to get the number of times sales are multiplied by to give the annual total.

Figure 7.3

Men's Specialty Shops Sales Index

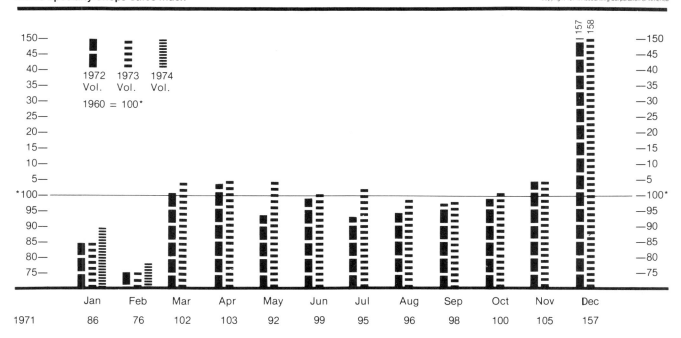

	Jan	Feb	Mar	Apr	May	Jun	Jul	Aug	Sep	Oct	Nov	Dec
1971	86	76	102	103	92	99	95	96	98	100	105	157

For example, if the sales for Zap Men's Clothing Store is $314,213 for the first seven months of the year, what is the annualized sales? 1209 ÷ 653 = 1.85. $314,213 × 1.85 = $581,294 Annual Sales

For annualization purposes, cost of sales is calculated by multiplying the interim statements (7/30/77) cost of sales percentage times the annualized sales. In the example, the cost of sales percentage of the 7/30/77 statement is 74.1% or 232,896 (cost of sales) ÷ 314,213 (sales) = 0.741.

You must assume that the cost of sales percentage for the annualized statement is the same as the interim statement (7/30/77), then—
0.741 × 581,294 annualized sales = 430,739 annualized cost of sales (See Fig. 7.4.). With this information in hand, one can now draw upon the historical data to predict future sales and expenses, in total.

Figure 7.4

	12/31/74 12 months Income Tax	12/31/75 12 months Income Tax	12/31/76 12 months Income Tax	7/30/77 7 months P & L	7/30/77 12 months Annualized
Sales	72,814	40,256	63,577	314,213	581,294
Cost of Sales	60,197	29,778	39,126	232,896	430,239
Gross Profit	12,617	10,478	24,451	81,317	150,555
Operating Expense	24,453	40,176	61,120	60,000	102,600
Net Profit	(11,836)	(29,698)	(36,669)	21,317	47,955

Expected Expenses, Cost of Sales and Owners Draw

If the applicant business is an existing business like Zap Men's Clothing, illustrated above, predicting future expenses is relatively easy. From annualization, you already know what the expected expenses for the year will be, assuming continued operations with no change, and the rest of the comparative data shows what your expenses in the past were. If you have a side-by-side expense comparison of the company, it would look like Figure 7.5. As you can see, the projected figures are close to the annualized figures, some are larger, some a little smaller. It is best to try to make your projected figures as close as possible to the last annual or annualized experience. In the example, advertising is projected lower than annualized because in the past it showed a trend of increasing, then decreasing the next year. Phone and miscellaneous expenses follow a similar reasoning. Most of the other expenses have shown continuous increases so they are projected higher. After you have projected these expenses based on past data, it is a good idea to go over each expense to see if they are reasonable. For instance, is rent going to remain the same? Are salaries likely to increase or decrease?

On the particular items of depreciation and interest, projected expense will probably be different than historical. Interest must be calculated based on the amount the business plans to borrow and depreciation will be affected by the amount of equipment and dollar amount of improvements the business will pay for from the loan proceeds. If the business will buy $10,000 worth of equipment from the loan proceeds, then the projected expenses will include present depreciation plus new depreciation.

Figure 7.5

	12/31/74 12 mos. Income Tax	12/31/75 12 mos. Income Tax	12/31/76 12 mos. Income Tax	7/30/77 7 mos. P & L	7/30/77 12 mos. Annualized	Projected 12 mos. 1st Yr.
Operating Expense:						
Salaries	10,000	20,000	35,000	32,748	56,000	56,000
Payroll Tax	830	1,660	2,905	2,717	4,648	4,648
Rent	6,000	6,000	9,000	5,672	9,700	9,700
Displays	150	250	200	888	1,520	1,500
Office Supplies	100	200	175	58	100	200
Bad Debt	-0-	150	220	268	460	500
Advertising	1,000	3,800	1,975	8,187	14,000	12,000
Depreciation	4,000	4,000	5,500	4,240	7,250	10,000
Utilities	200	260	285	166	275	300
Phone	500	700	650	512	875	700
Acct. & Legal	1,200	1,400	2,400	1,345	2,300	2,300
Auto & Travel	400	700	800	1,287	2,200	2,200
Miscellaneous	73	56	10	158	272	200
Interest	-0-	1,000	2,000	1,754	3,000	7,200
Total Operating Expense	24,453	40,176	61,120	60,000	102,600	107,448

The applicant business's owners should determine how much they would like to draw from the business so that we can later use this information in our cash flow projections. If the business is a corporation, of course, owners draw would be an expense. If the business is a proprietorship, the draw must come from net profits.

New Businesses

If the business applying for the loan is a new business, then expenses have to be calculated without having a historical basis. If the applicant has experience in this particular field he might be able to predict expenses fairly well. If the applicant doesn't know what the expenses would be, or he doesn't know what some of the expenses are, we can calculate these expenses from industry studies, discussed shortly. Some expenses, like rent, depreciation, and interest are already known in most cases. Rent is known because the business is going to move into a given store or factory and the cost of the rental is known from the rental agent. Depreciation is calculated on the equipment and improvements one expects to buy. Interest is calculated (discussed later in this chapter) according to how much one will borrow, and, therefore, have to pay interest on.

Figure 7.6

Description of Ratio Classification	Group 3 (*Nationally*) Annual Gross Vol. $100,000-$200,000 %		All Groups (*Nationally*) Average %	
	This Yr.	Last Yr.	This Yr.	Last Yr.
Sales	100.00	100.00	100.00	100.00
Cost of Sales	61.96	61.27	62.59	61.67
Gross Profit	38.04	38.73	37.41	38.33
Controllable Expenses Outside Labor	.10	.10	.10	.10
Operating Supplies	.72	.76	.80	.83
†Gross Wages	14.28	13.65	12.48	11.98
Repairs and Maintenance	.36	.36	.37	.37
Advertising	1.84	1.74	1.27	1.27
Car and Delivery	.41	.40	.43	.42
Bad Debts	.01	.01	.02	.02
Administrative and Legal	.39	.38	.42	.41
Miscellaneous Expense	.42	.45	.46	.49
Total Controllable Expenses	18.53	17.85	16.35	15.89
Fixed Expenses *Rent	2.55	2.55	2.70	2.69
Utilities	1.16	1.16	1.30	1.30
Insurance	.58	.58	.61	.60
Taxes and Licenses	.92	.92	.89	.90
Interest	.10	.10	.12	.12
Depreciation	1.05	1.05	1.08	1.08
Total Fixed Expenses	6.36	6.36	6.70	6.69
Total Expenses	24.89	24.21	23.05	22.58
Net Profit	13.15	14.52	14.36	15.75

†Does not include proprietor's wages.
*Adjusted to reflect exclusion of owned premises.

If you have a good idea of what sales will be, you can predict expenses by using industry data, like the Figure 7.6 from A.C.A.'s *Barometer of Small Business,* which shows expenses as a percentage of sales.

For example if sales were expected to be $100,000 per year, the calculations based on percentages illustrated in Figure 7.6 would look as follows:

Item	% of Sales	$
Sales	100.0	$100,000
Cost of Sales	61.96	61,960
Net Profit	38.04	38,040
Operating Expense:		
Outside labor	0.10 (.001 × 100,000=)	100
Operating supplies	0.72 (.0072 × 100,000=)	720
Gross wages	14.28 (etc.)	14,280
Repairs & Maint.	0.36	360
Advertising	1.84	1,840
Car & Delivery	0.41	410
Bad Debts	0.01	10
Admin. & Legal	0.39	390
Miscellaneous	0.42	420
Rent	2.55	2,550
Utilities	1.16	1,160
Insurance	0.58	580
Tax & License	0.92	920
Interest	0.10	100
Depreciation	1.05	1,050
Total Expense	24.89	24,890
Net Profit	13.15	13,150

Rent, depreciation, and interest, as I mentioned earlier, will be different than the national averages.

If the business is to be a manufacturing company, the national industry averages will probably be broken down into the components of: labor, material cost, shipping, and factory overhead.

Calculating Loan Repayment

The best way to calculate loan repayment is to use an interest table (available at libraries, savings and loans, real estate brokers, and so on. (See Fig. 7.7.)

If the applicant wanted to borrow $25,000 at 10 percent for five years, you would look down the far left column for the dollar amount of the loan, then move to your right to get the years. According to this interest table, the monthly payments, principal, and interest would then be $531.18, or rounded to the nearest dollar $531.00.

To get the annual payments multiply the monthly repayment by 12. In the example, that would be $531 × 12 = $6,372. Perhaps the best method for

Figure 7.7

10% — MONTHLY PAYMENT NECESSARY TO AMORTIZE A LOAN

TERM AMOUNT	1 YEAR	1½ YEARS	2 YEARS	3 YEARS	4 YEARS	5 YEARS	8 YEARS	10 YEARS	12 YEARS
$22500	1978.11	1351.29	1038.27	726.02	570.66	478.06	341.42	297.34	268.90
23000	2022.07	1381.32	1061.34	742.15	583.34	488.69	349.01	303.95	274.87
23500	2066.03	1411.35	1084.41	758.28	596.03	499.31	356.60	310.56	280.85
24000	2109.99	1441.37	1107.48	774.42	608.71	509.93	364.18	317.17	286.82
24500	2153.94	1471.40	1130.56	790.55	621.39	520.56	371.77	323.77	292.80
25000	2197.90	1501.43	1153.63	806.68	634.07	531.18	379.36	330.38	298.77
25500	2241.86	1531.46	1176.70	822.82	646.75	541.80	386.95	336.99	304.75
26000	2285.82	1561.49	1199.77	838.95	659.43	552.43	394.53	343.60	310.73
26500	2329.78	1591.52	1222.85	855.09	672.11	563.05	402.12	350.20	316.70
27000	2373.73	1621.55	1245.92	871.22	684.79	573.68	409.71	356.81	322.68
27500	2417.69	1651.57	1268.99	887.35	697.48	584.30	417.29	363.42	328.65
28000	2461.65	1681.60	1292.06	903.49	710.16	594.92	424.88	370.03	334.63
28500	2505.61	1711.63	1315.14	919.62	722.84	605.55	432.47	376.63	340.60
29000	2549.57	1741.66	1338.21	935.75	735.52	616.17	440.06	383.24	346.58
29500	2593.52	1771.69	1361.28	951.89	748.20	626.79	447.64	389.85	352.55
30000	2637.48	1801.72	1384.35	968.02	760.88	637.42	455.23	396.46	358.53
30500	2681.44	1831.75	1407.43	984.15	773.56	648.04	462.82	403.06	364.50
31000	2725.40	1861.77	1430.50	1000.29	786.25	658.66	470.40	409.67	370.48
31500	2769.35	1891.80	1453.57	1016.42	798.93	669.29	477.99	416.28	376.45
32000	2813.31	1921.83	1476.64	1032.55	811.61	679.91	485.58	422.89	382.43
32500	2857.27	1951.86	1499.72	1048.69	824.29	690.53	493.17	429.49	388.41
33000	2901.23	1981.88	1522.79	1064.82	836.97	701.16	500.75	436.10	394.38
33500	2945.19	2011.92	1545.86	1080.96	849.65	711.78	508.34	442.71	400.36
34000	2989.15	2041.94	1568.93	1097.09	862.33	722.40	515.93	449.32	406.33
34500	3033.10	2071.97	1592.00	1113.22	875.01	733.03	523.51	455.93	412.31
35000	3077.06	2102.00	1615.08	1129.36	887.70	743.65	531.10	462.53	418.28
36000	3164.98	2162.06	1661.22	1161.62	913.06	764.90	546.27	475.75	430.23
37000	3252.89	2222.12	1707.36	1193.89	938.42	786.15	561.45	488.96	442.18
38000	3340.81	2282.17	1753.51	1226.16	963.78	807.39	576.62	502.18	454.13
39000	3428.72	2342.23	1799.66	1258.43	989.15	828.64	591.80	515.39	466.09
40000	3516.64	2402.29	1845.80	1290.69	1014.51	849.89	606.97	528.61	478.04
41000	3604.56	2462.35	1891.95	1322.96	1039.87	871.13	622.15	541.82	489.99
42000	3692.47	2522.40	1938.09	1355.23	1065.23	892.38	637.32	555.04	501.94
43000	3780.39	2582.46	1984.24	1387.49	1090.60	913.63	652.50	568.25	513.89
44000	3868.30	2642.52	2030.38	1419.76	1115.96	934.87	667.67	581.47	525.84
45000	3956.22	2702.57	2076.53	1452.03	1141.32	956.12	682.84	594.68	537.79
46000	4044.13	2762.63	2122.67	1484.29	1166.68	977.36	698.02	607.90	549.74
47000	4132.05	2822.69	2168.82	1516.56	1192.04	998.61	713.19	621.11	561.69
48000	4219.97	2882.74	2214.96	1548.83	1217.41	1019.86	728.36	634.33	573.64
49000	4307.88	2942.80	2261.11	1581.10	1242.77	1041.11	743.54	647.54	585.59
50000	4395.80	3002.86	2307.25	1613.36	1268.13	1062.36	758.71	660.76	597.54
51000	4483.72	3062.92	2353.40	1645.63	1293.50	1083.60	773.89	673.97	609.49
52000	4571.63	3122.97	2399.54	1677.90	1318.86	1104.85	789.06	687.19	621.45
53000	4659.55	3183.03	2445.69	1710.16	1344.22	1126.10	804.24	700.40	633.40
54000	4747.46	3243.09	2491.83	1742.43	1369.58	1147.35	819.41	713.62	645.35
55000	4835.38	3303.14	2537.98	1774.70	1394.95	1168.59	834.58	726.83	657.30
56000	4923.29	3363.20	2584.12	1806.97	1420.31	1189.84	849.76	740.05	669.25
57000	5011.21	3423.26	2630.27	1839.23	1445.67	1211.09	864.93	753.26	681.20
58000	5099.13	3483.32	2676.41	1871.50	1471.03	1232.33	880.11	766.48	693.15
59000	5187.04	3543.37	2722.56	1903.77	1496.40	1253.58	895.28	779.69	705.10
60000	5274.96	3603.43	2768.70	1936.04	1521.76	1274.83	910.45	792.91	717.05
61000	5362.87	3663.49	2814.85	1968.30	1547.12	1296.07	925.63	806.12	729.00
62000	5450.79	3723.55	2860.99	2000.57	1572.49	1317.32	940.80	819.34	740.95
63000	5538.71	3783.60	2907.14	2032.84	1597.85	1338.57	955.98	832.55	752.90
64000	5626.62	3843.66	2953.28	2065.10	1623.21	1359.82	971.15	845.77	764.86
65000	5714.54	3903.72	2999.43	2097.37	1648.57	1381.06	986.33	858.98	776.81
67500	5934.33	4053.86	3114.79	2178.04	1711.98	1434.18	1024.26	892.02	806.68
70000	6154.12	4204.00	3230.15	2258.71	1775.39	1487.30	1062.20	925.06	836.56
72500	6373.91	4354.14	3345.51	2339.38	1838.79	1540.42	1100.13	958.10	866.44
75000	6593.70	4504.29	3460.87	2420.04	1902.20	1593.53	1138.07	991.14	896.31
80000	7033.28	4804.57	3691.60	2581.38	2029.01	1699.77	1213.94	1057.21	956.07
85000	7472.86	5104.86	3922.32	2742.72	2155.82	1806.00	1289.81	1123.29	1015.82
90000	7912.45	5405.14	4153.05	2904.04	2282.63	1912.24	1365.68	1189.36	1075.58
95000	8352.01	5705.43	4383.77	3065.39	2409.45	2018.47	1441.55	1255.44	1135.33
100000	8791.59	6005.71	4614.50	3226.72	2536.26	2124.71	1517.42	1321.51	1195.08

10% — MONTHLY PAYMENT NECESSARY TO AMORTIZE A LOAN

TERM AMOUNT	1 YEAR	1½ YEARS	2 YEARS	3 YEARS	4 YEARS	5 YEARS	8 YEARS	10 YEARS	12 YEARS
$50	4.40	3.01	2.31	1.62	1.27	1.07	.76	.67	.60
100	8.80	6.01	4.62	3.23	2.54	2.13	1.52	1.33	1.20
200	17.59	12.02	9.23	6.46	5.08	4.25	3.04	2.65	2.40
300	26.38	18.02	13.85	9.69	7.61	6.38	4.56	3.97	3.59
400	35.17	24.03	18.46	12.91	10.15	8.50	6.07	5.29	4.79
500	43.96	30.03	23.08	16.14	12.69	10.63	7.59	6.61	5.98
600	52.75	36.04	27.69	19.37	15.22	12.75	9.11	7.93	7.18
700	61.55	42.04	32.31	22.59	17.76	14.88	10.63	9.26	8.37
800	70.34	48.05	36.92	25.82	20.30	17.00	12.14	10.58	9.57
900	79.13	54.06	41.54	29.05	22.83	19.13	13.66	11.90	10.76
1000	87.92	60.06	46.15	32.27	25.38	21.25	15.18	13.22	11.96
1100	96.71	66.07	50.76	35.50	27.90	23.38	16.70	14.54	13.15
1200	105.50	72.07	55.38	38.73	30.44	25.50	18.21	15.86	14.35
1300	114.30	78.08	59.99	41.95	32.98	27.63	19.73	17.18	15.54
1400	123.09	84.08	64.61	45.18	35.51	29.75	21.25	18.51	16.74
1500	131.88	90.09	69.22	48.41	38.05	31.88	22.77	19.83	17.93
1600	140.67	96.10	73.84	51.63	40.58	34.00	24.28	21.15	19.13
1700	149.46	102.10	78.45	54.86	43.12	36.13	25.80	22.47	20.32
1800	158.25	108.11	83.07	58.09	45.66	38.25	27.32	23.79	21.52
1900	167.05	114.11	87.68	61.31	48.19	40.37	28.84	25.11	22.71
2000	175.84	120.12	92.29	64.54	50.73	42.50	30.35	26.44	23.91
2100	184.63	126.12	96.91	67.77	53.26	44.62	31.87	27.76	25.10
2200	193.42	132.13	101.52	70.99	55.80	46.75	33.39	29.08	26.30
2300	202.21	138.14	106.14	74.22	58.34	48.87	34.91	30.40	27.49
2400	211.00	144.14	110.75	77.45	60.88	51.00	36.42	31.72	28.69
2500	219.79	150.15	115.37	80.67	63.41	53.12	37.94	33.04	29.88
3000	263.75	180.18	138.44	96.81	76.09	63.75	45.53	39.65	35.86
3500	307.71	210.20	161.51	112.94	88.77	74.37	53.12	46.26	41.83
4000	351.67	240.23	184.58	129.08	101.45	85.00	60.70	52.87	47.81
4500	395.63	270.26	207.66	145.21	114.14	95.62	68.29	59.47	53.78
5000	439.58	300.29	230.73	161.34	126.82	106.24	75.88	66.08	59.76
5500	483.54	330.32	253.80	177.47	139.50	116.86	83.47	72.69	65.73
6000	527.50	360.35	276.87	193.61	152.18	127.49	91.05	79.30	71.71
6500	571.46	390.38	299.94	209.74	164.86	138.11	98.64	85.90	77.69
7000	615.42	420.40	323.02	225.88	177.54	148.73	106.22	92.51	83.66
7500	659.37	450.43	346.09	242.01	190.22	159.36	113.81	99.12	89.64
8000	703.33	480.46	369.16	258.14	202.91	169.98	121.40	105.73	95.61
8500	747.29	510.49	392.24	274.28	215.59	180.60	128.99	112.33	101.59
9000	791.25	540.52	415.31	290.41	228.27	191.23	136.57	118.94	107.56
9500	835.21	570.54	438.38	306.54	240.95	201.85	144.16	125.55	113.54
10000	879.16	600.58	461.45	322.68	253.63	212.48	151.75	132.16	119.51
10500	923.12	630.60	484.53	338.81	266.31	223.10	159.33	138.76	125.49
11000	967.08	660.63	507.60	354.94	278.99	233.72	166.92	145.37	131.46
11500	1011.04	690.66	530.67	371.07	291.67	244.35	174.51	151.98	137.44
12000	1055.00	720.69	553.74	387.21	304.36	254.97	182.09	158.59	143.41
12500	1098.95	750.72	576.82	403.34	317.04	265.59	189.68	165.19	149.39
13000	1142.91	780.75	599.89	419.47	329.72	276.22	197.27	171.80	155.37
13500	1186.87	810.78	622.96	435.61	342.40	286.84	204.86	178.41	161.34
14000	1230.83	840.80	646.03	451.74	355.08	297.46	212.44	185.02	167.32
14500	1274.79	870.83	669.11	467.88	367.76	308.09	220.03	191.62	173.29
15000	1318.74	900.86	692.18	484.01	380.44	318.71	227.62	198.23	179.27
15500	1362.70	930.89	715.25	500.15	393.13	329.33	235.21	204.84	185.24
16000	1406.66	960.92	738.32	516.28	405.81	339.96	242.79	211.46	191.22
16500	1450.62	990.95	761.40	532.41	418.49	350.58	250.38	218.05	197.19
17000	1494.58	1020.98	784.47	548.55	431.17	361.20	257.97	224.66	203.17
17500	1538.53	1051.00	807.54	564.68	443.85	371.83	265.55	231.27	209.14
18000	1582.49	1081.03	830.61	580.81	456.53	382.45	273.14	237.88	215.12
18500	1626.45	1111.06	853.69	596.95	469.21	393.08	280.73	244.48	221.09
19000	1670.41	1141.09	876.76	613.08	481.89	403.70	288.31	251.09	227.07
19500	1714.36	1171.12	899.83	629.22	494.58	414.32	295.90	257.70	233.05
20000	1758.32	1201.15	922.90	645.35	507.26	424.95	303.49	264.31	239.02
20500	1802.28	1231.18	945.98	661.48	519.94	435.57	311.08	270.91	245.00
21000	1846.24	1261.20	969.05	677.62	532.62	446.19	318.66	277.52	250.97
21500	1890.20	1291.23	992.12	693.75	545.30	456.82	326.25	284.13	256.95
22000	1934.15	1321.26	1015.19	709.88	557.98	467.44	333.84	290.74	262.92
22500	1978.11	1351.29	1038.27	726.02	570.66	478.06	341.42	297.34	268.90
23000	2022.07	1381.32	1061.34	742.15	583.34	488.69	349.01	303.95	274.87
23500	2066.03	1411.35	1084.41	758.28	596.03	499.31	356.60	310.56	280.85

getting annual interest payments, if this information isn't available from your interest table, is to multiply the total amount of the loan ($25,000 in the example) by the interest rate (10 percent in the example). This will give you a rough approximation of first year interest (although it won't be 100 percent accurate). In the example, the interest for the first year would be: $25,000 × 0.10 = $2,500.

Principal is calculated by merely taking the total annual loan payments and subtracting the interest portion. In the example: $6,372 principal and interest payments × years − $2,500 interest payments = $3,872 principal portion.

All the calculations together would look like Figure 7.8.

Figure 7.8

Monthly payments from interest table × 12 months

$$\begin{array}{r} \$ \ 531 \\ \underline{12} \\ \$6372 \end{array}$$

Annual payments

$$\begin{array}{rl} & 25,000 \text{ Total loan} \\ & \underline{0.10} \text{ Interest percentage} \\ \$ & 2,500 \text{ Years interest} \end{array}$$

$$\begin{array}{rl} & 6,372 \text{ Annual Payments} \\ - & \underline{2,500} \text{ Interest first year} \\ \$ & 3,872 \text{ Principal first year} \end{array}$$

Variable and Fixed Expenses

Variable costs are those expenses that vary directly as sales. For instance, cost of sales is generally a variable expense, because everything that you sell has a cost per item that increases as dollar volume. A German Luger deluxe water pistol sells at retail for $1.00. They cost 25¢ wholesale.

If you sell one water pistol, it costs you 25¢; if you sell ten pistols for $10.00, it costs you $2.50. In other words, variable expenses, such as cost of sales, will stay the same *percentage* of sales and will increase in dollar volume as sales increase.

If you are trying to project a new business and are using as your expenses items that are given as a percentage of sales in an industry average, you would treat these expenses as variable.

For the most part, however, expenses other than cost of sales and commissions are *fixed* in nature. Administrative salaries or rent will still be the same dollar amount no matter if sales are $100,000 or $80,000.

The fixed and variable expense concept is important so that you can do a cash break-even analysis for projection purposes.

Projected Financial Statement

An income statement reports how profitable a business has been. A projected income statement predicts how profitable a business will be. It shows how much money a business will clear over a given period of time.

Most sources of financing require a projected income statement for the first three years of operation. Second and third year projections are reasoned extensions of first year figures. Normally the sales volume increases in the succeeding years. However, expenses do not always grow at the same rate as sales. Some costs of doing business remain fixed or change very little. For example, in most manufacturing businesses, payroll grows at a rate similar to sales, but office expenses and the cost of professional services do not. In most retail businesses, advertising and promotional expenses vary directly with sales, but payroll and rent rise at a much slower rate.

In addition to the three years annual projections, the packager should project income statements for each of the first twelve months. Doing monthly calculations clarifies the relationship between sales and variable expenses and sales projections, it is a good practice to develop two levels of sales projections. One set of projections should show the expected level of sales and one set should show a more conservative level.

The most conservative projections are those at cash break-even sales, just discussed. For most purposes, projections should be done as conservative, as close to cash break-even, as possible.

From the information you have calculated—break-even sales; comparative historical data; expected expenses (from history, expectations or industry averages); and loan repayment (interest and principal)—you should be able to construct an annual profit and loss statement combined with a cash flow, that will be in the form shown in Figure 7.9.

Monthly Profit and Loss

When you have done the annual projected financial statement, illustrated in Figure 7.9, it can easily be changed into a monthly projected profit and loss and cash flow statement.

Annual expected sales for a new business can be calculated monthly by simply dividing by twelve months, then adjusting each month for growth. For instance, if sales for Zap Pyramid are $120,000 per year, dividing by twelve gives you average sales of $10,000 per month. If you wanted to adjust for growth, you simply multiply the average month by 0.8 the first two months of the projected year, 0.9 the next two, and so on, as illustrated in Figure 7.10.

By multiplying the average month by these factors, you get a gradual increase in monthly sales, appearing more realistic than $10,000 each month.

Most businesses have seasonal fluctuations from month to month. Retailers, for instance, experience their highest sales in the month of December. Because of these seasonal fluctuations, it is best to use a monthly sales index, like Figure 7.11, from A.C.A.'s *Barometer of Small Business*. The procedure for seasonally adjusted monthly sales with this index is fairly simple. Take the total dollar amount of sales and divide by the total index number, then multiply this resulting factor by each of the month's index number. Using the sales index in Figure 7.11 and $120,000 as the total annual sales, monthly (index-adjusted) sales can be calculated as in Figure 7.12.

Figure 7.9

First Year

Sales
  Cost of Sales
Gross Profit

Operating Expense
  Salaries
  Payroll Taxes
  Rent
  Supplies
  Acct. & Legal
  Advertising
  Travel
  Depreciation
  Interest
  Miscellaneous
Total Operating Expense

Net Profit

Add:
Depreciation

Total Cash In Flow (Net Profit + Depreciation)

Less:
Income Tax
Principal Loan Repayment
Owners Draw

Total Cash Out Flow (Income Tax + Loan Repayment + Owners Draw)

Cash Margin (Total Cash In Flow − Cash Out Flow)

Figure 7.10

$$\frac{\text{Total Annual Sales } \$120,000}{12 \text{ Months}} = \$10,000 \text{ Average Monthly Sales}$$

Months	Percentage Factors	Average Month		Monthly Sales	
1st & 2nd	0.8	×	10,000	=	8,000
3rd & 4th	0.9	×	10,000	=	9,000
5th thru 8th	1.0	×	10,000	=	10,000
9th & 10th	1.1	×	10,000	=	11,000
11th & 12th	1.2	×	10,000	=	12,000

8,000 + 8,000 + 9,000 + 9,000 + 10,000 + 10,000 + 10,000 + 10,000 + 11,000
+ 11,000 + 12,000 + 12,000 = 120,000 total annual sales.

Figure 7.11

Drug Stores Retail Sales Index

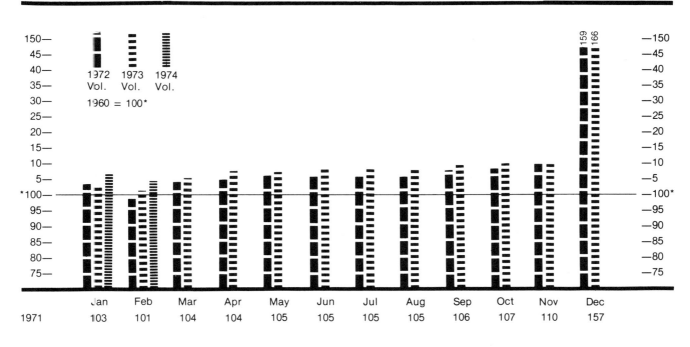

1971	Jan	Feb	Mar	Apr	May	Jun	Jul	Aug	Sep	Oct	Nov	Dec
	103	101	104	104	105	105	105	105	106	107	110	157

Figure 7.12

$$\frac{\text{Total Cash Break-Even Sales}}{\text{Total Index for Year}} = \text{Index-Adjusted Sales Factor}$$

$$\frac{120,000}{1,312} = 91.46$$

Month	Index #		Index-Adjusted Sales Factor	Monthly Sales	
January	103	×	91.46	$ 9,420	
February	101	×	91.46	9,237	
March	104	×	91.46	9,513	(9,512 + 1)
April	104	×	91.46	9,513	"
May	105	×	91.46	9,604	(9,603 + 1)
June	105	×	91.46	9,604	"
July	105	×	91.46	9,604	"
August	105	×	91.46	9,604	"
September	106	×	91.46	9,695	
October	107	×	91.46	9,786	
November	110	×	91.46	10,061	
December	157	×	91.46	14,359	
Total Sales				$120,000	

Because of rounding errors, the monthly index-adjusted sales will occasionally not add up to your break-even total annual sales. It is best in that case to just add (or subtract) equally from each month to make it accurate. In Figure 7.12, March and April multiplied equal 9,511.84, rounded to 9,512 and one is added, giving $9,513 and making it add up correctly. If the business is to be a new one or one that has to increase sales over the previous year, a combination of both the seasonal adjustment, above, and the percentage adjustment for growth, discussed previously is called for. Figure 7.13 is an illustration of the combination of methods: assuming $120,000 total annual sales.

Like the sales arrived at with the index-adjusted sales calculations (seasonal adjustment), the numbers are liable to come out slightly off so that they don't add up to the break-even cash sales total. In this case, each month should be adjusted so that it adds up to the break-even cash sales total ($120,000 in the example).

Cost of sales monthly is calculated by multiplying each monthly sales figure by the cost of sales percentage.

In the example, if the cost of sales percentage for Zap Pyramid was 75 percent, the January monthly sales of 7,436 would have a cost of sales of 5,577 (7,436 × 0.75). For February the cost of sales would be 7,290 times 0.75, or 5,468 and so on.

Operating expense monthly, which, as we said before, is considered for our purposes a fixed expense, is calculated by dividing total annual operating expense (or each yearly expense item) by twelve months (Fig. 7.14).

Figure 7.13

Month	Index #		Index-Adjusted Sales Factor		Percentage Factor		Monthly Sales Adjusted	
January	103	×	91.46	×	0.8	= $	7,536	$ 7,436
February	101	×	91.46	×	0.8	=	7,390	7,290
March	104	×	91.46	×	0.9	=	8,562	8,462
April	104	×	91.46	×	0.9	=	8,562	8,462
May	105	×	91.46	×	1.0	=	9,604	9,504
June	105	×	91.46	×	1.0	=	9,604	9,504
July	105	×	91.46	×	1.0	=	9,604	9,504
August	105	×	91.46	×	1.0	=	9,604	9,504
September	106	×	91.46	×	1.1	=	10,665	10,565
October	107	×	91.46	×	1.1	=	10,765	10,665
November	110	×	91.46	×	1.2	=	12,073	11,973
December	157	×	91.46	×	1.2	=	17,231	17.131
					Total		$121,200	$120,000

Figure 7.14

Expense	Annual			Monthly Expense
Rent	12,000	÷	12	$1,000
Interest	8,920*	÷	12	$ 743 for 8 mo. 744 for 4 mo.*
Accounting	600	÷	12	50
Depreciation	5,618*	÷	12	$ 468 for 10 mo. 496 for 2 mo.*
Utilities	900	÷	12	75
Travel	1,020	÷	12	85

*Some expenses such as interest and depreciation, cannot be evenly divided by 12. In these cases round the number, multiply by 12 and distribute the difference:

Annual Interest $\frac{\$8,920}{12}$ = $743.33 ($743 Rounded)

$743 × 12 = $8,916

Annual Interest $8,920
Less: 8,916
Difference   4

The first eight months will be $743, the last four months the figure will be $744.

$743 + 743 + 743 + 743 + 743 + 743 + 743 + 743 + 744 + 744 + 744 + 744 = $8,920 Annual Interest

Cash Flow

Cash flow, as the name suggests, is concerned with *cash* income and expenditures of the business.

On the income side cash income is the cash sales the business receives or the collection of receivables. Cash sales and collection of receivables is not the same thing as sales. You can sell $10,000 worth of goods one month on thirty days terms and have no cash income for that month. That $10,000 in sales is not cash income until it's paid thirty days later. Figure 7.15 is an illustration of the difference.

Figure 7.15

	Sold on 30-Day Terms	Cash Sales
Sales	$10,000	$10,000
Cash Income	-0-	10,000
Cost of Sales	5,000	5,000
Gross Profit (Cash)	(5,000)	5,000
Operating Expense (Cash)	4,000	4,000
Net Profit (Cash)	(9,000)	1,000

How do you know what the receivable collection period will be? The best way to find what the period will be is to use historical data (if available). One can determine receivable period from historical data by means of the average collection period ratio. The ratio looks like this:

Step 1. $\dfrac{\text{Net Sales (from P \& L)}}{\text{Days in the Accounting period}}$ = Average Sales per day

Step 2. $\dfrac{\text{Receivables (from Balance Sheet)}}{\text{Average sales per day}}$ = The average collection period in days

For example: Zap Black Ball Manufacturing has $120,000 in sales for the first six months of the year and has on its balance sheet receivables of $56,000. What is the average collection period in days?

Step 1. $\dfrac{\$120,000 \text{ (Net Sales)}}{180 \text{ (30 days x 6 mos)}}$ = $667 average sales per day

Step 2. $\dfrac{\$56,000 \text{ (Receivables)}}{\$667 \text{ (average sales days)}}$ = 84 days average collection

If the business is to be a new venture, and no historical data is available, there is information on receivable collection periods in the *Robert Morris Industry Averages* and other similar publications.

On the monthly cash flow projections format that follows, you will note that there are entries for cash sales and collection of receivables.

On the expense (or, more accurately, disbursement) side, all operating expenses except depreciation are cash disbursements. Cost of sales, if the merchandise is paid for in cash, is a cash expense. Principal loan repayment partnership or proprietorship owner's draw, and cash expenditures for equipment, fixtures and other assets are also cash disbursements, although they are not reported in the profit and loss statement as tax deductible expenses. Income tax is also a cash expense. It may or may not be reported in the profit and loss statement.

Depreciation is an odd-ball expense that is tax deductible as an expense on the profit and loss statement but is *not* a cash expense. As a matter of fact, if you do a cash flow, you subtract out depreciation from other operating expenses. In summary, the following are cash disbursements, counted as expenses subtracted from cash income in a cash flow projection.

—All operating expenses less depreciation
—Cost of sales paid for (Cost of sales might be composed of some inventory delivered but not paid for, i.e., inventory that the business owes the supplier for in the form of a trade payable. For our purposes, however, we consider that all cost of sales has been paid for in cash. If one wanted to make a completely accurate cash flow, cost of sales would be reduced by payables.)
—Principal loan repayment
—Partnership or proprietorship owner's draw

—Cash expenditures for assets
—Income Tax
—All otherwise unclassified cash expenditures

Monthly Profit and Loss and Cash Flow Projection Format

Figure 7.16 is the format for a projection used by the SBA. This format can generally be used with only minor adjustments.

Supporting Schedules

Sometimes in addition to the comparative and summary financial statements, schedule of operating expense, and monthly profit and loss, and cash flow, the proposal should have other supporting schedules, most notably, a schedule of cost of sales for a manufacturing company.

As you have seen in the different schedules and projections we have already discussed, cost of sales is usually given as one number (or a percentage) and is not broken down. In the case of retail businesses, a percentage is generally sufficient because the components of cost of sales for retail is only inventory (beginning inventory plus purchases minus ending inventory). Since you pay $.75 for an item and sell it for $1.00, the cost of sales is pretty straightforward.

For a manufacturing company, however, cost of sales is made up of many components—some are variable components and some are fixed expenses. Cost of sales for a manufacturing company is composed of the following elements:

—Beginning inventory (raw materials, work in process, and finished goods)
—Purchase of raw material
—Factory labor and payroll taxes
—Freight and shipping costs
—Subcontract work
—Factory attributable overhead
—Less: Ending inventory (raw materials, work in process, finished goods)

Sometimes beginning inventory plus purchases less ending inventory is expressed as a percentage of sales under the general heading "materials."

Because of the components involved in cost of sales, it is sometimes important to break each item down on a monthly basis. The sample loan proposal, later in this section, gives an example of cost of sales schedules. Basically, it only involves an enumeration of the above items on a monthly basis, with the total for each month transferred to the monthly profit and loss and cash flow.

Footnotes

All projections, operating expense schedules, supporting schedules, and so on must be footnoted. A projection without footnotes is worthless. Footnotes are designed to answer the questions: On what is sales based? What are expense items and cost of sales based on? How was depreciation calculated? How many

Figure 7.16

FORECAST OF PROFIT (LOSS)

	Start-up or Prior to loan	1st Month	2nd Month	3rd Month	4th Month	5th Month	6th Month	7th Month	8th Month	9th Month	10th Month	11th Month	12th Month	Total for Year
1. Total Sales (Net)														
2. Cost of Sales **														
3. Gross Profit (line 1 minus line 2)														
4. Expenses (operating)														
5. Salaries (other than owner)														
6. Payroll Taxes														
7. Rent														
8. Utilities (incl. phone)														
9. Insurance														
10. Professional Services (i.e., acct.)														
11. Taxes & Licenses														
12. Advertising														
13. Supplies (for business)														
14. Office Supplies (forms, postage, etc.)														
15. Interest (on loans, contracts, etc.)														
16. Depreciation														
17. Travel (incl. operating costs of veh.)														
18. Entertainment														
19. Dues & Subscriptions														
20. Other														
21.														
22. Total Expenses (add lines 5 thru 21)														
23. Profit Before Taxes (line 3 minus 22)														

FORECAST OF CASH FLOW

	Start-up or Prior to loan	1st Month	2nd Month	3rd Month	4th Month	5th Month	6th Month	7th Month	8th Month	9th Month	10th Month	11th Month	12th Month	Total for Year
24. Income (cash received)														
25. Cash Sales														
26. Collection of Accounts Receivable														
27. Other														
28. Total Income (add lines 25, 26 & 27)														
29. Disbursements (cash paid out)														
30. Owner's Draw														
31. Loan Repayments (principal only)														
32. Cost of Sales (line 2)														
33. Total Expenses (minus line 16)														
34. Capital Expenditures (equip., bldgs., veh., leasehold impr.)														
35. Reserve for Taxes														
36. Other														
37. Total Disbursements (add lines 30 thru 36)														
38. Cash Flow Monthly (line 28 minus 37)														
39. Cash Flow Cumulative (line 38 plus line 39 of previous month)														

people are employed at what rates that represent the total salary expense? On what is interest and principal based?

The following items are always footnoted:

—Sales
—Cost of sales
—Total operating expenses
—Collection of receivables
—Interest
—Salaries
—Payroll tax
—Principal repayment
—Depreciation
—Income tax
—Capital expenditures (cash purchase of assets or otherwise unclassified cash expenditures)

Besides the above, all projected items that differ from the historical data (i.e., utilities are $1,000 in 1975, $1,050 in 1976, then you project $3,000 for the projected year) must be footnoted and explained.

Footnotes in a loan proposal explain the logical reasons behind the elements you have used. If you did a lot of work collecting data to justify the projected sales, for instance, this should be spelled out in detail in the footnotes. If you use any formulas to calculate expenses, receivables, or inventory write out the formulas and explain.

Pro Forma Balance Sheet

What will the applicant's balance sheet look like when he gets the money, or "at disbursement?" This is what a pro forma balance sheet is designed to answer.

If the business is a new one the pro forma balance sheet is easy—it just shows those items the business wants to use the money for (the "use of funds" statement) and how much money is being put into the venture (the owner's equity). This is illustrated in Figure 7.17.

If the business applying for the loan is an existing business the pro forma balance sheet would equal the use of funds statements added to the current balance sheet as illustrated in Figure 7.18.
Note: net worth is the same in the current balance sheet and the pro forma balance sheet. The only time net worth will be different is if the applicant puts in cash plus borrows money, which is an extraordinary case. In most cases, assets and debt increase, but only when extra cash is put into the business from a nondebt source will the net worth increase.

Sometimes money is borrowed to pay off debts that already exist. In this case everything will be the same as previously illustrated but the liabilities that are paid off won't appear on the pro forma balance sheet. Figure 7.19 illustrates this.

Figure 7.17

Use of Loan Funds		Pro Forma Balance Sheet	
		Current Assets:	
Working capital	$10,000	Cash	$10,000
Inventory	20,000	Inventory	20,000
Prepayments*	5,000	Prepayments	5,000
		Total Current Assets	$35,000
		Fixed Assets:	
Equipment	15,000	Equipment	15,000
Improvements	5,000	Improvements	5,000
		Total Fixed Assets	$20,000
		Other Assets:	
Deposits†	5,000	Deposits	5,000
		Total Other Assets	$ 5,000
Total Funds Required	$60,000	Total Assets	$60,000
Funds to come from:			
(1) Loan (First yr.)		Current Liabilities:	
Loan Repayment ††	$11,500	Current portion Debt	$11,500
Repayment after 1st year ††	$49,500	Long-Term Liabilities Long-term debt	$49,500
Total Loan	$50,000	Total Liabilities	$50,000
(2) Owner's Equity Injection	$10,000	Net Worth	$10,000
Total Funds	$60,000	Total Liabilitity and Net Worth	$60,000

*If prepayments are amounts paid for the first year, they are considered a current asset.
†Deposits that won't be refunded or used up in one year are considered other assets. Goodwill and licenses are also considered other assets.
††The principal portion of the first year's payments on the debt are equivalent to the current portion of a long-term debt. Interest payments are considered expenses items, and don't show up on the balance sheet.

Figure 7.18

Current Balance Sheet		Use of Funds		Pro Forma Balance	
Current Assets					
Cash	$10,000	Working Cap.	$ 5,000	$ 15,000	Cash
Receivables	15,000		-0-	15,000	Receivables
Inventory	14,000	Inventory	10,000	24,000	Inventory
Total Current Assets	$39,000			$ 54,000	
Fixed Assets					
Land & Bldgs.	50,000		-0-	$ 50,000	Land & Bldgs.
Equipment	10,000	Equipment	15,000	25,000	Equipment
Improvements	6,000	Improvements	5,000	11,000	Improvements
Total Fixed Assets	$66,000			$ 86,000	
Total Assets	$105,000	**Total Funds**	$35,000	$140,000	**Total Assets**

(continued)

Current Balance Sheet		Use of Funds		Pro Forma Balance	
Current Liabilities					
Trade Payables	20,000		-0-	20,000	Trade Payables
Current Portion Debt	-0-	Principal Repayment	12,000	12,000	Current Portion Debt
Current Portion Mortgage	3,000		-0-	3,000	Current Portion Mortgage
Total Current Liabilities	$ 23,000			$ 35,000	Total Current Liabilities
Long-Term Liabilities:		Repayment after 1st Yr.			
Mortgage	38,000			38,000	Mortgage
Loan	-0-		23,000	23,000	Loan
Total Long-term Liabilities	$ 38,000	Total Debt	35,000	$ 61,000	Total Long-Term Liabilities
Total Liabilities	$ 61,000			$ 96,000	Total Liabilities
Net Worth	$ 44,000		-0-	$ 44,000	Net Worth
Total Liabilities & Net Worth	$105,000			$140,000	Total Liabilities & Net Worth

Figure 7.19

Current Balance Sheet		Use of Funds		Pro Forma	
Current Liabilities					
Trade Payables	$20,000	Pay off Debt	$20,000	-0-	
Current portion Debt	-0-	Prin. Repayment	12,000	12,000	CPD
Current portion Mortgage	3,000			3,000	CPM
Total Current Liabilities	$23,000			$15,000	TCL

Of course, if this sum was paid out of the loan illustrated above, the loan amount would be $20,000 higher. Again, it will not change net worth to use debt to pay off debt.

Ratios

Along with your other financial statements projections and pro forma, the lender would generally like to see the calculations of two ratios: the debt-to-worth ratio and the current ratio. Both these ratios are calculated from balance sheet items and usually it is best to put the ratios right after the pro forma balance sheet. The present ratios from the current balance sheet and the projected ratios from the pro forma balance sheet should be used in the loan proposal. The ratios are as follows:

Debt-to-worth ratio = Total debt ÷ Net Worth

Current ratio = Current assets ÷ Current Liabilities

Using the figures from the previous example's current balance sheet (Fig. 7.18), total debt is $61,000 (total liabilities), net worth is $44,000, current assets are $39,000, and current liabilities are $23,000.

Debt to worth = $61,000 ÷ $44,000 = 1.39

Current ratio = $39,000 ÷ $23,000 = 1.7

When the company borrows more money and adds to their assets and liabilities, these ratios change. From Figure 7.18 illustrated pro forma balance sheet; debt = $96,000, net worth = $44,000, current assets = $54,000, and current liabilities = $35,000.

Debt to worth ratio = $96,000 ÷ $44,000 = 2.18

Current ratio = $54,000 ÷ $35,000 = 1.54

What do these ratios mean? The debt-to-worth ratio shows a lender how highly "leveraged" the business is, that is, how much debt they have in relation to their equity in the business. If this number gets higher, it indicates to the bank that the business has much more of other peoples' money in the business than the owner has in it. For instance the debt-to-worth ratio of 1.39 means that the owner owes 1.39 times more than he has invested (which isn't bad, incidentally), but when he borrows the loan, the ratio changes to 2.18, or he now would owe 2.18 times more than he has invested. Small debt-to-worth ratios are all right, but you can see as the ratio approaches 10 to 15, the lender would be concerned because the owner doesn't have much to lose if the business goes under.

The current ratio indicates if a business can use current assets (those that can be liquidated within one year) to pay off current liabilities (those due within one year). The higher this number, the better, because it assures the bank that for the next year the company can cover its existing debt. If the number is less than one (1), it means that the company can't cover its short-term debt out of its current assets.

The Presentation Format

All the items we discussed in previous chapters—the market study, use of funds, financial data, business history, owner's history and personal finances, and all the back-up data—must now be put into a format.

The format that will be used is one that I have developed over the years by practical experience and by borrowing ideas from every major bank in California. The format puts all the information that has been developed into a reasonable, logical order.

The format is divided into three areas: the package summary, the exhibits, and the agency forms. The package summary is the most important of the three areas and includes: application, ownership purpose, use of funds, repayment and finance, personal data, collateral summary, pro forma balance sheet, market study, and business history. Because the package summary is so important, it is included in its entirety.

The exhibits are the necessary back-up data such as: personal income tax of owners, business financial statements, purchase estimates, market support documents, leases, property titles, corporation or partnership papers, buy-sell agreements, complete reserves, and copies of any indexes used for the projections.

The following pages are a sample loan proposal package with a contents page. The exhibits and agency forms listed on the contents page are not included in the sample proposal. After the package summary is a discussion of each major section and some sample government forms.

Sample Loan Proposal
Contents

Package Summary

Application
Ownership
Purpose and Use of Funds
Repayment
Figure 1 Comparative and Projected Financial Statements
Figure 2 Projected Profit and Loss and Cash Flow Monthly—Year 1
Figure 3 Projected Profit and Loss and Cash Flow Quarterly—Years 2 and 3
Comments re Projected Items
Market Analysis
Other Operating Figures
Figure 4 Comparative and Projected Operating Expense and Manufacturing Overhead
Comments re Operating and Manufacturing Overhead
Figure 5 Increased Operating and Manufacturing Overhead
Figure 6 Monthly Projected Cost of Sales—Years 1, 2, and 3
Comments re Projected Cost of Sales
Personal Data
Figure 7 Personal Financial Statement
Collateral
Figure 8 Pro Forma Balance Sheet
Footnotes to Pro Forma Balance Sheet
Business History

Exhibit I   Income tax statements, last three years; current profit and loss and balance sheet of Tie-Top Tennies, Inc.

Exhibit II   New York Times article; industry studies; and company advertising material

Exhibit III   Personal income tax, last three years, T. Tie and H. Sat

Exhibit IV   Incorporation papers for Tie-Top Tennies

Exhibit V   Lease of company premises

Exhibit VI   Written estimates of required equipment

Forms   SBA forms 912, 413, 4 Schedule A, and 159

Theodore Tie

Tie Top Tennies, Inc.
20 Tennies Boulevard
Tie Top, California 90000
218/362-4833

Application	$350,000 partially secured term loan payable for six (6) years, payable as follows: in eighty-two monthly installments of $6,755.00 including interest of 11.% per annum. An SBA guarantee of 90% ($315,000) is requested under 7(a) program. A guarantee fee of 1% ($3,150) is requested of the bank by the SBA.	

The owner's wives will be required to sign the note and all loan documents.

The bank shall obtain their standard credit terms and conditions agreement, containing the usual convenants and restrictions together with specific provisions asked by the bank.

Ownership

The ownership of Tie Top Tennies, Inc. is as follows: (See Exhibit IV for Corporation papers):

	Title	Ownership
Theodore Tie	President	50%
Hiram Sat	V. Pres.	35%
Ron Halfwack	Sec./Trea.	15%

Purpose and Use of Funds

To financially assist Tie Top Tennies to expand its present manufacturing facilities (more than doubling manufacturing capacity) by providing capital for equipment, raw materials, debt repayment and working capital. The limited size of the present facility, lack of additional equipment, and working capital has kept the Company from expanding to its full market potential.

The Loan Proceeds will be used as follows:

Raw Material	29,000	(1)
Equipment	45,300	(2)
Repay Debt	100,000	(3)
Working Capital	175,700	(4)
Total Loan Required	350,000	

(1) Raw Materials represents one month's supply for the expansion operation.

(2) Equipment required is as follows:

2 Clickers	11,300
6 Pfaff 911's	9,150
1 Skinner	1,250
1 Final	4,250
Shelves	1,350
18 Shoe Molds	18,000
Total	45,300

(continued)

(3) Star Bank Loan—Original Balance 148,000
Balance as of 12/30/75 100,000
Interest & Term:
16.2% - 1 year
Expected Balance at Disbursement 100,000

(4) Because of two elements, i.e., rapid planned expansion and 90-day receivables, this amount of working capital is absolutely necessary. According to the cash flow projections, following, the actual amount of working capital required is $191,224. However, since short-term resources (i.e., accounts receivable financing) should be available and some of the receivables might be paid in a shorter term than 90 days, the requested amount should be sufficient.

Figure 1 Comparative and Projected Financial Statements

	12/30/73 12 mos. Income Tax	12/30/74 12 mos. Income Tax	12/30/75 12 mos. Income Tax	9/30/76 9 mos. P & L
Sales	72,814	40,256	63,577	314,213
Cost of Sales	60,197	29,778	39,126	232,896
Gross Profit	12,617	10,478	24,451	81,317
Operating Expense	24,453	40,176	61,120	62,697
Net Profit	(11,836)	(29,698)	(36,669)	18,620
Add:				
Depreciation & Amort.	630	1,978	3,423	5,277
Officers' salaries	6,000	12,000	16,400	15,200
Interest Income	N/A	N/A	N/A	31
Cash in Flow	(5,206)	(15,720)	(16,846)	39,128
Less:				
Income Tax	—0—	—0—	—0—	1,600
Loan Repayment	—0—	—0—	—0—	—0—
Officers' salaries	6,000	12,000	16,400	15.200
Cash Out Flow	6,000	12,000	16,400	16.800
Cash Margin	(11,206)	(27,720)	(33,246)	22.328
Commonsized (%)				
Sales	100.0	100.0	100.0	100.0
Cost of Sales	82.6	73.9	61.5	74.1
Gross Profit	17.4	26.1	38.5	25.9
Operating Expense	33.5	99.8	96.1	19.9
Net Profit	(16.1)	(73.7)	(57.6)	6.0

	9/30/76 Annualized (X1.333)	Projected 12 mos. 1st Year		Projected 12 mos. 2nd Year	Projected 12 mos. 3rd Year	
Sales	418,846	1,263,168	(1)	1,904,222	2,380,278	(1a)
Cost of Sales	310,450	859,842	(2)	1,253,831	1,544,501	(2b)
Gross Profit	108,396	403,326		650,391	835,777	
Operating Expense	83,575	227,840	(3)	255,642	303,028	
Net Profit	24,821	175,486		394,749	532,749	(3a)
Add:						
Depreciation & Amort.	7,034	12,748		12,748	12,748	
Officers' salaries	20,262	34,731		38,204	42,024	
Interest Income	41	41	(4)	41	41	(4)
Cash In Flow	52,158	223,036		447,742	587,562	
Less:						
Income Tax	2,133	70,194	(5)	197,375	266,375	(5a)
Loan Repayment	—0—	43,032	(6)	48,251	54,099	(6)
Officer's salaries	20,262	34,731	(7)	38,204	42,024	(7)
Cash Out Flow	22,395	147,957		283,830	362,498	
Cash Margin	29,763	75,079		161,912	225,064	
Commonsized (%)						
Sales		100.0		100.0	100.0	
Cost of Sales		68.1		65.8	64.9	
Gross Profit		31.9		34.2	35.1	
Operating Expense		18.0		13.4	12.7	
Net Profit		13.9		20.8	22.4	

Figure 2 Projected Profit & Loss and Cash Flow Monthly—Year 1

	1977 March	April	May	June	July	Aug.	Sept.
Gross Sales (1)	52,632	65,016	77,400	89,784	102,168	114,552	126,936
Cost of Sales (2)	41,369	48,495	55,621	62,747	69,872	76,998	84,124
Gross Profit	11,263	16,521	21,779	27,037	32,296	37,554	42,812
Fixed Operating Expense (3)	11,618	11,618	11,618	11,618	11,618	11,618	11,618
Commissions (7% of sales)	3,684	4,551	5,418	6,285	7,152	8,019	8,886
Total Operating Expense	15,302	16,169	17,036	17,903	18,770	19,637	20,504
Net Profit	(4,039)	352	4,743	9,134	13,426	17,917	22,308

Projected Cash Flow

	1977 March	April	May	June	July	Aug.	Sept.
Receivables Collected (8)	47,508	47,508	52,632	52,632	65,016	77,400	89,784
S.B.A. Loan Proceeds	350,000						
Total Cash Available	397,508	47,508	52,632	52,632	65,016	77,400	89,784
Disbursements:							
Operating Expense (less Depr.) (3)	15,265	16,132	16,999	17,865	18,833	19,600	20,467
Cost of Sales (less Depr.) (2)	40,683	47,809	54,935	62,061	69,186	76,312	83,438
Principal Payments—SBA	3,586	3,586	3,586	3,586	3,586	3,586	3,586
Reserve for Taxes (5)	5,849	5,849	5,849	5,849	5,849	5,849	5,850
Capital Disbursement (8)	174,300						
Total Disbursements	239,683	73,376	81,369	89,362	97,354	105,347	113,341
Cash Flow Monthly	157,825	(25,868)	(28,737)	(36,730)	(32,338)	(27,947)	(23,556)
Cash Flow Cumulative (9)	170,825	144,957	116,220	79,490	47,152	19,205	(4,351)

	Oct.	Nov.	Dec.	1978 January	February	Total 1st Year
Gross Sales (1)	126,936	126,936	126,936	126,936	126,936	1,263,168
Cost of Sales (2)	84,123	84,123	84,123	84,123	84,122	859,841
Gross Profit	42,812	42,812	42,812	42,813	42,814	403,327
Fixed Operating Expense (3)	11,618	11,618	11,618	11,619	11,619	139,418
Commissions (7% of Sales)	8,886	8,886	8,886	8,885	8,885	88,422
Total Operating Expense	20,504	20,504	20,504	20,504	20,504	227,940
Net Profit	22,309	22,309	22,309	22,309	22,310	175,487

Projected Cash Flow

	Oct.	Nov.	Dec.	1978 January	February	Total 1st Year
Receivables Collected (8)	102,168	114,552	114,552	126,936	126,936	1,030,008
S.B.A. Loan Proceeds						350,000
Total Cash Available	102,168	114,552	114,552	126,936	126,936	1,380,008
Disbursements:						
Operating Expense (less Depr.) (3)	20,467	20,467	20,467	20,467	20,466	227,395
Cost of Sales (less Depr.) (2)	83,436	83,436	83,438	83,436	83,436	851,605
Principal Payments—SBA	3,586	3,586	3,586	3,586	3,586	43,032
Reserve for Taxes (5)	5,850	5,850	5,850	5,850	5,850	70,194
Capital Disbursement (8)						174,300
Total Disbursements	113,339	113,339	113,339	113,339	113,338	1,366,526
Cash Flow Monthly	(11,173)	1,213	1,213	125,597	12,598	
Cash Flow Cumulative (9)	(15,524)	(14,311)	(13,098)	10,884	23,482	

Figure 3 Projected Profit & Loss And Cash Flow Quarterly—Years 2 & 3

	1978 3 mos. Mar.–May	3 mos. June–Aug.	3 mos. Sept.–Nov.	1978–1979 3 mos. Dec.–Feb.	Total 2nd Year
Gross Sales (1a)	418,889	456,970	495,050	533,313	1,904,222
Cost of Sales (2a)	280,563	302,476	324,388	346,404	1,253,831
Gross Profit	138,326	154,494	170,662	186,909	650,391
Fixed Operating Expense (3a)	30,586	30,586	30,587	30,587	122,346
Commissions	29,322	31,988	34,654	37,332	133,296
Total Operating Expense	59,908	62,574	65,241	67,919	255,642
Net Profit	78,418	91,920	105,421	128,990	394,749

Projected Cash Flow

	1978 3 mos. Mar.–May	3 mos. June–Aug.	3 mos. Sept.–Nov.	1978–1979 3 mos. Dec.–Feb.	Total 2nd Year
Receivables Collected (8a)	380,808	418,889	456,970	495,050	1,751,717
Disbursements:					
Oper. Expense (less Depr.) (3a)	59,065	61,731	64,397	67,074	252,267
Cost of Sales (less Depr.) (2a)	278,504	300,417	322,329	344,344	1,245,594
Prin. Payments—SBA	12,063	12,063	12,063	12,062	48,251
Reserve for Taxes (5a)	49,344	49,344	49,344	49,343	197,375
Total Disbursements	398,976	423,555	448,133	472,823	1,743,487
Cash Flow Monthly	(18,168)	4,666	8,837	22,227	
Cash Flow Cumulative	5,314	648	9,485	31,712	

	1979 3 mos. Mar.–May	3 mos. June–Aug.	3 mos. Sept.–Nov.	1979–1980 3 mos. Dec.–Feb.	Total 3rd Year
Gross Sales (1a)	582,718	588,894	601,245	607,421	2,380,278
Cost of Sales (2a)	379,018	382,571	389,679	393,233	1,544,501
Gross Profit	203,700	206,323	211,566	214,188	835,777
Fixed Operating Expense (3a)	34,102	34,102	34,102	34,103	136,409
Commissions	40,790	41,223	42,087	42,519	166,619
Total Operating Expense	74,892	75,325	76,189	76,622	303,028
Net Profit	128,808	130,998	135,377	137,566	532,749
Projected Cash Flow					
Receivables Collected (8a)	533,313	582,718	588,894	601,245	2,306,170
Disbursements:					
Oper. Expense (less Depr.) (3a)	74,853	75,288	76,152	76,594	302,583
Cost of Sales (less Depr.) (2a)	376,959	380,512	387,620	391,173	1,536,264
Principal Payments—SBA	13,525	13,525	13,525	13,524	54,099
Reserve for Taxes (5a)	66,594	66,594	66,594	66,593	266,375
Total Disbursements	531,931	535,919	543,891	547,884	
Cash Flow Monthly	1,382	56,799	45,003	53,361	
Cash Flow Cumulative	33,094	89,893	134,896	188,259	

Repayment

See the cash flow as demonstrated in Figure 1 of Comparative and Projected Financial Statements.

Comments Re Projected Items

(1) Sales $1,263,168: Represents a 201.6% increase over annualized 9/30/76 sales. However, this is not unreasonable in view of increases in sales in the past years.

Increase in Sales

Year		Sales		Chg. from Prev. Yr.
1973		72,814		N/A
1974		40,256	(−)	44.8%
1975		63,577	(+)	57.9%
1976	(Est.)	418,846	(+)	558.8%
1977	(Proj)	1,263,168	(+)	201.6%

Although it might be easy to dismiss the 1973 to 1974 increase as a freak fluctuation, there are several factors that would indicate otherwise:

(a) 1975 was the first full year of production. (In 1973 and 1974, the Company imported shoes. The dollar devaluation in 1974 made importing unprofitable, so the Company started manufacturing operations. However, production was slow because they had not yet developed their improved one piece sole, nor set up their manufacturing operation for maximum efficiency.)

(b) The trend for increased tennis shoe sales, in particular, expensive tennis shoe sales, in the general market is up (see "market" section, following).

(c) The Company had to turn down more orders than they filled in 1975.

(d) The Company is primarily selling on the West Coast now, although they have new sales agreements set up in the East Coast, Midwest, and South. The Company has not been the deliverer to these areas because of limited production and cash flow problems caused by 90-day receivables. The sales organizations in the South area expects initial sales available of 24,000 pairs per year. The New York area expects initial sales at 12,000 per year. The Midwest has potential for 50,000 pairs per year. (Projected production for $1,263,168 in sales is 87,720 pairs).

(e) Potential minimum sales penetration for the West Coast are 100,000 pairs/year. (Adidas sells 700,000 pairs, and Puma sells 500,000 per year).

(f) Tie Top shoes are a quality, higher than/or as high as, all the imports (Adidas, Puma, Tre-Torn, Dunlop, etc.) and costs $5.00 per pair on the average less than these competitors.

(g) The Company has been approached by two large shoe chains to make private label shoes, a market that Tie Top does not contemplate entering, but a market that has not even been explored by the Company.

(h) Tie Top the name, is, as Pro Illustrated's, January 12, 1976, article "Tennis Fashion", says, "no novice in the tennis shoe market". Tie Top was the first imported hemp tennis shoe marketed in the United States.

(i) The Company has their own patented design for an advanced, more durable high-rise sole. Furthermore, with the new equipment and the modifications in the machines planned, the Company will be the largest and most automated company in their field in the U. S. Support for the first year's projected sales can be more graphically illustrated by the following market study.

Market Analysis

General Market — The total market for all tennis shoes (canvas, leather and hemp) in the U. S. is $1-billion per year or 220 million pairs according to a June 16, 1974 *New York Times* article appearing in the "Business and Finance Section", entitled "Sneaking Up on Status". Twenty percent (20%) of all shoes sold in the United States in 1973 were tennis shoes. Gross amounts of shoes increased 15% over 1973 and are expected to increase in the double digits in 1975, despite the recession (or because of it).

Currently, there are three strong elements working in favor of increased sales, elements which should persist for at least the next year:

(a) The United States has moved consistently to more casual wear over the past decades and away from more formal attire. For instance, it is now perfectly acceptable for a large percentage of professional and managerial persons to wear open-necked shirts (or pants in the case of women) and very few social events are formal. More specifically, while it was unacceptable only a decade ago for "grown men" to wear tennis shoes in public, in my personal estimation, now fully 30% of the men seen in shopping centers, movies and at social events wear tennis shoes. This is especially so for the leather tennis shoe.

(b) Outdoor life (hiking, camping, golf, tennis, etc.) has undergone a renaissance within the past 10 years. Tennis, in particular, has grown in popularity geometrically within the past two years. Bicycling, jogging and hand ball are also very popular. Needless to say, all these sports require the use of tennis shoes.

(c) Leather and hemp tennis shoes have become a status symbol for the young and a must for the more affluent tennis players, joggers, etc., which will be discussed in the following "Leather and Hemp Tennis Shoe Market" section.

Leather and hemp tennis shoes in the United States are imported. Tie Top's competitors include Puma and Adidas, manufactured in Germany and France, Head (made for Head by Adidas), Tre Torn, manufactured in Sweden, and Claussures Ours, manufactured in Europe. Other major competitors notably Pro-Keds and Converse, both U. S. manufacturers, make expensive shoes $15.00 up, but they have nylon or cloth uppers, not leather or hemp.

There were 66 million pairs of tennis shoes imported into the United States in 1973, double the tennis shoe imports in 1965. All but 7 million were inexpensive shoes imported from Hong Kong or Formosa. The 7 million that were not from Hong Kong or Formosa were mostly those expensive shoes mentioned above. Adidas sold 1.5 million pairs in 1973, Puma sold 1 million and Tre Torn sold 750,000. The other expensive shoes accounted for 3.75 million pairs.

Tie Top, if they produce 87,720 pairs as projected, will account for only 1.25% of the 1973 market for hemp shoes. If the expensive shoe market expanded by 15% in 1975, and will expand by 15% in 1976, as expected, (growing from 7 million in 1973 to 9.258 million in 1975), Tie Top's production will account for only 0.95 of the total market in the U.S. in 1977, Tie Top's production will represent 0.03% (three hundred of one percent) of the total market.

The status-fadish aspects of the hemp shoes market can't be ignored. According to the *New York Times* article cited previously, "As for teenagers, many can't afford lavish status symbols so they are forced to settle for sneakers, which became a modest, yet flashy, status symbol. And in that limited domain, they'll too, prefer the status of hemp tennis shoes to conventional tennis shoes."

The fact that leather or hemp tennis shoes have only been available in any numbers for five years, tends to indicate that the market is far from reaching its potential.

Because all of Tie Top's competitors are imported, Tie Top has logistical advantages. Orders of the competitors' shoes take two months for delivery, whereas Tie Top's takes two weeks. Because imported shoes have to be ordered a long time in advance and warehoused, they cannot be as flexible in the market place as Tie Top. If the new style becomes red and blue uppers for example, Tie Top can be producing and delivering up to six months in advance of the competition, who would have to convince the headquarters office to produce this item, dispose of already inventoried shoes, and order two months in advance.

Also, due to dollar fluctuations, costs for imported goods are never certain from month to month. Moreover, the present dollar trend especially against the German Mark and Swedish Kronin, is devaluating, making these competitors progressively more expensive.

(a) Sales have been increased rapidly at Tie Top in the last two years.

(b) The tennis shoe market, particularly the expensive shoe market, is very large and expanding rapidly.

(c) Tie Top has tapped but a small percentage of its readily available market.

(d) Tie Top is an established name, and holds exclusive patents.

(e) Tie Top shoes are as high in quality as the competitors, all of which are imported and take less time for delivery and are cheaper in price.

(f) With projected production, Tie Top's sales will only account for 0.95% of the expensive shoe market, 0.03% of the total market, a very conservative expectation.

The sales figures represent 82.9% of projected one shift capacity.

Sales in the monthly projected profit and loss statement were determined by adding 40 shoes per day production for each successive month until one shift capacity of 410 pairs per day is reached in the seventh month, September, 1975, then production is continued at the rate for the balance of the projected year.

Other Operating Figures

1a) *Second Year Sales—$1,904,222—Third Year Sales—$2,380,278.* In the second year, the Company will fill its one shift capacity and add other shifts. The second year's sales represent a modest (compared to historical) 50.75% increase over the first year, and represent only a slight increase in market penetration from 0.95% first year to 1.23% second year. Total production is 131,326 pairs 509 pairs per day or 62% of two shift capacity. The third year's sales represents a 25% increase in sales over the second year, a production of 164,157 pairs, 636 pairs per day, or 77.56% of two shift capacity. Market penetration would increase to 1.34%.

2) *Cost of Sales—$859,842—*See Schedule of Cost of Sales, following Operating Expense schedule.

2a) *Cost of Sales—$1,253,831—*(2nd. Yr) and $1,544,501 (3rd Yr), see

Cost of Sales schedule, years two and three, following Comparative and Projected Operating Expense schedule.

3) *Operating Expense—$277,840—*See following schedule "Comparative and Projected Operating Expense."

Operating expense in the monthly projected cash flow is less depreciation, a non cash expense.

3a) *Operating Expense—$255,642—*(2nd Yr) and $303,028 (3rd Yr) See "Comparative and Projected Operating Expenses" following. Operating expenses, for projection purposes, were increased 10% in the second year and 10% in the third year, except commissions, maintained at 7% of gross sales and depreciation which, naturally, stayed the same.

Operating expenses in the monthly projected cash flow is exclusive of depreciation.

4) *Interest Income—$41—*based on annualized 9/30/76 statement.

5) *Income Tax $70,194—*represents 40% of net profit for State and Federal income tax.

5a) *Income Tax—$197,375 (2nd Year),* and *$266,375 (3rd Year),* represent 50% of net profit for State and Federal income tax.

6) Represents only principal portion of SBA loan; interest portion is included in operating expense.

7) Officers salaries include an increase over the present levels and takes into consideration salaries both attributed to manufacturing and operating overhead. In years two and three, officers' salaries were increased 10% per annum.

8) *Capital Disbursements—$174,300* included in monthly projected cash flow, includes:

Equipment	$ 45,300
Debt Repayment	$100,000
Raw Material	$ 29,000

9) *Cash Flow Cumulative* includes $13,000 in initial funds as per the Cash in the 9/30/74 Balance Sheet, Exhibit I.

Figure 4 Comparative & Projected Operating Expense and Manufacturing Overhead

	12/31/72 12 mos. Income Tax	12/31/73 12 mos. Income Tax	12/31/74 12 mos. Income Tax	9/30/75 9 mos. P & L	9/30/76 Annualized (X 1.333)
Operating Expense					
Advertising	1,358	949	1,028	2,366	3,154
Auto, Travel/Entertainment	4,230	3,220	2,851	4,164	5,551
Depreciation	537	1,885	3,330	334	445
Insurance	663	384	1,702	639	852
Interest	1,100	903	4,258	12,448	16,593
Legal & Accounting	1,572	2,512	2,751	3,023	4,030
Office Expense	147	1,033	—0—	917	1,222
Officers Life Insurance	—0—	—0—	—0—	154	205
Payroll Taxes & Welfare	—0—	1,195	105	933	1,244
Rent	1,375	3,160	12,721	557	742
Repairs & Maintenance	746	1,309	1,349	289	385
Salaries:					
Office		2,749	—0—	3,200	4,266
Officers	6,000	12,000	16,400	7,600	10,131
Sales Commissions & Discounts	1,806	376	4,391	21,414	28,545
Tax & Licenses	275	275	6,682	200	267
Telephone & Utilities	957	950	1,679	853	1,137
Bad Debt	855	2,083	—0—	3,606	4,807
Amortization	93	93	93	—0—	—0—
Promotion	618	—0—	—0—	—0—	—0—
Moving Expense	200	—0—	—0—	—0—	—0—
Supplies	696	—0—	1,618	—0—	—0—
Outside Labor	1,255	—0—	—0—	—0—	—0—
Dues & Subscriptions	—0—	100	—0—	—0—	—0—
Franchise Costs	—0—	5,000	—0—	—0—	—0—
Miscellaneous	—0—	—0—	162	—0—	—0—
Total Operating Expense	24,453	40,176	61,120	62,697	83,575
Manufacturing Overhead					
Equipment Rental				3,699	4,931
Supplies				1,178	1,570
Insurance				1,917	2,555
Depreciation				1,893	2,523
Payroll Taxes				8,393	11,188
Rent				5,017	6,688
Repairs & Maintenance				2,600	3,466
Salaries:					
Officers				7,600	10,131
Supervisory				7,000	9,331
Tax & Licenses				1,978	2,637
Telephone & Utilities				854	1,138
Patent Expense				3,050	4,066
Total Manufacturing Overhead				45,179	60,224

Figure 4 (cont.) Comparative & Projected Operating Expense and Manufacturing Overhead

	Projected 12 mos. 1st year		Projected 12 mos. 2nd year	Projected 12 mos. 3rd year	
Operating Expense					
Advertising	8,700		9,570	10,527	
Auto, Travel, Entertainment	10,400		11,440	12,584	
Depreciation	445	(A)	445	445	(A)
Insurance	2,050		2,255	2,481	
Interest	38,028	(B)	32,809	26,961	(B)
Legal & Accounting	8,400		9,240	10,164	
Office Expense	4,850		5,335	5,869	
Officers Life Insurance	205		226	249	
Payroll Taxes & Welfare	2,890	(C)	3,179	3,497	(C)
Rent	14,240		15,664	17,230	
Repairs & Maintenance	770		847	932	
Salaries:					
Office	11,500		12,650	13,915	
Officers	17,400		19,140	21,054	
Sales Commissions & Discounts	88,422	(D)	133,296	166,619	(D)
Tax & Licenses	275		306	337	
Telephone & Utilities	3,600		3,960	4,356	
Bad Debt	4,800		5,280	5,808	
Amortization	—0—		—0—	—0—	
Promotion	—0—		—0—	—0—	
Moving Expense	—0—		—0—	—0—	
Supplies	—0—		—0—	—0—	
Outside Labor	—0—		—0—	—0—	
Dues & Subscriptions	—0—		—0—	—0—	
Franchise Costs	—0—		—0—	—0—	
Miscellaneous	—0—		—0—	—0—	
Total Operating Expense	227,840		255,642	303,028	
Manufacturing Overhead					
Equipment Rental	6,731		7,404	8,144	
Supplies	3,370		3,707	4,078	
Insurance	4,955		5,471	5,996	
Depreciation	8,237	(A2)	8,237	8,237	(A2)
Payroll Taxes	35,382	(C)	51,568	58,483	(C)
Rent	14,368		15,805	17,386	
Repairs & Maintenance	4,906		5,397	5,937	
Salaries:					
Officers	17,331		19,064	20,970	
Supervisory	26,131		28,744	31,618	
Tax & Licenses	4,000	(E)	4,400	4,840	(E)
Telephone & Utilities	3,538		3,892	4,281	
Patent Expense	4,066		4,473	4,920	
Total Manufacturing Overhead	133,015		158,142	174,890	

Comments Re Operating & Manufacturing Overhead

Note: All projected operating expense and manufacturing overhead are based on historical data plus the company's estimate of expected new expenses. Expenses that were increased were calculated as in Figure 5.

Figure 5

Increased Operating and Manufacturing Overhead

Expense	Annualized	Increase	Total
Operating Expense			
Advertising	1,500	7,200	8,700
Auto & Travel	5,600	4,800	10,400
Insurance	850	1,200	2,050
Legal & Acctg.	4,000	4,400	8,400
Office Expense	1,250	3,600	4,850
Rent*	12,800	1,360	14,240
Repairs & Maintenance	390	380	770
Salaries:			
Office	4,300	6,200	11,500
Officers	10,200	7,200	17,400
Telephone & Utilities	1,200	2,400	3,600
Manufacturing Overhead			
Equipment Rental	4,931	1,800	6,731
Supplies	1,570	1,800	3,370
Insurance	2,555	2,400	4,955
Rent*	6,688	7,680	14,368
Repairs & Maintenance	3,466	1,440	4,906
Salaries:			
Officers	10,131	7,200	17,331
Supervisors	9,331	16,800	26,131
Telephone & Utilities	1,138	2,400	3,538

*Rent includes new facility, old facility and warehouses.

A) *Depreciation*—$455 is equal to 9/30/76 annualized.

A2) *Depreciation*—$8,237 is based on the following schedule:

Value	Item	Salvage	Life	Method	Annual
$45,300	Equipment Old	$5,300	7 yrs.	S/L	$5,714

B) *Interest* is for the SBA loan, 11.5% for six years, principal—$350,000. Interest, naturally, is less for each succeeding year.

C) *Payroll Taxes*—represents 10% of operating expense salaries in the Operating Expense schedule, all three years. In the manufacturing overhead schedule, payroll taxes are 10% of manufacturing overhead salaries *plus* ten percent (10%) of labor in Cost of Sales (Projected Cost of Sales schedule, following).

Figure 6 Monthly Projected Cost of Sales—Years 1, 2, and 3

	1977 Mar.	Apr.	May	June	July	Aug.	Sept.	Oct.
Cost of Sales-First Year								
Inventory (I)	15,184	18,757	22,330	25,903	29,475	33,048	36,621	36,621
Labor (II)	12,932	15,974	19,017	22,060	25,103	28,145	31,188	31,188
Freight (III)	2,168	2,679	3,189	3,699	4,209	4,720	5,230	5,230
Manufacturing Overhead (IV)	11,085	11,085	11,085	11,085	11,085	11,085	11,085	11,084
Total Cost of Sales	41,369	48,495	55,621	62,747	69,872	76,998	84,124	84,123

	1977 Nov.	Dec.	1978 Jan.	Feb.	Total 1st Yr.
Cost of Sales-First Year					
Inventory (1)	36,621	36,621	36,621	36,621	364,424
Labor (II)	31,188	31,188	31,188	31,188	310,360
Freight (III)	5,230	5,230	5,230	5,230	52,043
Manufacturing Overhead (IV)	11,084	11,084	11,084	11,084	133,015
Total Cost of Sales	84,123	84,123	84,123	84,123	859,842

	1978 Mar/May	Jun/Aug.	Sept/Nov.	1978—79 Dec/Feb.	Total 2nd Year
Cost of Sales-Second Year Third Year					
Inventory (I)	168,114	169,896	173,459	175,241	686,710
Labor (II)	143,174	144,691	147,726	149,243	584,834
Freight (III)	24,008	24,262	24,771	25,026	98,067
Manufacturing Overhead (IV)	43,722	43,722	43,722	43,723	174,890
Total Cost of Sales	379,018	382,571	389,679	393,233	544,501

	1979 Mar—May	Jun—Aug	Sept—Nov	1979—80 Dec—Feb	Total 3rd Year
Cost of Sales-Second Yr. Third Yr.					
Inventory (1)	120,849	131,836	142,822	153,861	549,368
Labor (II)	102,921	112,278	121,634	131,035	467,867
Freight (III)	17,258	18,827	20,396	21,972	78,454
Manufacturing Overhead (IV)	39,535	39,535	39,536	39,536	158,142
Total Cost of Sales	280,563	302,476	324,388	346,404	1,253,831

D) *Sales Commissions and Discounts*—represents seven percent (7%) of sales.

E) *Tax & License*—an additional $1,363 was added to the previous year's tax and license by the packager. The increase was not suggested by the Company. Second and Third year tax and license were increased by 10% per year.

Comments Re Projected Cost of Sales

(I) Inventory material was based on 28.85% of sales and includes beginning inventory plus purchases minus ending inventory each month. Inventory was 30.85% in 1974, but because of increased volume and larger purchasing power, the Company expects it to drop two percentage points in the projected year.

(II) *Labor* was based on 24.57% of sales, in line with historical costs. Cost of labor, however, might be cut with the new automated equipment the Company is purchasing and due to the fact that the present employees will have more experience (the longest any employee has worked now is 1½ years). Labor does not include factory supervisors' wages, included in manufacturing overhead.

(III) *Freight* is calculated at 4.12% based on historical data.

(IV) *Manufacturing Overhead* is based on the Comparative and Projected Manufacturing Overhead Schedule, preceding.

Personal Data

The following is a summary of the resumes of Theodore Tie, President and Hiram Sat, Vice President.

Resume

Theodore Tie, President
1425 Wahaakan Avenue
Gold, California 91623
Phone: 286-3220

Born:	July 4, 1950 in Los Angeles, California
Marital Status:	Married, no children
Education:	University of California (Los Angeles) BA—Marketing
Experience:	1972—Present, President—Tie Top Tennies
	1970–1972—Marketing Assistant, Goodwill Mexican Imports, San Diego, California.

Resume

Hiram Sat, Vice President
24 Gringo Trail
Gold, California 91623

Born:	January 12, 1948 in San Diego, California
Marital Status:	Married with two children
Education:	BA—Political Science (University of California, San Diego, 1969)

| Experience: | 1972 to Present—Vice President, Tie Top Tennies, Inc. |
| | |

Experience:

1972 to Present—Vice President, Tie Top Tennies, Inc.

1971 to 1972—Production Manager, Tacky Tennis Shoe Manufacturers, Phoenix, Arizona

Responsible for production scheduling and raw material ordering.

1969 to 1971—Production Assistant, Campo Tent Company, Tucson, Arizona. In charge of tent sewing operation

Personal Financial Statement

Figure 7 is a personal financial statement, dated 9/30/76 on SBA Form 413, attached.

Figure 7

Personal Financial Statement—Tie and Sat

	T. Tie	H. Sat
Assets		
Cash (1)	3,800	15,000
U.S. Bonds	—0—	200
Real Estate (2)	60,000	50,000
Auto (3)	4,200	6,000
Business (4)	39,797	27,858
Other Assets	4,000	3,000
Total Assets	111,797	112,058
Liabilities & Net Worth		
Loan—Auto (3)	2,800	4,000
R. E. Mortgage (2)	32,000	31,000
Total Liabilities	34,800	35,000
Net Worth	76,997	77,058
Total Liabilities & Net Worth	111,797	112,058

Footnotes:
(1) Cash includes:

	Amount	Acct. #	Institution
T. Tie	800	Check 486-91113	Bank of Amer.
	3000	Sav. 628-16-3418	Home Sav. & L.
H. Sat	1200	Check 318-12-92	Sec. Pac. Bk.
	12000	Sav. 628-12-3831	Home Sav. & L.
	1800	Sav. 782-321186	Glendale S & L

(2) Real Estate includes:

	Address	Purchased	Pres. Val.	Balance Owed	Mortgage Held By
T. Tie	1425 Wahaakan Ave. Gold, Ca. 91623	1972 for $39,500	$60,000	$32,000	Gold Valley S&L Gold, Cal.
H. Sat	24 Gringo Trail Gold, Cal, 91623	1976 for $43,000	$50,000	$35,000	Glendale S&L Los Angeles, Ca.

(3) Automobiles include:

	Year and model	Pres. Val.	Balance Owed	Financed by
T. Tie	76 Impala	$4,200	$2,800	Bank of America, Gold, Ca.
H. Sat	76 Volvo	$6,000	$4,000	Security Pacific, Gold, Ca.

(4) Includes percentage of net worth in Tie Top Tennies, Inc. as of 9/30/76

Collateral

(1) The bank will be provided with a security in all machinery and equipment, including furniture and fixtures now owned or hereafter acquired.

(2) The bank will obtain a security interest in all inventory and supplies now owned or hereafter acquired and all accounts and other rights to payments of any kind now existing or hereafter arising (Subject to trade suppliers).

(3) The bank will receive the right to assignment to beneficial interest of life insurance in the minimum amount of $350,000.

Summary of Collateral

Equipment & Improvements	$ 65,664
Receivables+	108,026
Inventory*	136,559
Total	$310,249

*Includes 9/30/74 assets plus proposed asset purchases
+As per 9/30/74 statement

Figure 8

Pro Forma Balance Sheet

	9/30/76 P & L	Pro Forma at Disbursement
Current Assets	231,946	436,646
Current Liabilities	173,815	95,040
Cash	12,902	188,602
Current Ratio	1.334	4.594
Contingent Liabilities	173,815	404,812
Net Worth	79,593	98,593
Debt to Worth Ratio	2.184	4.106
Cash	12,902	188,602
Accounts Receivable	108,026	108,026
Inventory	107,559	136,559
Prepaid	3,459	3,459
Total Current Assets	231,946	436,646
Real Estate & Building (net)	565	565
Machinery, Fixtures & Equipment	27,821	73,121
Prepaid Charges		
Goodwill, Patents, etc.	1,098	1,098
Accumulated Depreciation	(8,022)	(8,022)
Total Assets	253,408	503,408
Notes Payable SBA		43,032
Notes Payable—Other Banks	3,457	3,457
Notes Payable—Other	119,000	—0—
Accounts Payable	20,497	20,497
Federal Inc. & Other Taxes	4,868	4,868
Miscellaneous Accruals	20,429	20,429
Due Officers, Partners, Etc.	2,397	2,397
Other		
Total Current Liabilities	171,008*	95,040*
Bonded or Mortgage Debt	2,807	2,807
Long Term SBA		306,968
Total Liabilities	73,815	404,815
Capital Stock	84,240	84,240
Surplus	56,504	56,504
Difference*		19,000*
R. Earnings	(61,151)	(61,151)
Net Worth	79,593	98,593
Total	253,408	503,408

*See following page

Footnotes to Pro Forma Balance Sheet

*There is a $360.00 addition error on the 9/30/76 current liabilities, instead of $171,008 it should be $170,648. However, since I am not an accountant, I have elected to carry on the error over the pro forma so it will balance. Furthermore, since I have allocated only $100,000 to pay off the debt recorded at $119,000 (because by the time the loan is disbursed, the loan should be reduced to this amount), there will be an additional $19,000 difference. I have taken the $19,000 difference and added it to net worth.

I calculated the pro forma current liabilities total by the following formula:

9/30/74 Current Liabilities	171,008
Less: $119,000 debt retired	(119,000)
Sub-total	52,008
Plus: $43,030 current portions SBA Note	+43,032
	95,040

Business History

Tie Top Tennies, Inc., is a California corporation and the trade name Tie Top is registered with the patent office. The Company has been under continuous operation since 1972.

Tie Top was formed by Theodore Tie and Hiram Sat in 1972.

Tie Top was the first hemp tennis shoe introduced into this country. The business grew from $40,000 in 1972 to $314,000 for the nine months ending 9/30/76.

Because of the prevailing buy USA philosophy, Tie Top decided to raise some capital and go into their own manufacturing of the shoe. Advantages of such a project would be greater profit margin and potential, greater control over quality, better flexibility, and greater control of quantity required to meet the market demand. The shoe has very high level of acceptance with the public and the demand for it is very large. Currently, the Company has been telling their sales force not to take large orders in order that the Company may have and keep good deliveries. Tie Top has a unique design with its red, white, and blue stripes and white star lace findings to give the shoe that extra support that is needed in a quality shoe. Tie Top Tennies is the owner of the trademark Tie Top ® and also of the stars and stripes identification symbol appearing on its tennis shoe and other athletic shoes as well. The shoes are a result of a carefully planned ad campaign in High Times magazine and elsewhere, and are fast becoming one of the best known shoes in the field, and, in fact, have a reputation of being generally superior. It is the considered opinion of the management that now is the time for Tie Top to expand fast with the market of tennis players steadily increasing at a very high rate.

Presently, there are 35 million players, and projections are for 60 million players in 1977. A very big increase that will assure us of a big increase in sales.

Major Sections of Proposal

Application explains how much money the applicant business wishes to borrow, for what time period, and how much is to be paid back each month, each quarter, or each year. The application section also explains what kind of loan and, in the case of the sample, what government program (SBA) the loan is for, if any.

The application also explains that the business is subject to cosignatures of spouses (in the state of California and other states) and also subject to the bank (or lender's) "credit terms and loan agreement."

If there are any special things the lender should know about a company, such as the fact that it hasn't been operational for the previous four months or was just purchased by one partner from another, this should also be included in the application section.

Ownership spells out who owns the company, the officers, and what percentage they own.

Purpose briefly states the reasons for the loan (to expand, purchase).

Use of Funds shows how the funds borrowed are to be used and makes a note of further information about each item.

Repayment includes comparative and projected financial statements, comparative and projected operating expenses, monthly projections, supporting schedules, and footnotes.

The repayment section is the heart of the loan proposal and is the section on which lenders usually base most of their decision to approve the loan. You may, as I often do, include your market study under the footnotes to sales in this section. If your market study, however, exceeds several pages, I suggest you put it in a separate section called "Market Study."

Personal Data includes a resume and personal financial statement (with footnotes) for each owner.

Pro Forma Balance Sheet includes the pro forma and comparative balance sheets and notes, if applicable.

Collateral includes a summary of those assets a bank or lender can take as collateral for the loan.

Market Study includes an indepth study of the business' market. If the market study is short it should be included as a footnote to the projections in the repayment section.

Business History gives a brief history of the business—when started, basic philosophy, and so on.

Exhibits attached to the package summary should include the following.

—Business financial statements, last three years and current (The existing business or "buy-outs" of existing businesses, only. Does not apply to new businesses.)

—List of major customers and suppliers

—Aging of Accounts Receivable and Payable

—Personal income tax, resumes, and last three years from any person who has 20 percent or more ownership of the company

—Present or proposed lease of business
—Copies of any large contracts the business may have successfully bid that would affect future sales
—Corporation or partnership papers
—Lengthy market studies (a synopsis *only* should go in the package summary)
—Any other documents that might be pertinent to understanding of the business or its future operations
—SBA or other government agency forms

Exhibits are basically support data for your package summary. The exhibits sort of "flesh out" the overview of your company. Besides which, bankers and lenders usually want to look at these original documents with their own *eyes*, even though it has been summarized.

Government Forms. The good thing about government forms is that they usually give very specific directions on how to fill them out, on the form itself. (Sometimes they get boring, they are so specific). If you read the forms and you've done your homework (the rest of the loan proposal) the forms should be fairly easy to fill out.

The three important things to remember when filling out government application forms are:

1. Read the instructions *very* carefully.

2. Fill *everything* out *completely*. If there is a blank space or question that does not apply to you write "N/A", not applicable, in the space.

3. If you don't understand something or it doesn't make sense, don't ignore it, call the agency and ask them about it.

I have seen complete loan packages turned back, without being read, because a couple of the items on the government application form were left blank.

Following are some sample SBA loan application forms filled out. They should give you an idea of government forms in general.

United States of America

SMALL BUSINESS ADMINISTRATION

STATEMENT OF PERSONAL HISTORY

PLEASE READ CAREFULLY

Each member of the small business concern requesting assistance or the development company must submit this form in TRIPLICATE for filing with the SBA application This form must be filled out and submitted

1. If a sole proprietorship, by the proprietor.
2. If a partnership, by each partner.
3. If a corporation or a development company, by each officer, director, and additionally, by each holder of 20% or more of the voting stock.
4. Any other person, including a hired manager, who has authority to speak for and commit the borrower in the management of the business.

Name and Address of Applicant (Firm Name) (Street, City, State and ZIP Code)	SBA Office (City)
Joe Smith Trucking, Inc. 1622 West End Avenue Nashville, Tennessee 37203	Nashville, Tennessee
	Amount Applied for. $25,000.00

1. Personal Statement of: (State name in full, if no middle name, state (NMN), or if initial only, indicate initial) If married include name of spouse. List all former names used, and dates each name was used. Use separate sheet if necessary.

First	Middle	Maiden	Last
Joseph	James		Smith

Name of Spouse: (Include former married names and maiden name)
Ellen Harrison Smith

2. Date of Birth: (Month, day and year)

May 8, 1934

3. Place of Birth: (City & State or Foreign Country)

Louisville, Kentucky

4. Give the percentage of ownership or stock owned or to be owned in the small business concern or the Developement Company.   50%

Social Security No.

401 07 7442

5. Present residence address.

From	To	Address
7-4-68	Present	4702 Stonewood Drive Nashville, Tennessee 37205

Immediate past residence address.

From	To	Address
2-1-61	7-4-68	2707 Wanderlust Road Nashville, Tennessee 37205

6. Are you presently under indictment, on parole or probation?

☐ Yes ☒ No   If yes, furnish details in a separate exhibit. List name(s) under which held, if applicable.

7. Have you ever been charged with or arrested for any criminal offense other than a minor motor vehicle violation?

☐ Yes ☒ No   If yes, furnish details in a separate exhibit. List name(s) under which charged, if applicable.

8. Have you ever been convicted of any criminal offense other than a minor motor vehicle violation?

☐ Yes ☒ No   If yes, furnish details in a separate exhibit. List name(s) under which convicted, if applicable.

9. Name and address of participating bank

Fifth National Bank
2941- 49th Street, Nashville, Tennessee 37203

The information on this form will be used in connection with an investigation of your character. Any information you wish to submit, that you feel will expedite this investigation should be set forth.

Whoever makes any statement knowing it to be false, for the purpose of obtaining for himself or for any applicant any loan, or loan extension by renewal, deferment or otherwise, or for the purpose of obtaining, or influencing SBA toward, anything of value under the Small Business Act, as amended, shall be punished under Section 16(a) of that Act, by a fine of not more than $5000, or by imprisonment for not more than 2 years, or both.

Signature	Title	Date
(signed) Joseph J. Smith	President	Feb. 1, 1973

It is against SBA's policy to provide assistance to persons not of good character and therefore consideration is given to the qualities and personality traits of a person, favorable and unfavorable, relating thereto, including behavior, integrity, candor and disposition toward criminal actions. It is also against SBA's policy to provide assistance not in the best interests of the United States, for example, if there is reason to believe that the effect of such assistance will be to encourage or support, directly or indirectly, activities inimical to the Security of the United States.

SBA FORM 912 (1-72) REF: ND 510-1A PREVIOUS EDITIONS ARE OBSOLETE

1. This copy to be submitted to:

SBA, OFFICE OF SECURITY AND INVESTIGATIONS.
1441 L ST. WASHINGTON, D.C. 20416
Exhibit 3

APPLICATION FOR LOAN

(See Instructions on Page 2)

SBA LOAN NUMBER

1. **APPLICANT** (Show official name without abbreviations unless an abbreviation is a part of the official name. For proprietor or partnership, show name(s) followed by d/b/a and trade name used, if any)

Name	Street
Artic Freeze Lockers, Inc.	519 South 4th Street

City	County	State	ZIP Code	Tele. No.
Appleton	Orange	Virginia	24600	DE 6-3214

Employer's I.D. Number	Date of Application	Amount of Loan Requested	Maturity Requested
00-0000000	June 6, 1972	$55,000.	10 years

Type of Business	Date Established	Number of Employees (Including subsidiaries and affiliates).
Service	September 1961	At Time of Application _____ 16
	[X] Existing Business	If Loan is Approved _____ 18
	[ ] New Business	

Franchise	[ ] Yes	[X] No	If Yes, Submit Copy

2. **Use of Proceeds:**

Land Acquisition	$_____	Acquisition and/or repair of machinery and equipment	$ 42,700.00
New Building or plant construction	$_____	Working Capital	$_____
Debt Payment	$ 12,300.00	Other	$_____
		Total	$ 55,000.00

3. **SUMMARY OF COLLATERAL OFFERED** (Attach detailed list of collateral offered - See Item 8(16), page 2)

	Cost	Net Book Value (Cost Less Depreciation)	Present Liens Or Mortgage Balance, If Any
Land and Buildings	$29,416.65	$ 22,873.46	$ 6,300.00
Business machinery and equipment. .	120,218.80	38,814.96	6,000.00
Business furniture and fixtures	15,333.67	5,699.13	
Accounts receivable			
Inventory			
Other (specify) Auto/.equip...	16,608.01	7,971.16	

4. **AS ADDITIONAL SECURITY, PAYMENT OF THE LOAN WILL BE GUARANTEED BY:**

Name and Address (Include ZIP Code and Social Security Number of Guarantors) (Each principal must submit a signed personal balance sheet as of the same date as the applicant's balance sheet)	Net Worth Outside Of Interest In Applicant Company
John Richard Adams, 3134 Prospect Street, Boston, Mass. 01304 000-00-000	$ 83,350.00
Ollie P. Jefferson, 2134 South 19th Street, Tulsa, Okla 20605 000-00-000	18,680.00

5. **DISCLOSURE OF SPECIAL INFORMATION REGARDING PRINCIPALS:** (a) List below the names of any SBA employees or SBA advisory board members who are related by blood, marriage or adoption to, or who have any present or have had any past, direct or indirect, financial interest in or in association with, the applicant, or any of its partners, officers, directors or principal stockholders (such interest to include any direct or indirect financial interest in any other business entity or enterprise); (b) When the proprietor, or any of its partners, officer, director, or person who holds 10 percent or more of the applicant's stock is an investor in a licensed Small Business Investment Company, or a proposed investor in an SBIC which has filed for a license, detailed information shall be submitted with this application; and (c) Likewise, if any person identified in (b) above, or their spouse, is an employee of the U.S. Government (including members of the armed forces), detailed information shall be submitted with this application. (Use separate sheet if necessary).

If none, check here: [X] (a)   [X] (b)   [X] (c)

Name and Address (Include ZIP Code)	Details of Relationship or Interest

6. **MANAGEMENT** (1) Names of all owners, officers, directors or partners and their annual compensation, including salaries, fees, withdrawals, etc. (complete all columns). (2) Names and compensation of all employees receiving in excess of $17,500 annually. (3) All stockholders having a 20% or more interest in applicant (complete all columns except annual compensation). (4) Hired manager.

Name (List first, middle, maiden & last.) (If no middle name, so state) Home Address (Include ZIP Code)	Office Held	Annual Compensation	Percent Ownership	Personal Guaranty Offered (Yes or No)	Insurance Carried for Benefit of Applicant*
John R. Doe 518 South 4th Street, Appleton, Va.	President	$8,400.00	85%	Yes	$50,000.00
Robert G. Times, 700 Herald Street, Appleton, Va.	Vice Pres.	7,600.00	None	Yes	20,000.00
Grace L. Doe 518 South 4th Street, Appleton, Va.	Secretary	None	15%	Yes	None

*Life insurance on owner(s) or principal(s) will be required ONLY when specifically included as a condition of an approved loan.

7. **RECENT EFFORTS TO OBTAIN CREDIT** (For Direct Loan Applicants Only): The SBA is authorized to make loans to business enterprises only when the financial assistance is not otherwise available on reasonable terms. SBA is also empowered to make loans in cooperation with banks or other lending institutions through agreement to participate on an immediate or guaranty basis. Therefore, applicant must furnish the information required below regarding efforts made within 60 days preceding the filing of this application to obtain credit from banks or other sources. Letters declining to extend credit as well as declining to participate with SBA must be obtained from the following lending institutions: (a) The applicant's bank of account; and (b) if the amount of the loan applied for is in excess of the legal lending limit of the applicant's bank or in excess of the amount that the bank normally lends to any one borrower, then a refusal from a correspondent bank or from any other lending institution whose lending capacity is adequate to cover the loan applied for (c) letters from two banks are required if applicant is located in a city with a population in excess of 200,000. These letters must contain date of application, amount of loan requested and reasons for refusal, and be attached to this application.

CREDIT INFORMATION - Applicant expressly authorizes disclosure of all information submitted in connection with this application and any resulting loan to the financial institution agreeing below to participate in such loan or, if none, to its bank(s) of account and (Insert name of other financial institution if desired) _____

PARTICIPATION - Will any lending institution participate with SBA in the loan requested? [X] Yes [ ] No. If "Yes" institution shall execute Application For Participation or Guaranty Agreement at bottom of page 4

SBA FORM 4 (11-71) REF: ND 510-1A REPLACES APPLICATION FOR LOAN PARTS OF SBA FORMS 4 PART 1, 4A, 6B, 527, 528A, AND 751 ALL OF WHICH ARE OBSOLETE. ALSO INCORPORATES REQUIREMENTS CONTAINED IN FORMS 394, 652 AND 652B.

Exhibit 2

8. INSTRUCTIONS TO APPLICANT

Direct Loans - Submit one copy of this form and all supporting documents to SBA.

Participation Loans - Submit two copies of this form and all supporting documents to the participating bank.
All attachments must be signed and dated.

(1) SBA Form 912 must be submitted in quadruplicate by the proprietor, if a sole proprietorship; by each partner, if a partnership; by each officer, director, and each holder of 20 percent or more of the voting stock, if a corporation; and other person, including a hired manager, who has authority to speak for and commit the borrower in the management of the business. In addition, applicant must submit a signed copy of SBA Form 641, "Request for Counseling," with the application.

(2) Attach to application a brief description and history of the business.

(3) Comment briefly on the benefits the business will receive if the loan is obtained.

(4) Attach a schedule on all installment debts, contracts, notes and mortgages payable, showing to whom payable, original amount, original date, present balance, rate of interest, maturity date, monthly payment, security and whether current or delinquent. (Amounts on this schedule should agree with the figures on the applicant's financial statement.) Indicate by an asterik (*), items to be paid by loan proceeds and reason for paying same.

(5) If construction is involved, state the estimated cost, source of any additional funds which may be required to complete the construction and whether temporary financing for the construction is available. Furnish preliminary plans and specifications with the application. Final plans and specifications must be submitted for SBA/Lender approval prior to commencement of construction if loan is approved.

(6) Where loan funds will be used for construction purposes, and the contract or subcontracts are in excess of $10,000, the Applicant must execute and submit with the application "Applicant's Agreement of Compliance," SBA Form 601, which is a non-discrimination agreement issued pursuant to Executive Order 11246.

(7) Where purchase of machinery and equipment is involved, furnish a detailed list of items to be purchased and the estimated cost thereof.

(8) For each person listed in "Management" give brief description of education, technical training, employment and business experience.

(9) Attach balance sheets for the past 3 fiscal years.

(10) Attach balance sheet dated within 90 days from date of filing application with aging of accounts receivable and payable.

(11) Attach Profit and Loss Statement for past three fiscal years and for as much of current year as is available. (If operating statements are not available, explain why not and enclose corresponding Federal income tax returns in lieu thereof.) If past earnings do not show ability to repay proposed loan and existing obligations, attach an estimated profit and loss statement for at least one full year.

(12) Reconciliation of net worth shall be provided for items (9) and (10) above.

(13) If new business, furnish earnings projection (estimated profit and loss statement) for at least one full year.

(14) Personal Financial Statements must be submitted for proprietors, each partner, each officer, and each stockholder with 20% or more ownership. (For this purpose the enclosed SBA Form 413 may be used.)

(15) Details must be given of any pending litigation, whether applicant be plantiff or defendant or any litigation that involves management of the applicant.

(16) A description of collateral is required. Attached SBA Forms may be used for this purpose. SBA/Bank may require submission of an appraisal.

(17) SUBSIDIARIES AND AFFILIATES - List on an attached sheet the names and addresses of (1) all concerns that may be regarded as subsidiaries of the applicant, including concerns in which the applicant holds a controlling (but not necessarily a majority) interest, and (2) all other concerns that are in any way affiliated, by stock ownership or otherwise, with the applicant. The applicant should comment briefly regarding the trade relationship between the applicant and such subsidiaries or affiliates, if any, and if the applicant has no subsidiary or affiliate, a statement to this effect should be made. Signed and dated balance sheets, operating statements and reconcilement of net worth must be submitted for all subsidiaries and affiliates.

(18) PURCHASE AND SALES RELATIONS WITH OTHERS - Does applicant buy from, sell to, or use the services of, any concern in which an officer, director, large stockholder, or partner of the applicant has a substantial interest? ☐ Yes ☒ No If "Yes" give names of such officers, directors, stockholders, and partners, and names of any such concern on attached sheet.

(19) RECEIVERSHIP - BANKRUPTCY - Has applicant or any officer of the applicant or affiliates or any other concern with which such officer has been connected ever been in receivership or adjudicated a bankrupt? ☐ Yes ☒ No If "Yes" give names and details on separate sheet.

(20) Previous Government Financing - List assistance received, or requested and refused, and any pending applications.

Name of Agency or Department (including SBA)	Amount Approved or Requested	Date of Approval or Request	Present Balance	Status (Current, Delinquent, Maturity Accelerated)
None				

9. POLICY AND REGULATIONS CONCERNING REPRESENTATIVES AND THEIR FEES An applicant for a loan from SBA may obtain the assistance of any attorney, accountant, engineer, appraiser or other representative to aid him in the preparation of his application to SBA; however, such representation is not mandatory. In the event a loan is approved, the services of an attorney may be necessary to assist in the preparation of closing documents, title abstracts, etc. SBA will allow the payment of reasonable fees or other compensation for services performed by such representatives on behalf of the applicant.

There ar no "authorized representatives" of SBA, other than our regular salaried employees. Payment of any fee or gratuity to SBA employees is illegal and will subject the parties to such a transaction to prosecution.

SBA Regulations (Part 103, Sec. 103.13-5(c)) prohibit representatives from charging or proposing to charge any contingent fee for any services performed in connection with an SBA loan unless the amount of such fee bears a necessary and reasonable relationship to the services actually performed; or to charge any fee which is deemed by SBA to be unreasonable for the services actually performed; or to charge for any expenses which are not deemed by SBA to have been necessary in connection with the application. The Regulations (Part 122, Sec. 122.19) also prohibit the payment of any bonus, brokerage fee or commision in connection with SBA loans.

In line with these Regulations SBA will not approve placement or finder's fees for the use or attempted use or influence in obtaining or trying to obtain an SBA loan, or fees based solely upon a percentage of the approved loan or any part thereof.

Fees which will be approved will be limited to reasonable sums for services actually rendered in connection with the application or the closing, based upon the time and effort required, the qualifications of the representative and the nature and extent of the services rendered by such representative. Representatives of loan applicants will be required to execute an agreement as to their compensation for services rendered in connection with said loan.

It is the responsibility of the applicant to set forth in the appropriate section of the application the names of all persons or firms engaged by or on behalf of the applicant. Applicants are required to advise the SBA Field Office in writing of the names and fees of any representatives engaged by the applicant subsequent to the filing of the application.

Any loan applicant having any question concerning the payment of fees, or the reasonableness of fees, should communicate with the Field Office where the application is filed.

10. NAMES OF ATTORNEYS, ACCOUNTANTS, AND OTHER PARTIES. The names of all attorneys, accountants, appraisers, agents, and all other parties (whether individuals, partnerships, associations or corporations) engaged by or on behalf of the applicant (whether on a salary, retainer or fee basis and regardless of the amount of compensation) for the purpose of rendering professional or other services of any nature whatever to applicant, in connection with the preparation or presentation of this application to Bank in which SBA may participate or any loan to applicant as a result of this application; and all fees or other charges or compensation paid or to be paid therefor or for any purpose in connection with this application or disbursement of the loan whether in money or other property of any kind whatever, by or for the account of the applicant, together with a description of such services rendered or to be rendered, are as follows:

Name and Address (Include ZIP Code)	Description of Services Rendered and to be Rendered	Total Compensation Agreed to be Paid*	Compensation Already Paid*
ABC Accounting Service Redstone, Virginia 246003	Monthly and Annual Reports	$50 per month	Current - $50 monthly

* Enter specific dollar amounts. "Unknown," "Undetermined" or other emprecise terms are not sufficient.

11. AGREEMENT OF NONEMPLOYMENT OF SBA PERSONNEL. In consideration of the making by SBA to applicant of all or any part of the loan applied for in this application, applicant hereby agrees with SBA that applicant will not, for a period of two years after disbursement by SBA to applicant of said loan, or any part thereof, employ or tender any office or employment to, or retain for professional services, any person who, on the date of such disbursement, or within one year prior to said date, (a) shall have served as an officer, attorney, agent, or employee of SBA and (b) as such, shall have occupied a position or engaged in activities which SBA shall have determined, or may determine, involve discretion with respect to the granting of assistance under the Small Business Act, or Economic Opportunity Act or said Acts as they may be amended from time to time.

12. CERTIFICATION, I hereby certify that:

(a) The Applicant has read SBA Policy and Regulations concerning representatives and their fees (#9 above) and has not paid or incurred any obligation to pay, directly or indirectly, any fee or other compensation for obtaining the loan hereby applied for.

(b) The applicant has not paid or incurred any obligation to pay to any Government Employee or special Government employee any fee, gratuity or anything of value for obtaining the assistance hereby applied for. If such fee, gratuity, etc. has been solicited by any such employee, the applicant agrees to report such information to the Office of Security and Investigations, SBA, 1441 L Street, N. W., Washington, D. C. 20416.

(c) All information contained above and in exhibits attached hereto are true and complete to the best knowledge and belief of the applicant and are submitted for the purpose of inducing SBA to grant a loan or to participate in a loan by a bank or other lending institution to applicant. Whether or not the loan herein applied for is approved, applicant agrees to pay or reimburse SBA for the cost of any surveys, title or mortgage examinations, appraisals, etc., performed by non-SBA personnel with consent of applicant.

(d) The applicant hereby covenants, promises, agrees and gives herein the Assurance as required by 13 CFR 112.8 and CFR 113.4 that in connection with any loan to applicant which SBA may make, or in which SBA may participate or guaranty as a result of this application, it will comply with the requirements of Parts 112 and 113 of SBA Regulations and Title VI of Civil Rights Act of 1964 to the extent that said Parts 112 and 113 are applicable to such financial assistance, and further agrees that in the event it fails to comply with said applicable Parts 112 and 112, SBA may call, cancel, terminate, accelerate repayment or suspend in whole or in part the financial assistance provided or to be provided by SBA, and that SBA, or the United States Government may take any other action that may be deemed necessary or appropriate to effectuate the nondiscrimination requirements in said Parts 112 and 113, including the right to seek judicial enforcement of the terms of this ASSURANCE OF COMPLIANCE. These requirements prohibit discrimination on the grounds of race, color or national origin by recipients of federal financial assistance, including but not limited to employment practices, and require the submission of appropriate reports and access to books and records; these requirements are applicable to all transferees and successors in interest.

Artic Freeze Lockers, Inc.
(Individual, general partner, trade name or corporation)

Corporate Seal

Attest (Signed) Grace L. Doe
(Title)
Secretary

By (Signed) John R. Doe
Title President
Date Signed: June 6 , 19 72

Whoever makes any statement knowing it to be false, or whoever willfully overvalues any security, for the purpose of obtaining for himself or for an applicant any loan, or extension thereof by renewal, deferment of action, or otherwise, or the acceptance, release, or substitution of security therefor, or for the purpose of influencing in any way the action of the SBA, or for the purpose of obtaining money, property, or anything of value, under the Small Business Act, as amended, shall be punished under Section 16(a) of the Small Business Act, as amended, by fine of not more than $5,000 or by imprisonment for not more than two years, or both.

SBA FORM 4 (11-71)

PAGE 3 OF 4

13. APPLICATION FOR PARTICIPATION OR GUARANTY AGREEMENT

(For use only by bank or other financial institution)

Bank Transit No.

We propose to make a (check one):

[X] Guaranteed loan Bank Share __25__ %, SBA Share __75__ %.

[ ] Immediate participation loan with bank to make and service, Bank Share _____ %, SBA Share _____ %.

To the Applicant named on page 1 of this application. We hereby make application for the type of participation agreement checked above subject to the following loan conditions (use separate sheet if necessary):

(1) Terms and Conditions:

(a) Term of loan __10__ years. Monthly payments, including lender's interest at __6½__ % per annum, simple, in the amount of $ __625.00__ .

(b) Collateral and lien position.

1. First mortgage on land and buildings located at 519 South 4th Street, Appleton, Virginia.

2. First lien on machinery and equipment (including automotive), and furniture and fixtures located at above address.

(c) Guarantors

John Richard Adams, and spouse
Ollie P. Jefferson, and spouse
John R. Doe, and spouse (Grace L. Doe)
Robert G. Times, and spouse

(d) Insurance: Life, Hazzard, Federal Flood.

$50,000 term life insurance on John R. Doe
20,000 "   "   "   " Robert G. Times
70,000 hazard insurance

(e) Other

(2) Participation: SBA prefers that a lender participate beyond the total existing debts owed the lender which are to be refinanced through the loan. Existing obligations owed to the lender may be refinanced through the loan, in accordance with the minimums set forth below, only when the lender certifies in writing that such debt is in good standing (payments and other obligations handled substantially as agreed) and is satisfactory in all respects. Lenders minimum share of a loan shall be:

(a) Guaranty - 10% for SBA loans and as currently applicable for Economic Opportunity Loans.

(b) Immediate Participation - 25% provided the legal lending limit permits; 10% for Economic Opportunity Loans.

(3) Interest Rate: Lender may establish its own interest rate provided it is legal and reasonable, subject to SBA's approval. If lender's interest exceeds 8 percent per annum (simple) on a guaranteed loan SBA will pay accrued interest to the date of purchase on its guaranteed portion at the simple annual rate of 8 per cent without any future adjustment for unpaid accrued interest in excess of this effective rate. Lender may use an add-on interest provided (i) State law permits; (ii) the face of the SBA Note shows the principal amount of the actual dollar amount disbursed or to be disbursed to the borrower under the loan and all other SBA documents show this amount of principal; (iii) interest is converted to a simple annual interest rate and such converted rate is shown on all SBA documents other than the note (The add-on interest rate should be specified on the Note, if necessary, to comply with State law; otherwise show the simple interest rate.)

(4) Comments of the Bank, which may be in the form of a letter or memorandum, shall:

(a) include an evaluation of ability of Applicant's management, its past record of handling obligations, your expression as to what the loan will do for applicant, applicant's repayment ability, and other pertinent information. If Applicant or any of its officers have been adjudicated a bankrupt or connected with a receivership or been involved in any criminal, or other legal proceedings, give details. Also include an appraisal of the collateral if available and your evaluation of its adequacy to secure the loan.

(b) state whether any officer, director or substantial stockholder of Bank has a financial interest in Applicant and, if so, the extent thereof;

(c) indicate whether Applicant, its subsidiaries or affiliates, is indebted to the Bank, the amount, terms, and how secured, including any guaranties, and whether applicant's loans have been met substantially as agreed. (Include all such loans made during the past 12 months, showing high and low credit by months. If no loans were made during the period, so state.)

(5) Without the participation of SBA to the extent applied for we would not be willing to make this loan. In our opinion, the financial assistance applied for is not otherwise available on reasonable terms.

The Bank of Newport
Name and address of bank (Include ZIP Code)
Newport, Virginia 24600

Telephone No. __DE 00000__

Date __June 10,__ , 19__72__

(Signed) __John C. Smith, President__
Authorized Officer

SBA FORM 4 (11-71)   GPO : 1971 O - 450-824   PAGE 4 OF 4

<table>
<tr><td colspan="2">PERSONAL FINANCIAL STATEMENT

As of_____ , 19 ___.</td><td>Return to:
Small Business Administration</td><td>For SBA Use Only
SBA Loan No.</td></tr>
</table>

Name and Address, Including ZIP Code *(of person and spouse submitting Statement)*	This statement is submitted in connection with S.B.A. loan requested or granted to the individual or firm, whose name appears below:
SOCIAL SECURITY NO. _____ **Business** *(of person submitting Statement)*	**Name and Address of Applicant or Borrower, Including ZIP Code**

Please answer all questions using "No" or "None" where necessary

ASSETS	LIABILITIES
Cash on Hand & In Banks . . . . $ _____ _____	Accounts Payable . . . . $ _____
Savings Account in Banks . . . . _____	Notes Payable to Banks . . . . _____
U. S. Government Bonds . . . . _____ _____	*(Describe below - Section 2)*
Accounts & Notes Receivable . . . . _____ _____	Notes Payable to Others . . . . _____
Life Insurance-Cash Surrender Value Only . . _____	*(Describe below - Section 2)*
Other Stocks and Bonds . . . . _____ _____	Installment Account (Auto) . . . . _____
(Describe - reverse side - Section 3)	Monthly Payments $ _____
Real Estate . . . . _____	Installment Accounts (Other) . . . . _____
(Describe - reverse side - Section 4)	Monthly Payments $ _____
Automobile - Present Value . . . . _____	Loans on Life Insurance . . . . _____
Other Personal Property . . . . _____ _____	Mortgages on Real Estate . . . . _____
(Describe - reverse side - Section 5)	*(Describe - reverse side - Section 4)*
Other Assets . . . . _____	Unpaid Taxes . . . . _____ _____
(Describe - reverse side - Section 6)	*(Describe - reverse side - Section 7)*
	Other Liabilities . . . . _____
	(Describe - reverse side - Section 8)
	Total Liabilities . . . . _____
	Net Worth . . . . _____
Total . . . . $ ___ _____	Total . . . . $ _____

Section I. Source of Income	CONTINGENT LIABILITIES
(Describe below all items listed in this Section)	
Salary . . . . $ _____	As Endorser or Co-Maker . . . . $ _____
Net Investment Income . . . . _____	Legal Claims and Judgments . . . . _____
Real Estate Income . . . . _____	Provision for Federal Income Tax . . . . _____
Other Income *(Describe)* . . . . _____	Other Special Debt . . . . _____

Description of items listed in Section I ____ _____

_____

_____

_____

_____

_____

_____

Life Insurance Held *(Give face amount of policies - name of company and beneficiaries)* _____

_____

_____

_____

_____

_____

SUPPLEMENTARY SCHEDULES

Section 2. Notes Payable to Banks and Others

Name and Address of Holder of Note	Amount of Loan		Terms of Repayments	Maturity of Loan	How Endorsed, Guaranteed, or Secured
	Original Bal.	Present Bal.			
	$	$	$		

SBA FORM 413 (8-67) REF: ND 520-1   EDITION OF 1-67 MAY BE USED UNTIL STOCK IS EXHAUSTED   (OVER)

Section 3 Other Stocks and Bonds. Give listed and unlisted Stocks and Bonds (Use separate sheet if necessary)

No. of Shares	Names of Securities	Cost	Market Value Statement Date	
			Quotation	Amount

Section 4 Real Estate Owned. (List each parcel separately. Use supplemental sheets if necessary. Each sheet must be identified as a supplement to this statement and signed). (Also advises whether property is covered by title insurance, abstract of title, or both).

Title is in name of	Type of property

Address of property (City and State)	
	Original Cost to (me) (us) $ _____
	Date Purchased _____
	Present Market Value $ _____
	Tax Assessment Value $ _____

Name and Address of Holder of Mortgage (City and State)	
	Date of Mortgage _____
	Original Amount $ _____
	Balance $ _____
	Maturity _____
	Terms of Payment _____

Status of Mortgage, i.e., current or delinquent. If delinquent describe delinquencies

Section 5. Other Personal Property (Describe and if any is mortgaged, state name and address of mortgage holder and amount of mortgage, terms of payment and if delinquent, describe delinquency.)

Section 6. Other Assets. (Describe)

Section 7. Unpaid Taxes. (Describe in detail, as to type, to whom payable, when due, amount, and what, if any, property a tax lien, if any, attaches)

Section 8 Other Liabilities. (Describe in detail)

(I) or (We) certify the above and the statements contained in the schedules herein is a true and accurate statement of (my) or (our) financial condition as of the date stated herein. This statement is given for the purpose of: (Check one of the following)

☐ Inducing S.B.A. to grant a loan as requested in application, of the individual or firm whose name appears herein, in connection with which this statement is submitted.

☐ Furnishing a statement of (my) or (our) financial condition, pursuant to the terms of the guaranty executed by (me) or (us) at the time S.B.A. granted a loan to the individual or firm, whose name appears herein.

Signature	Signature	Date

GPO 1967 O -

Summary of Collateral

OFFERED BY APPLICANT AS SECURITY FOR LOAN AND SBA APPRAISER'S VALUATION REPORT

	EMPLOYER ID NO.
Name and Address of Applicant: (Include Zip Code) _____	
	SBA LOAN NO.

IMPORTANT INSTRUCTIONS FOR PREPARING THE LISTING OF
COLLATERAL OFFERED AS SECURITY FOR LOAN

Page 1. Summary Of Collateral Offered By Applicant As Security For The Loan: This is a summarization of the detailed listing on SBA Form 4, Schedule A. If collateral is to be acquired, with proceeds of loan describe the collateral in detail *on an attachment* to Schedule A with the notation "To be acquired".

Show exact cost. If assets were acquired from a predecessor company at a price other than cost less depreciation.

The figures to be entered in the net book value column must agree with the figures shown in the balance sheet, on page 2 of the application, except for the assets, if any, not being offered as collateral and non-business assets, if any, which are being offered to secure guarantees.

If a recent appraisal has been made of the collateral offered, it should be submitted with the application.

Any leases on land and buildings must be described, giving date and term of lease, rental, name and address of owner.

Page 2. Real Estate:

Item 1 - Land And Improvements: (a) legal description from deed on the land - location - city where deed is recorded. Book and page numbers of Official Records. Describe the land improvements such as paving, utilities, fence, etc. (b) cost of land when purchased.

Item 2 - Buildings: (a) general description, describe each building or structure on the land. Include size, type of construction, number of stories, date erected, use and condition. (b) amount of taxes and the assessed value from tax bills. (c) total amount of income received by owner from rental of the described property. (d) cost of building when purchased.

INADEQUATE OR POORLY PREPARED LOAN APPLICATION AND LISTING OF COLLATERAL ON PAGE 3 WILL CAUSE DELAY IN THE PROCESSING OF LOAN APPLICATIONS.

Page 3 - It is most **IMPORTANT** that applicants make an **ACTUAL PHYSICAL INVENTORY OF THE EQUIPMENT** being offered as collateral. **DO NOT TAKE FROM BOOK RECORDS.** Actually list each in accordance with the classification, e.g.: 1. Machinery and Equipment; 2. Automotive Equipment; 3. Office furniture and equipment; 4. Other— jigs, dies, fixtures, airplanes, etc.

Page 4 - Is a continuation of Equipment being offered.
Group items in accordance with the above classifications

Show: manufacturer or make, model and serial numbers, size, year, whether purchased new, used, or rebuilt.
BE SURE ITEMS LISTED CAN BE **READILY INSPECTED** BY SBA APPRAISERS.

SUMMARY			
Item	Cost	Net Book Value	Not to be used by applicant
1. Land and land improvements			
2. Buildings			
3. Machinery and Equipment			
4. Automotive Equipment			
5. Office furniture and equipment			
6. Other			
7. Total			
8. Real and chattel mortgages (Not to be paid from SBA loan req.) Attach details	X X X X		
9. Equity	X X X X		
10. To be acquired (Cost)		X X X X	
11. Total			

THE APPRAISER CERTIFIES that he has personally and thoroughly inspected the collateral as listed in this Report. Furthermore, as of _____ the market values shown in the above Summary are fair and reasonable as of that date. Additional comments are attached to this Report.

_____
SBA Appraiser's Signature   Date of Report

SBA Form 4 Schedule A (8-66) REF ND 510-1A previous editions of sheets 1, 2 and 3 are obsolete.

Real Estate

OFFERED BY APPLICANT AS SECURITY FOR LOAN AND SBA APPRAISER'S VALUATION REPORT

Name and Address of Applicant (include Zip Code)	Parcel number _____	SBA LOAN No.
	Title data: ☐ Title Insurance ☐ Abstract ☐ Other (indicate)	
Address of Realty Offered _____	Realty in name of _____	
	Recorded Book_____ Page_____ County_____	

1. **Land and land improvements** (Do not include buildings - see Sec. 2 below)

   Cost_____   date acquired_____

   Legal description (Attach if too long) *

* If available, attach plat survey.

2. **Improvements**   Cost (If separate from land) $_____

   Building description: List each building separately with brief description and dimensions.

Income if Applicable.

Rent $_____ Month ☐ Annually ☐ Lease ☐ ___ ___ Term.

Assessed Value	
Land	_____
Improvements	_____
Taxes	_____

SBA Form 4 Schedule A (8-66) previous editions are obsolete

Personal Property (Chattels)

OFFERED BY APPLICANT AS SECURITY FOR LOAN AND SBA APPRAISER'S VALUATION REPORT

The following described chattels are located or headquartered at (include Zip Code)

	EMPLOYER ID NO.
Above location is owned ( ) leased ( )	SBA LOAN NO.

It is most **IMPORTANT** that applicants make an **ACTUAL PHYSICAL INVENTORY OF THE EQUIPMENT** being offered as collateral. **DO NOT TAKE FROM BOOK RECORDS.** Actually list each item in accordance with the classification. e.g.:* 1. Machinery and Equipment 2. Automotive Equipment 3. Office furniture and equipment 4. Other - jigs, dies, fixtures, airplanes, etc.

Show: manufacturer or make, model and serial numbers, size, year, whether purchased new, used or rebuilt.

List chattels at different locations on separate sheets. * Description of _____	Model	Serial Number	New Used Rebuilt	NOT TO BE USED BY APPLICANT	
				Cond.	Market Value
Carry Totals of Each Classification to Page 1 (Summary) Lines 3, 4, 5, and 6.				Total	

INADEQUATE OR POORLY PREPARED LOAN APPLICATION AND LISTING OF COLLATERAL WILL CAUSE DELAY IN THE PROCESSING OF LOAN APPLICATIONS. BE SURE ALL ITEMS CAN BE READILY INSPECTED BY SBA APPRAISER.

I, _____ ,
　　　　(Signature of owner, partner, or corporation officer)　　　　　　　　　(Title)

of the _____
　　　　　　　　　　　　　(Name of Firm)

certify that the above machinery and equipment listing represents an *actual physical inventory* taken on (date) _____.
Mark items (in column 2) with an asterisk if they are subject to conditional bills of sale or chattel mortgages the balance of which will not be paid off from an SBA loan. Carry total of such balances to line 8, page 1 (Summary).

SBA Form 4 Schedule A (8-66) previous editions are obsolete

COMPENSATION AGREEMENT FOR SERVICES IN CONNECTION WITH
APPLICATION AND LOAN FROM (OR IN PARTICIPATION WITH)
SMALL BUSINESS ADMINISTRATION

This undersigned representative (attorney, accountant, engineer, appraiser, etc.) hereby agrees that the undersigned has not and will not, directly or indirectly, charge or receive any payment in connection with the application for or the making of the loan except for services actually performed on behalf of the Applicant. The undersigned further agrees that the amount of payment for such services shall not exceed an amount deemed reasonable by SBA (and, if it is a participation loan, by the participating lending institution), and to refund any amount in excess of that deemed reasonable by SBA (and the participating institution). This agreement shall supersede any other agreement covering payment for such services.

A general description of the services performed, or to be performed, by the undersigned and the compensation paid or to be paid are set forth below. If the total compensation in any case exceeds $300 (or $50 for: (1) regular business loans of $15,000 or less; (2) all disaster home loans; or (3) all economic opportunity loans; or if SBA should otherwise require, the services must be itemized showing each date services were performed, time spent each day, and description of the service rendered on each day listed. If necessary, the statement of services may be continued on the reverse side of this form, or attached as a rider hereto.

The undersigned Applicant and representative hereby certify that no other fees have been charged or will be charged by the representative in connection with this loan, unless provided for in loan authorization specifically approved by SBA.

DESCRIPTION OF SERVICES

Amount Heretofore Paid $ _____

Additional Amount to be Paid $ _____

Total Compensation $ _____

(Parts 103, 104, and 122 of Title 13 of the Code of Federal Regulations contain provisions covering appearances and compensation of persons representing SBA applicants. Section 103.13-5 authorizes the suspension or revocation of the privilege of any such person to appear before SBA for charging a fee deemed unreasonable by SBA for the services actually performed, charging of unreasonable expenses, or violation of this agreement. In addition, whoever commits any fraud, by false or misleading statement or representation, or by conspiracy. shall be subject to the penalty of any applicable Federal or State statute.)

Dated_____, 19____

_____
(Representative)

By_____

The Applicant hereby certifies to SBA that the above representations, description of services and amounts are correct and satisfactory to Applicant.

Dated_____, 19____

_____
(Applicant)

By_____

The participating lending insitution hereby certifies that the above representations of service rendered and amounts charged are reasonable and satisfactory to said lender.

Dated_____, 19____

_____
(Lender)

By_____

NOTE: Foregoing certificate must be executed, if by a corporation, in corporate name by duly authorized officer and duly attested; if by a partnership, in the firm name, together with signature of a general partner.

**SBA REVIEW BY_____ TITLE_____DATE_____

SBA FORM 159 (10-74) REF SOP 20 50 PREVIOUS EDITIONS ARE OBSOLETE.

WHITE TO SBA, YELLOW TO BORROWER, PINK TO BORROWER'S REPRESENTATIVE

GPO 895-748

Appendix

Analog
of a Loan
Proposal

The 'analog of a loan proposal' that follows is the *how* of doing a loan proposal. It shows step-by-step the calculations involved in comparing historical data, annualizing current financial statements, and how to do a cash break-even and projected profit and loss statement. The analog of a loan proposal is a set of instructions as one would give an analog computer. All the exercise requires is that the reader do the calculations. There is no consideration given to why you are doing the calculations or what they represent.

Info:

Exhibits 1–4 represent the profit and loss statements for New Liquor for the past three years and currently.

On your work sheet label column #1 "12/30/73," column #2 "12/30/74," and so on in relation to the dates on the profit and loss statements.

Along the left hand side of the page write in the items from the P & L's, i.e., sales, cost of sales, net profit, salaries, and so on.

Put the figures from the P & L's under their respective columns and beside their respective items, e.g. salaries for 1973 go under the first column, beside the item "salaries", salaries for 1974 go in the second column beside the 1973 salaries.

Info:

Chart 1, entitled "Liquor Store Operations" shows seasonal variations in sales. Add up the index numbers at the bottom of the chart.

Chart 1   Liquor Stores Retail Sales Index

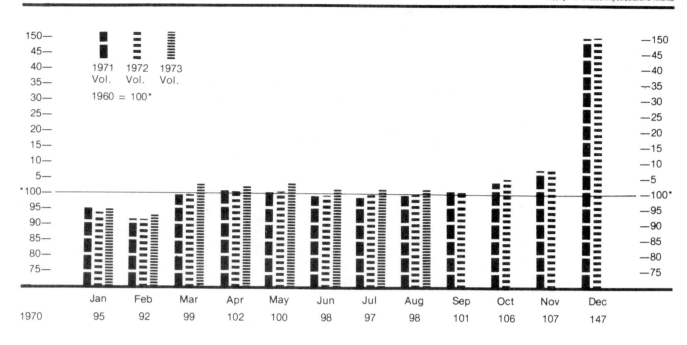

| 1970 | Jan 95 | Feb 92 | Mar 99 | Apr 102 | May 100 | Jun 98 | Jul 97 | Aug 98 | Sep 101 | Oct 106 | Nov 107 | Dec 147 |

Liquor Stores
Sales Trends by Geographical Area
1960 = 100

Area	August 1973	1972 Average	1971 Average	1970 Average
1 New England	103.8	106.0	105.5	105.5
2 New York Pennsylvania, New Jersey	106.4	107.3	107.1	107.2
3 Wisconsin, Illinois, Indiana Michigan, Ohio	103.2	105.2	104.8	105.0
4 North Dakota, South Dakota, Kansas Nebraska, Minnesota, Iowa, Missouri	101.6	103.6	103.6	103.6
5 Florida, Georgia, South Carolina, North Carolina, Virginia, West Virginia, Maryland	101.5	103.1	102.9	103.0
6 Tennessee, Kentucky Mississippi, Alabama	99.5	100.2	100.3	100.2
7 Oklahoma, Arkansas, Texas, Louisiana	99.4	100.7	101.0	101.2
8 New Mexico, Idaho, Arizona, Nevada, Utah Colorado, Wyoming, Montana	98.2	100.8	100.4	100.4
9 California, Oregon, Washington	104.3	106.2	105.2	105.4
Composite National Average	102.0	103.8	103.4	103.5

Answer A   *February* is the month ending for the current statement. Add up the index numbers for *January* to *February*.

Answer B   Divide Answer (A) by Answer (B) to four decimal places.

Answer C   Multiply the total sales of the 2/28/76 statement column 4 by Answer C.

Answer D   Enter the answer under "sales" in the next column (5). The current statement is for 2 months. Divide the number of months of the current statement by 12.

Answer E   Multiply all current expense items and total in column (4) by Answer E. Enter the answers in column 5.

Info: Exhibit 5 represents a list of what your client, John Brown, expects some of his expenses will be and how much he wants to take as a salary.

Take these expense items and enter them in the proper item space in column (6). Put Brown's salary on a separate sheet of paper and label it "Owner's Draw".

For *every* expense item in columns 1,2,3, and 5 except those items from Exhibit 5, depreciation, and interest, multiply on the following basis:

Column #	Multiply By (Weight):	Answer
1	0.10	_____
2	0.20	_____
3	0.45	_____
5	0.25	_____

Add the answers for each expense item to get a new figure for that item.

Answer F
Info: Exhibit 6, entitled "Use of Funds", shows what the total cost of going into business will be and the amount of the loan required.

Make a chart as follows:

Item	Value	Life	Salvage	Method	Annual

Place fixtures, equipment, and leasehold improvements as separate items under the "Item" heading. Enter the amount each costs under the "Value" heading. Under the "Life" column enter fifteen years for improvement and fixtures and seven years for equipment. Multiply each item's value by 0.2 and enter that number under the "salvage" column for each item. Write "S.L." under the "Method" column for each item.

Subtract the figure under the "Salvage" column from the figure under the "Value" column for each item.

Answer G	Divide Answer G for each item by the number under "Life" for each item and enter the answers under the "Annual" column.
Answer H	Add all Answer H.
Answer I	Put Answer I in column (6) under "Depreciation". Take the items from the Use of Funds, Exhibit 6, and multiply as follows:

Items	Value	Multiply By	Answer J
Fixtures, Leasehold Improvements	$_____	× 15	
Equipment	$_____	× 7	
Deposits, Working Capital, Inventory, Licenses Minus the owners' injection	$_____	× 5	

Add up the answers thus arrived at.

Answer K	Divide Answer K by the amount of the loan.
Answer L	Answer L represents the number of years the loan will be for. Round to a whole number.
Info:	Chart 2 is an interest table. Go down the left hand side to find the number of years the loan will be for. Go across the top to 10.75 percent interest. Where the parallel and horizontal columns coverage is a factor. Multiply this factor by the total loan amount and round to dollars.
Answer M	Answer M represents the total monthly repayment—interest and principal. Multiply Answer M by 12.
Answer N	Answer N represents the total annual loan repayment. Multiply the total loan amount by 0.1075.
Answer O	Answer O is the total interest the first year. Enter this number under "interest" in column (6). Subtract Answer O from Answer N.
Answer P	Answer P is the total annual principal the first year. Write this figure on a separate sheet of paper and entitle it "Annual Principal". Add the expenses in column (6) to get "Total Operating Expense".
Answer Q	Write Answer Q on a separate sheet and entitle it "Total Operating Expense".

Go to the bottom of your work paper and write the following headings:
Commonsized (%)
(Indent) Sales
        Cost of Sales
        Gross Profit
        Operating Expense
        Net Profit
Take the sales figures in columns 1, 2, 3 and 4. Write them down.

Answers R 1, R 2, R 3, R 4   Write down the Cost of Sales figures for columns 1, 2, 3, and 4.

Answers S 1, S 2, S 3, S 4   Write the total Operating Expense figures for columns 1, 2, 3 and 4.

Answers T 1, T 2, T 3, T 4   Divide Answers S 1, S 2, S 3, and S 4 by Answers R 1, R 2, R 3 and R 4, respectively to four decimal places.

Answers U 1, U 2, U 3, U 4   Enter the Answers U in their respective column, moving the decimal two places to the right, under "Commonsized (%) Cost of Sales".

Add all the Cost of Sales percentages from the first four columns and divide by 4.

Answer V   Answer V represents the average Cost of Sales percentage for the last four statements. Write Answer V on a separate sheet of paper and title it "Average Cost of Sales Percentage", and also put in column (6) under "Commonsized Cost of Sales".

For "Commonsized (%) Sales" put 100.00 in columns 1, 2, 3, 4 and 6.

Divide Answers T 1, T 2, T 3 and T 4 by Answers R 1, R 2, R 3 and R 4, respectively.

Answers W 1, W 2, W 3, W 4   Enter the Answers W in their respective column, moving the decimal two places to the right, under "Commonsized (%) Operating Expense".

In each column subtract Commonsized Cost of Sales from Commonsized Sales to get Commonsized "Gross Profit". Subtract Commonsized Operating Expense from Commonsized Gross Profit to get Commonsized Net Profit.

Go to your separate sheet of paper and add total Operating Expense plus total Annual Principal plus Owner's Salary minus Depreciation.

Answer X   Divide Answer X by one minus the Cost of Sales percentage (in decimal equivalent).

Answer Y   Add Owner's Salary plus Principal minus Depreciation.

Answer Z

Info:

Exhibit 7 is a schedule of expected Income Tax percentages.

Find where Answer Z falls in the schedule and write down the corresponding Income Tax percentage.

Divide Answer Z by one minus the Cost of Sales percentage and multiply the resulting number by the Income Tax percentage.

Answer AA

Add Answer Y and Answer AA

Answer BB

Answer BB is your Break-Even Sales for the business. Put this under sales in column (6) *unless* the last full year's sales are higher. *If* the last full year's sales are higher place *that* sales figure in column (6).

Multiply the sales figure in column (6) by the Cost of Sales percentage you have entered under "Commonsized Cost of Sales" in column (6).

Answer CC

Enter this figure under Cost of Sales in column (6).

Entitle column (6) "Projected 12 Months".

Subtract Cost of Sales in columns 5 and 6 from sales. Write the answers under "Gross Profit" in the respective columns.

Subtract "Total Operating Expense" in columns 5 and 6 from "Gross Profit". Enter the answers under "Net Profit" in the respective columns. Write 100.00 in column (6) under "Commonsized Sales".

Divide Operating Expense in column (6) by sales in column (6).

Answer DD

Enter Answer DD under Commonsized Operating Expense in column (6).

In the column (6) Commonsized Section, subtract the Cost of Sales from Sales to get Gross Profit and subtract Operating Expense from Gross Profit to get Net Profit.

	1	2	3	4	5	6

Exhibit 1

New Liquor
Profit and Loss 12 Months Ending 12/30/73

Sales	250,000
Cost of Sales	187,500
Gross Profit	62,500
Expense:	
Salaries	13,750
Payroll Tax	1,375
Supplies	2,050
Legal & Acct.	1,200
Repairs & Maintenance	900
Advertising	1,572
Delivery	1,150
Miscellaneous	950
Rent	7,500
Utilities	2,575
Insurance	1,275
Tax & Licenses	3,050
Interest	250
Depreciation	2,000
Total Expense	39,597
Net Profit	22,903

Exhibit 2

New Liquor
Profit and Loss 12 Months Ending 12/30/74

Sales	285,000
Cost of Sales	216,600
Gross Profit	68,400
Expense:	
Salaries	15,675
Payroll Tax	1,568
Supplies	2,337
Legal & Acct.	1,368
Repairs & Maintenance	1,026
Advertising	1,796
Delivery	1,311
Miscellaneous	1,083
Rent	7,500
Utilities	2,936
Insurance	1,454
Tax & License	3,477
Interest	285
Depreciation	2,000
Total Expense	43,816
Net Profit	24,584

Exhibit 3

New Liquor
Profit and Loss 12 Months Ending 12/30/75

Sales	310,000
Cost of Sales	231,260
Gross Profit	78,740
Expense:	
Salaries	17,000
Payroll Tax	1,700
Supplies	2,542
Legal & Acct.	1,488
Repairs & Maintenance	1,116
Advertising	1,953
Delivery	1,426
Miscellaneous	1,178
Rent	9,600
Utilities	3,193
Insurance	1,581
Tax & Licenses	3,782
Interest	230
Depreciation	2,400
Total Expense	49,189
Net Profit	27,551

Exhibit 4

New Liquor
Profit and Loss 2 Months Ending 2/28/76

Sales	51,192
Cost of Sales	38,189
Gross Profit	13,003
Expense:	
Salaries	2,816
Payroll Tax	282
Supplies	420
Legal & Acct.	245
Repairs & Maintenance	184
Advertising	323
Delivery	235
Miscellaneous	194
Rent	1,600
Utilities	527
Insurance	263
Tax & Licenses	625
Interest	38
Depreciation	400
Total Expense	8,152
Net Profit	4,851

Exhibit 5

Expected Expenses—John Brown Annual	
Rent	9,600
Salaries	15,000
Payroll Tax	1,500
Advertising	600
Insurance	1,600
My Salary	13,000

Exhibit 6

Use of Funds

Purchase Price:			
Fixtures & Signs		10,000	
Equipment		7,500	
Leasehold Improvements		20,500	
Liquor License		27,000	65,000
Inventory			22,000
Start-Up Expense:			
ABC Transfer Fee	1,270		
Rent Deposit	1,600		
Utility Deposits	500		
Sparten Deposit	1,070		
Business Lic. & Misc.	100		4,540
Working Capital			3,460
Money Required			95,000
Less: Owner's Cash Inj.			19,000
Loan Required			76,000

Exhibit 7

Expected Income Tax Percentages

If owner's Draw + Principal − Depreciation Equals			The Income Tax Percentage Is
1	to	10,000	10%
10,001	to	20,000	15%
20,001	to	35,000	20%
35,001	to	50,000	25%
50,001	to	65,000	30%
65,001	to	80,000	35%
80,001	to	100,000	40%
100,000	.....Plus		45%

Chart 2

Term of Loan Yrs.	Mos.	Number of Payments	MONTHLY INSTALLMENT PER DOLLAR INCLUDING INTEREST				
			@ 10 1/4%	@ 10 1/2%	@ 10 3/4%	@ 11%	@ 11 1/4%
8	10	106	.004 378	.014 514	.014 651	.014 788	.014 926
8	11	107	.014 296	.014 432	.014 569	.014 706	.014 844
9	0	108	.014 214	.014 351	.014 488	.014 626	.014 764
9	1	109	.014 135	.014 272	.014 409	.014 547	.014 686
9	2	110	.014 057	.014 194	.014 332	.014 470	.014 609
9	3	111	.013 981	.014 118	.014 256	.014 394	.014 534
9	4	112	.013 906	.014 043	.014 181	.014 320	.014 460
9	5	113	.013 832	.013 970	.014 108	.014 247	.014 387
9	6	114	.013 760	.013 898	.014 037	.014 176	.014 316
9	7	115	.013 689	.013 827	.013 966	.014 106	.014 247
9	8	116	.013 619	.013 758	.013 897	.014 037	.014 178
9	9	117	.013 551	.013 690	.013 830	.013 970	.014 111
9	10	118	.013 484	.013 623	.013 763	.013 904	.014 045
9	11	119	.013 418	.013 558	.013 698	.013 839	.013 980
10	0	120	.013 354	.013 493	.013 634	.013 775	.013 917
10	1	121	.013 290	.013 430	.013 571	.013 712	.013 855
10	2	122	.013 228	.013 368	.013 509	.013 651	.013 793
10	3	123	.013 167	.013 307	.013 449	.013 591	.013 733
10	4	124	.013 107	.013 248	.013 389	.013 531	.013 674
10	5	125	.013 048	.013 189	.013 330	.013 473	.013 616
10	6	126	.012 990	.013 131	.013 273	.013 416	.013 559
10	7	127	.012 933	.013 074	.013 216	.013 359	.013 503
10	8	128	.012 877	.013 018	.013 161	.013 304	.013 448
10	9	129	.012 822	.012 964	.013 106	.013 250	.013 394
10	10	130	.012 767	.012 910	.013 053	.013 196	.013 341
10	11	131	.012 714	.012 857	.013 000	.013 144	.013 289
11	0	132	.012 662	.012 804	.012 948	.013 092	.013 238
11	1	133	.012 610	.012 753	.012 897	.013 042	.013 187
11	2	134	.012 560	.012 703	.012 847	.012 992	.013 137
11	3	135	.012 510	.012 653	.012 798	.012 943	.013 089
11	4	136	.012 461	.012 604	.012 749	.012 894	.013 041
11	5	137	.012 412	.012 556	.012 701	.012 847	.012 993
11	6	138	.012 365	.012 509	.012 654	.012 800	.012 947
11	7	139	.012 318	.012 463	.012 608	.012 754	.012 901
11	8	140	.012 272	.012 417	.012 563	.012 709	.012 857

EFFECTIVE DATE	PAGE
6-8-72	117

index

Accounting Corporation of America's Small Business Barometer, 112, 116, 119, 121
accounts receivable financing, 18, 19, 21, 26–27, 28, 29

balance sheet, 81, 82, 127–30
banks (commercial), and Eximbank, 61–62, 63, 64–8; and Federal Reserve Board, 71; as loan source, 4–13, 15, 17, 18, 19, 20, 21, 23, 24, 25; and SBA, 49, 50, 52, 56; vs government, 38
break-even analysis, 106–10, 118, 119, 122, 167, 171
business analysis, for loan proposal, 100–04; vs market analysis, 100
Business Week, 10

capital, debt, 3–4; equity, 3, 4, 15; injection, 3; seed, 3
cash flow, 83, 123, 124, 125, 135–37, 141
character loans, 16
collateral, 5, 14, 15, 16, 17, 18, 20, 21, 23, 26, 29, 52, 53, 85, 148, 151; and EDA loans, 59; and SBA loans, 53, 58
comaker, 18, 25, 26

Commercial Bank Exporter Guarantee Program, 61–62, 63–64
commercial banks, see banks
commercial financial lenders, 22, 23, 24, 25, 26–8; vs government, 38
Commercial Financing, 29–30
commercial paper houses, 33
commercial time sales companies, 26
Commodity Credit Corp., 40–1, 68
consumer finance companies, see finance companies, personal
Consumer Protection Loans, 55, 58
credit rating, 4, 7, 12, 16, 23, 24, 25, 33; service, 25
credit unions, 22, 23, 33
current ratio, 12, 129–30

debt-to-worth ratio, 12, 129–30
default, 3
depreciation, 84, 107, 108, 109, 114, 115, 116, 124, 144, 169, 170
disaster loans, 49, 55–6
Displaced Business Loans, 54, 58
Dun and Bradstreet, Inc., 15

Economic Development

Administration (EDA), 39, 57–61; requirements, 59–60
Economic Injury Disaster Loan (EIDL), 56, 58
Economic Injury Loan (EIL), 49, 54–5
Economic Opportunity Loan (EOL), 49, 53–4, 57
endorser, 18
equity capital, 3, 4, 15
Estes, Billy Sol, 27–8
Export-Import Bank of the United States (Eximbank), 39–40, 61–8; and banks, commercial, 61–2, 63, 64–8
Exporter Credit Insurance Program, 61

factor, 19, 22, 26, 27, 29
factoring, 19, 20, 29
Farm Credit Administration, 42, 68–9
Farmers Home Administrations (FHA), 41–2, 69–71
federal government, loan process, 36–8; loan source, 5–6, 7, 10, 34–74;
Federal Reserve Board, as loan source, 42, 71–2
finance companies, personal, 22, 23, 24, 25, 26
financial institutions, 5–6

financial projection, 111–15; for new businesses, 115–18
financial statement, 79, 85, 112, 134–5, 151; projected, 118–19, 120–29, 134–35
fixed asset loans, 18, 20, 21
Foreign Credit Insurance Association (FCIA), 61, 62–3
funds statement, 106, 107, 127, 131, 133, 151, 169, 176

guarantor, 16, 18

Handicapped Assistance Loans (HAL), 49, 57

income statement, 118–19
industrial time sales financing, 27
installment loans, 16, 17
insurance, 5, 16, 18
interest, 3, 4, 8, 9, 16, 17, 19, 22, 23, 25, 26, 28, 29, 33, 116–18, 169, 170; EDA loans, 59; Eximbank loans, 66; Farm Credit Union, 68; Federal Reserve Board, 71; SBA loans, 53, 56, 57, 58, 73; table, 177
Internal Revenue Service (IRS), 79
inventory loans, 18, 20, 21, 26, 28

Journal of Commercial Bank Lending, 11, 12

Kiyawa, Daniel, 11

leasing, 26, 30–2
leverage, 4, 130
life insurance companies, 22, 23, 25, 26, 32

lines of credit, 16, 17; revolving, 49, 57
loan analysis, see loan proposal
loan proposal, analog of, 167–177; contents, 77–8, 85–6, 87–130; format, 131–52
loan-to-deposit ratio, 10, 52
loans, see term loans, secured loans, etc.
Local Development Company (LDC), 73–74

Maritime Administration, 42, 43, 72
market analysis, for loan proposal, 85, 87, 89–100, 103, 138–40, 151; competition study, 87, 89, 97–9; location, 87, 89, 90–1, 95, 98, 100; market share, 87, 89–90; population study, 87, 89, 95–7, 102–03, 105–06; traffic patterns, 87, 89, 91–3, 102–03; vs business analysis, 100

National Association of Credit Management, 15
Natural Resource Loans, 42, 43

Occupational Safety and Health Loans, 55
Overseas Private Investment Corp., 39, 40

pension funds, 22, 23, 33, 52
personal credit, 33
physical disaster loans, 56, 58
private financial companies, see finance companies, personal

Pro Forma balance sheet, 127, 128–29, 131, 149–50, 151
product disaster loan, 56–57, 58
profit and loss statement, 79–81, 85, 111, 119–20, 125, 126, 135–36, 167, 174–75

reconciliation of net worth statement, 82–3
revolving loans, 14

sales projections, 100–04
secured loans, 17–19, 21, 26, 28
Small Business Act, 47, 53
Small Business Administration (SBA), 18, 20, 35, 38–9, 44–57, 72, 73, 74, 82, 125, 133, 151, 152, SBA 7(a) loan, 49, 52–3
Small Business Reporter, 81, 82
Smith, Victor D., 12
State Development Company (SDC), 72–3

term loans, 13–16, 20, 21, 26; agreement, 15–16; intermediate-, 13–15, 19, 21; long-, 13–15, 17, 20, 21, 23; short-, 13–15, 17, 18, 21, 32
trade credit, 23, 32–33

unsecured loans, 14, 16–17, 21, 26, 32
U.S. Department of Agriculture, types of loans, 40–2, 68
U.S. Department of Interior, 72

Veterans Administration, 42–3, 72

Wall Street Journal, 10